Cinematic Skepticism

Cinematic Skepticism

Across Digital and Global Turns

JEROEN GERRITS

Cover: Hatice Aslan in *Three Monkeys* (2008), directed by Nuri Bilge Ceylan.
Credit: Mongrel Media/Photofest

Published by State University of New York Press, Albany

© 2019 State University of New York

All rights reserved

No part of this book may be used or reproduced in any manner whatsoever without written permission. No part of this book may be stored in a retrieval system or transmitted in any form or by any means including electronic, electrostatic, magnetic tape, mechanical, photocopying, recording, or otherwise without the prior permission in writing of the publisher.

For information, contact State University of New York Press, Albany, NY
www.sunypress.edu

Library of Congress Cataloging-in-Publication Data

Names: Gerrits, Jeroen, 1975– author.
Title: Cinematic skepticism : across digital and global turns / Jeroen Gerrits.
Other titles: Lubricious objects
Description: Albany : State University of New York Press, [2019] | Revision of author's thesis (doctoral)—Johns Hopkins University, 2011, titled Lubricious objects : skepticism, cinema, poetry. | Includes bibliographical references and index.
Identifiers: LCCN 2018056831 | ISBN 9781438476636 (hardcover : alk. paper) | ISBN 9781438476643 (pbk. : alk. paper) | ISBN 9781438476650 (ebook)
Subjects: LCSH: Skepticism in motion pictures.
Classification: LCC PN1995.9.S5533 G47 2019 | DDC 791.4301—dc23
LC record available at https://lccn.loc.gov/2018056831

10 9 8 7 6 5 4 3 2 1

*To Wout Gerrits and Martha Valke-De Witte,
in loving memory*

Contents

List of Illustrations		ix
Acknowledgments		xiii
Introduction: A "Still" New "Moving" Image of Skepticism?		1
Chapter 1	Broken Links: A Cavello-Deleuzian Approach to Film	17
Chapter 2	Renoir's Key to Cinematic Skepticism	41
Chapter 3	What Cinema Calls Believing, or: Deleuze beyond Skepticism?	53
Chapter 4	A Seem-less Digital Skepticism in *Grizzly Man* and *Amélie*	73
Chapter 5	Digital, Global, Ontological Turns	109
Chapter 6	Reveiling the Gap in *The Headless Woman* and *Three Monkeys*	127
Conclusion: The Digital Will or a New Romanticism?		175
Notes		183
References		203
Index		215

Illustrations

The figures listed below are frame captures taken (in order of appearance) from *Amélie*, *Grizzly Man*, *The Rules of the Game*, *It Happened One Night*, *The Headless Woman*, and *Three Monkeys*, as listed in the references.

Figures 1.1, 1.2	Antipodal characters	11
Figure 2.1	Schumacher halfway up the stairs	45
Figures 2.2, 2.3	Marceau (left) and Lisette (right) fleeing through a crack in the crystal	49
Figure 4.1	Herzog's text over Treadwell's footage	77
Figure 4.2	Treadwell reached out	77
Figure 4.3–4.5	Capra's shift of focus in *It Happened One Night*	88
Figure 4.6–4.11	At the Gare de Lyon	90–91
Figure 4.12	*"Toujours lui!"*	92
Figure 4.13	Going "woo" in the ghost train	93
Figures 4.14, 4.15	Allegories of cinema at the Square Louise Michel	95
Figures 4.16, 4.17	Body, text, and photo-copy-graph	97
Figure 4.18	Through the transparent screen	97
Figure 4.19	Nino squats down at the photomaton as the luggage train arrives	99

x / Illustrations

Figure 4.20–4.25	Amélie and Saïd: different turn	100–101
Figures 4.26, 4.27	Magical resonance	103
Figures 4.28, 4.29	Proliferating screens	104
Figure 6.1	A literally headless woman	130
Figure 6.2, inset	The rear window shot showing a dog "in the middle of the road"	131
Figure 6.3	Aldo ("Harelip") and his dog	135
Figure 6.4	Indexical signs on the side window	137
Figure 6.5	"Watch those fingers"	137
Figure 6.6	Vero reaches for the phone in her purse just before the accident	138
Figures 6.7, 6.8	Calling for Elisabeth Andrade	142
Figure 6.9	Vero witnessing Elisabeth Andrade through the mirror next to "ours"	143
Figure 6.10, 6.11	Vero turns toward the literally marginalized people in her life	144
Figures 6.12, 6.13	From the margin to the signifying zone of the image	145
Figures 6.14, 6.15	Vero avoiding the indigenous gaze	146
Figures 6.16, 6.17, inset	Indexical, symbolic, illegible: passing by Changuila in El Cruce	148
Figure 6.18	Vero at the party behind the slightly ajar door of translucent glass	151
Figure 6.19, 6.20	Servet just before the accident	152
Figure 6.21	An indistinct body lying in the middle of the road	153

Figures 6.22, 6.23	Oscillating between subjective and objective shots	155
Figures 6.24, 6.25	Servet leaving the scene of the accident	156
Figures 6.26, 6.27	Eyüp hears a train pass by	159
Figures 6.28, 6.29	False reverse shot	159
Figures 6.30–6.32	Hacer entering her own POV	163
Figures 6.33, 6.34	The cut to the framed view	164
Figure 6.35	The drowned boy: Ishmael's brother	169

Acknowledgments

This project reflects my passionate research interests, which have continued to grow over the past fifteen years. My fascination for Stanley Cavell and Gilles Deleuze's idiosyncratic styles of doing philosophy germinated while I was a master's student of philosophy at the University of Amsterdam and continued as I pursued a PhD at the Johns Hopkins Humanities Center. Paola Marrati's teaching, mentorship, and friendship have been decisive throughout my graduate career: I cannot thank her enough. I also want to single out Hent de Vries for his personal and professional support during my years at the Humanities Center.

The Humanities Center encouraged and enabled me to foster crucial working relations with some of the scholars in the fields of film and philosophy whose work I value most. These included, in particular, D. N. Rodowick, who welcomed me at the Visual and Environmental Studies Department at Harvard (which he chaired at the time), and Sandra Laugier, who invited me for lectureships and conference contributions at Université de Picardie Jules Verne, Amiens and later at Paris-Sorbonne. I thank them deeply for their generosity and inspiration.

Although the theoretical framework for the current study stems from my PhD dissertation, its actual shape and direction did not occur until my appointment at Binghamton University (SUNY), first as visiting assistant professor and, as of 2013, as junior faculty. I am incredibly grateful for having the opportunity to conduct my research and to teach courses on film and new media in the best possible environment: a theoretically oriented comparative literature department. Of my many heart-warming and intellectually stimulating colleagues, I want to thank Luiza Moreira and Brett Levinson in particular for their guidance, support, feedback, and trust.

I want to extent my gratitude to the bright and diverse student body at Binghamton University as well. Student responses to much of the material I present here was indispensible. Two graduate students, Tomas Guerrero Diaz and Basak Bingol Yuce, deserve special mention for the excellent research they conducted on *The Headless Woman* and *Three Monkeys*, as well as for sharing their insights.

The Humanities Center at JHU generously continued to host me during the various summers I spent working on this book. I am especially grateful to Marva Philip for this hospitality. And I want to thank Binghamton University for awarding me a most welcome research leave as well as a fellowship from the Institute for Advanced Studies in the Humanities, both of which propelled this project when it needed it most.

I thank Beth Bouloukos and Rafael Chaiken at SUNY Press for their continuous interest in this book project and for their guidance in preparing the manuscript.

I am grateful to my family for their unwavering support of my pursuits, in particular, my parents. I have dedicated this book to the memory of Wout Gerrits and Martha Valke-De Witte, whose love for life I carry with me. My dear friends Ron Griffin and Shaun Carrick have made me feel at home on the American side of the Atlantic. I hope to have them both near me for much longer; may Whistle Stop continue to bemuse my writings. My final words of gratitude are for Elham Hatef, my partner in life, whose determination, emotional strength, and profound love have humbled and inspired me throughout the writing process. This book would not exist without her.

Introduction

A "Still" New "Moving" Image of Skepticism?

The term "cinematic skepticism" speaks of films that deal in audiovisual ways with the problem of skepticism: How does one cope with a sense of distance to the world? "Dealing with" the skeptical problem is different from illustrating a philosophical argument: it rather indicates a manner of struggling or of finding and inventing ways through a problem, using the tools and means specific to the medium. But films do deal (cope, struggle) with a problem philosophy also deals with, using different means (as does literature). What *is* this problem?

In philosophy, the skeptic is usually taken to occupy a radical epistemological position by undermining not a specific knowledge claim, but the very possibility of knowing as such; not this or that belief, but the power to believe at all. The skeptic asks such questions as: How can we exclude the possibility that we are dreaming when we believe we are awake? Or how can we be certain that what we take to be real won't turn out to be a simulation? Under the weight of the skeptic's hyperbolic doubt, the very ground of reality is called into question, just as the foundations of language and rationality may be found to crack. Indeed, it may drive a wedge between mind and world, thus severing our sense of presentness and connectedness to the world. As a consequence of these radical skeptical conclusions, we may feel inclined to either withdraw in isolation or be willing to violate the limitations of the human condition, if that is what it takes to overcome the skeptic's assault. This, then, constitutes the problem of skepticism: given the absence of ground as well as our sense of being at a distance, (how) can we establish new connections to a world without recourse to violence?

Because of its own enigmatic way of relating to the world, film has a privileged relation to the problem of skepticism. Be it in fiction or documentary, the medium's use of automatically captured audiovisual recordings of the world has from the outset provoked ontological and epistemological questions. If early film theorists celebrate the cinema for overcoming skeptical doubt about the power of human vision, recent film philosophers argue that our postphotographic, digital cinema is heading toward a general acceptance of skepticism, as though nothing on screen has anything to do with reality any longer. Without denying relevant changes and variations throughout film history and theory, my take on cinematic skepticism challenges both these views, hence also the idea of a linear historical development from one to the other.

The formal qualities of film constitute a second, if related, reason to conceive cinema as helping us deal with the problems of skepticism and of finding ways to relate to the world. If photographic images, being *of* the world, already evoke anxieties of an ontological nature, their organization *into* a film world puts further pressure on questions of relations among (sounds and) images themselves and of their relations to the viewer. That is, aesthetic choices concerning cinematic techniques such as perspective or focalization, and especially formal experimentation with montage, can be used to express or inspire ways of creating or crossing gaps.

Taking the problem of skepticism beyond an epistemological concern of knowledge and challenging the inside-outside dichotomy it assumes, this study turns skepticism into an ethical concern instead and argues for its pervasiveness throughout film history. It shows how films deal, in their specifically cinematic manner, with this problem of skepticism by bringing together formal invention, creative modes of storytelling, and reflections on the medium. It also discusses the will to manipulate stories and images as a new tendency or dimension within this prevailing problem of how cinema thinks and invents ways of dis/connecting to the world.

My take on cinematic skepticism emerges from the interaction between Stanley Cavell and Gilles Deleuze's film philosophies. The former, in particular, is well known for drawing out the relation between film and skepticism. Let me introduce his take on the issue by elaborating on the following statement from a text entitled "What Photography Calls Thinking": "The name skepticism speaks, as I use it, of some new, or new realization of, human distance from the world, or some withdrawal of the world" (Cavell and Rothman 2005, 117). Both the title of this text and the quote I am pulling from it are, I take it, meant to provoke.

Cavell's title itself alludes to a title of one of Heidegger's later texts—*What Is Called Thinking?* (1952)—which in the German original (*Was heißt Denken?*) also evokes the idea that thinking is called *for*. As Heidegger explains in these collected lectures, thinking is called *into* being (say: provoked) as a response to a call issued *from* Being, or the nature of things. Hence the way Cavell names (*heißt*) *his* essay suggests that *photography* has the capacity to issue this call, to call forth or provoke thinking, and by extension has a privileged relation to Being. Yet the title equally suggests that what *photography* calls thinking may not be the same as what others (read: what philosophy) calls it.

The citation I pulled from this text speaks of a name that speaks of something *new*, yet what it names—skepticism—is about as old as (Western) philosophy itself; just consider the importance of the Phyrronian and Academic schools of skepticism in ancient Greece. And Cavell himself has frequently argued that the foregrounding of skepticism as the central preoccupation of philosophical inquiry marks the advent of *modern* philosophy in the Renaissance. Descartes and, later, Kant *acknowledge* the skeptical impetus in the very act of trying to overcome this "scandal of philosophy" (a point I discuss in the next chapter). So what, we may wonder, is *new* about skepticism? And what does photography—or film as a photographic medium—have to do with this?

In the essay, Cavell offers the following suggestion, which he brings up in the course of arguing against the idea that photography has changed the way we see—a statement that strikes him as equally untrue as the one that asserts that photographs always lie ("To say that photographs lie implies that they might tell the truth; but the beauty of their nature is exactly to say nothing, neither to lie nor not to"):

> People who say that photography has changed the way we see, typically, in my experience, find this a good thing . . . But . . . photography could not have impressed itself so immediately and pervasively on the European (including the American) mind unless that mind had at once recognized in photography something that had already happened to itself. What happened to this mind, as the events are registered in philosophy, is its fall into skepticism, together with its efforts to recover itself, events recorded variously in Descartes and Hume and Kant and Emerson and Nietzsche and Heidegger and Wittgenstein . . . Since for me philosophy is still . . . finding

> its way in the question of skepticism, and since for me the question of photography is bound up with the question of skepticism, I am not likely to regard any proposal as illuminating the one that does not illuminate the other. (Cavell and Rothman 2005, 117)

On the relatively slow-moving time-scale of philosophy, Cavell suggests here, the fall into skepticism is *still* new: philosophy has not yet recovered from it since Descartes. Indeed, it is "still" trying to find its way in its "question"—which is worse, in a way, than being at loss for an answer. But one of Cavell's major philosophical contributions to the question of skepticism precisely consists in his insistence that such a final answer, or a full recovery, is not to be expected. Even the desire for it, while human, is undesirable if it requires the overcoming of the human (and its limited forms of knowing). Such a "drive to the inhuman," as Cavell calls it elsewhere, may well cause another fall, requiring a recovery of its own (Cavell 1988, 26).

Even though the mind's fall into skepticism has "already happened," it is not a particular historical event situated in the past. To Cavell, it is intrinsically related to the very condition of being human. In that sense, it is not unlike the fall the Bible speaks of—the one into sin—which has always already happened and yet happens again to each one of us: we continue to struggle for a recovery from that discovery. Likewise, the peculiar lineage of thinkers Cavell mentions in the passage above (which, beyond Descartes and Kant, includes Hume, Emerson, Nietzsche, Heidegger, and Wittgenstein, though Cavell discusses many more candidates throughout his oeuvre) *do not overcome* skepticism as much as work their ways through a recovery from their own fall into it. Skepticism, we could say, is a self-renewing struggle, one that continues to be new every time it gets at us. Even if we recognize it as having already happened, skepticism continues to be new (or provokes "a new realization").

Then again, when Cavell interrupts himself, saying that skepticism speaks "of some new, *or new realization of*, human distance from the world," we may also take him to suggest that there are perhaps new or other *ways* of realizing this distance. Photography, in particular, seems to provide such a new realization, as the longer passage I quote above suggests. "Since for me the question of photography is bound up with the question of skepticism," Cavell writes there, "I am not likely to regard any proposal as illuminating the one that does not illuminate the other." That photography is *bound up* with skepticism just *is* a new realization of it. That is, photography establishes our distance to the world *automatically*. This is a temporal, or even metaphysical (rather than spatial), distance, as I will elaborate in the first chapter, and it is one of the crucial reasons for Cavell to call the cinema (as a photographic medium in movement) a *moving image of skepticism*; its privileged relation to ontological questions and anxieties is another one.

I will develop or derive my take on cinematic skepticism in that first chapter not only from the Cavellian idea of a "moving" image of skepticism, but from Deleuze's account of the time-image as well. Like Cavell, Deleuze perceives cinema as being bound up with a broken link between humans and the world. It thus addresses the same distance or gap of which the name skepticism speaks, albeit with the important qualification that cinema, for Deleuze, does not do so *automatically*: it is only with the crisis of the movement image that he finds the broken sensory-motor links of the modern cinema's protagonists to correlate on a higher level with a break between humans and the world. Or perhaps we could argue that the movement image seeks to cover or cross the break, whereas the time image rather insists on it (with the gap notably changing its name from *the interval* in the first volume to *the interstice* in the second). Deleuze calls on modern cinema to film, "not the world, but belief in this world" in order to restore this link (Deleuze 1989, 272).

This at once provides the most interesting and the most challenging connection between Cavell and Deleuze. Reading their works on cinema together has the crucial benefit of framing the concept of cinematic skepticism as an ethical or moral problem rather than an epistemological one. If Cavell holds that the world on screen is present to us while we are not present to it (which points at the moral responsibilities we bear in our ordinary lives to establish our "presentness" or our connections to the world), Deleuze extends the responsibility for establishing new connections to the cinema itself. To him, viewers of modern film are not merely outside of the world on screen; they are connected through it to an outside "more distant than any external world" (Deleuze 1989, 178). I will explain that this new connection to the outside implies a new sense of subjectivity and a new image of thought, an image that includes the unthought, or the impower of thought. As is the case for Cavell, at any rate, (photographic) film thus has a privileged relationship with thought generally, and with skepticism in particular.

At the same time, many commentators have interpreted Deleuze's call for belief as an attempt to *overcome* skepticism. In the third chapter of this study, I discuss several such interpretations in order to make the case that Deleuze rather acknowledges the standing threat of the skeptical impetus, even while trying to avoid the skeptical conclusion (as Cavell does in his philosophical works).

My Cavello-Deleuzian inflected take on cinematic skepticism is thus crucially based on Cavell's distinction between three positions: the *skeptical impetus* (which acknowledges the *de jure* limitations of human subjectivity and its ways of knowing, hence the world's "stand-offishness"); the radical *skeptical conclusion* (which infers from the impetus the idea that we have *no* way of knowing the world—it may just as well not exist at all—which implies our complete isolation from it); and the ultimate *defeat of skepticism* (which requires that we ground certain knowledge of the world by overcoming the limitations of human subjectivity, thus implying violence). These latter two radical positions on skepticism—its conclusion and its defeat—are intrinsic to the medium of analog film. However, the name cinematic skepticism, as I use it, speaks of those films that deal with the continuous negotiation between or struggle with these positions as it is played out on the level of the film's narrative and in the use of specific cinematic techniques.

Given this general idea, I feel compelled to add a disclaimer: I will not focus on the many films emerging since the 1990s that center on the discovery by their protagonists that what they took to be their world turns out to be an illusion, a simulation, or different in nature from some hardcore reality. I will explain why, for example, *The Matrix* (1999), *The Thirteenth Floor* (1999), or *The Truman Show* (1998)—films that feature in Philipp Schmerheim's recent book *Skepticism Films* (2016), which I discuss in chapter 4—do not constitute convincing candidates for my take on cinematic skepticism, despite their apparently explicit staging of the skeptical problem.

Instead of these seemingly obvious candidates for a case study in cinematic skepticism, I present comparative analyses of four contemporary films that will, I hope, not immediately strike one as being *about* skepticism at all. Rather, these films *are* cinematic renditions of it. Before introducing these films, let me briefly return to the relation between photography/film and philosophy, which has been picked up with renewed vigor in recent scholarship.

Thomas Elsaesser acknowledged Deleuze's cinema books (along with the simultaneous advent of digitization and Bordwell and Carroll's attack on "grand theory"), as important catalysts for the "philosophical turn" in film studies (Elsaesser 2009a; Elsaesser and Hagener 2015, 216).¹ The recent publications of John Mullarkey, Stephen Mulhall, D. N. Rodowick, Robert Sinnerbrink, and others have in various ways addressed the importance of Cavell in this context, and some (the latter two, notably) explore a connection to Deleuze as well.² All of these studies at once reject the idea of a general theory *of* cinema that does not take the specificity of particular films into account *and* philosophical approaches that reduce films to mere illustrations of pre-existing, abstract ideas. Deleuze has been particularly explicit about this, claiming that film itself thinks, as does philosophy. But whereas the latter does so by creating concepts, film thinks by way of audiovisual creation. Or better still, through its specific images and signs, the cinema does generate concepts, but, as Deleuze writes, "Cinema's concepts are not given in cinema. And yet they are cinema's concepts, not theories about cinema . . . Cinema itself is a new practice of images and signs, whose theory philosophy must produce as conceptual practice" (1989, 280). In other words, it is up to the philosopher to distill the concepts of cinema from it and to render them in a conceptual rather than audiovisual form and framework. Film philosophy, in short, does not impose ideas, but it emerges from the films.

It thus follows that the name "cinematic skepticism" does not speak of a different kind of skepticism than the one philosophical skepticism speaks of. But it knows, expresses, and responds to skepticism differently, just as literature would know and express it in *its* own way. Cavell indeed writes about his take on this relation between philosophy and literature:

> I am not here going to make a move toward deriving the skeptical threat philosophically. My idea is that what in philosophy is known as skepticism (for example as in Descartes and Hume and Kant) is a relation to the world, and to others, and to myself, and to language, that is known to what you might call literature, or anyway responded to in literature. (Cavell 1988, 155)

Like philosophy, then, literature knows skepticism (or it knows what is known as skepticism in philosophy), but Cavell's point here is that, in discussing literature, he is not going to *derive* it philosophically. For literature has its own, literary way of responding to the distance implied in the skeptical conception of our relation to the world, and the same could be said of film.³ In fact, we have already discussed that *more* should be said when it comes to that medium because unlike literature (and other traditional arts), Cavell argues that film, as a photographic medium, is *intrinsically* bound to address skeptical dilemmas. Yet it remains up to the filmmaker, the critic, and the philosopher to turn images ("whose nature," we recall, "is exactly to say nothing") into *moving* images—that is, into images that move us, speak to us, call upon us, make us respond to their call.[4]

～

My study in cinematic skepticism, including the choice of films selected for close analysis, is inspired by two interrelated challenges to a Cavello-Deleuzian take on cinema. First, if the philosophical turn in film studies coincided with the digital turn, as Elsaesser suggested above, an important question remains whether or not a "moving" image of skepticism is "still" new. For digitization attenuates the automatic analogical causation that ties photographic media to their subjects (or objects), as D. N. Rodowick has argued. If analog film is bound up with skepticism because it "withholds reality before us" (to use one of Cavell's powerful phrases I will unpack later), the digital either undermines or doubles down on its force, as we no longer know the nature of what is at once screened for and from us. I will argue in chapter 5 that the *ontological turn*, which Elsaesser takes to be a trademark of contemporary (world) cinema, had in fact already taken place before the digital turn.

Yet I am not merely claiming that cinema continues with business as usual. Based on a combined reading of D. N. Rodowick and Thomas Elsaesser's interpretations of the "virtual life of film" as well as my own experiences in viewing, researching, and teaching contemporary world cinema, I will suggest that "post-photographic" or "post-epistemological film" (the phrases are Elsaesser's) provides a different—say new—expression to a fall that has already happened.

The second challenge has already surfaced in my response to the first. Along with the philosophical/ontological/digital turn, world cinema added another turn of the screw in the 1990s. Until then, world cinema had primarily been conceived as either an international third (world) cinema or a succession of national cinemas and new waves (a second cinema as counted by the third), each of which self-identified over and against Hollywood. The global turn has led to a more transnationally organized film world, which does not conceive of itself over and against Hollywood as such; indeed, it includes many films from its more mainstream directors (and not only its renegades, as in the case of the Hollywood Renaissance). Or perhaps the dichotomy between mainstream popular movies and independent art films (or between a first, second and third cinema) is no longer the most pertinent one to draw (though Cavell already suggested as much in the 1970s).[5]

Although the "new cinemas" that have appeared with the global turn are still often identified by country—such as the New Argentine Cinema and the New Turkish Cinema, from which I discuss examples in the last chapter—the filmmakers associated with them actively pursue transnational forms of production, exhibition, and distribution. More important, perhaps, are the various shared or overlapping aesthetic, theoretical, and thematic concerns that traverse these new cinemas. These tend to be self-reflective: films aiming at a global (niche) audience often feature themes such as migration, physical and metaphysical border crossing, queer sexuality, and other tropes that undermine dichotomies in various ways. Digitization and the idea of simulated minds and worlds also prevail. In line with this, world cinema has, since the 1990s, explored new or newly reconceived subgenres such as the following:

- Border- and genre-crossing road movies (*Leningrad Cowboys Go America*, dir. Aki Kaurismäki, 1989; *Happy Together*, dir. Wong Kar-wai, 1997; *Y Tu Mamá También*, dir. Alfonso Cuarón, 2001)

- Mafia and gangster movies centering on transnationally organized crime and human trafficking (*Gomorrah*, dir. Matteo Garrone, 2008; *Sin Nombre*, dir. Cary Jôji Fukunaga 2009; *Dheepan*, dir. Jacques Audiard, 2015)

- Home-invasion films (*Funny Games*, dir. Michael Haneke, 1997, USA remake 2007; *Lost Highway* (dir. David Lynch, 1997; *3-Iron*, dir. Kim Ki-duk, 2004)

While such genres in world cinema thus tend to undermine dichotomies, the simultaneous digital turn could also be said to reintroduce a new one. For, on the one hand, we find big-budget movies that excel in spectacular, CGI-enhanced, 3D special effects—call it a cinema of simulation. On the other hand, the digital ushered a tendency toward a *new realism*. It acknowledges that the digital image may have attenuated analogical causation, yet this, to put it in the words of Lúcia Nagib, "has not prevented filmmakers across the globe from resorting to the digital for realistic ends" (2011, 7). Nagib perceives a current "resistance to simulation," not by avoiding but by embracing digital technology. Digital technology facilitates amateur or independent filmmakers in terms of both cost efficiency and bulky, cumbersome equipment, and thus it has "enabled the shooting of films on locations and among populations which would otherwise be inaccessible to audiovisual reproduction, as eloquently illustrated by the Inuit film *Atanarjuat, the Fast Runner* (Zacharias Kunuk, 2001)" (ibid.).

The global turn might be seen as a challenge to a Cavello-Deleuzian approach to cinema, given Cavell's qualification, in the longer passage I cited above, of the mind on which photography impressed itself immediately and pervasively: it concerned "the European (including the American) mind." I do not know whether other than European minds managed to avoid the fall into skepticism, although David Martin-Jones appears to imply as much in his discussion of the "masala-image." Martin-Jones, to be sure, does not write about Cavell, but he applies the challenge of world cinemas to Deleuze, writing:

> Approaching world cinemas, using Deleuze, requires care. To attempt to validate Deleuze's ideas through their application to films from around the world would run the risk of imposing already Eurocentric conclusions onto cinemas that belong to very different, context-specific cultures and aesthetic traditions . . . Thus it is not the aim of this book to homogenize world cinemas, grouping together, for example, Argentine films with popular Indian movies as though they were all peas from the same pod. (2011, 2)

Even if I am yet to be convinced by Martin-Jones's claim that Deleuze indeed draws "Eurocentric conclusions" (as well as by his suggestion that the categories he proposes to add to the movement and time image, such as the "attraction image" or the "masala image," effectively call into question the "totalizing conclusions of Deleuze's taxonomy"), I take his lead in warning (myself) against a homogenization of world cinemas (Martin-Jones 2011, 43). If I still group together, for example, an Argentine film with a Turkish one (chapter 6) "as though they were peas from the same pod," it is precisely because they provide *locally specific expressions of global concerns*, as my allegorical reading of the films will show.

If cinema is not a homogenous phenomenon, and if the task of the film philosopher consists in drawing out concepts from the films themselves, as Cavell and Deleuze suggested and recent film scholarship is affirming, then the questions of selection and categorization of course become all the more important.

I selected four contemporary films for discussion, which I present in two comparative analyses (chapters 4 and 6), each pairing two films. Needless to say, these four films are not going to represent the whole of world cinema in the digital age, yet they work to bring together a matrix of concerns. Let me, by way of concluding this introduction, account for my choices.

~

The first comparative analysis, entitled "A Seem-less Digital Skepticism" (chapter 4), connects Jean-Pierre Jeunet's *Amélie* (*Le fabuleux destin d'Amélie Poulain* 2001) to Werner Herzog's *Grizzly Man* (2005). These films can be associated, respectively, with the two opposing tendencies in cinema ushered by the digital turn, discussed above. Whereas *Amélie* takes us in the direction of a fantasy world augmented through digital special effects, *Grizzly Man* exploits the new realism instigated by relatively manageable and affordable digital technologies. The protagonists of the respective films, Amélie Poulain (Audrey Tautou) and Timothy Treadwell, would seem to be antipodal characters as well, as can be gathered anecdotally by the brunette and blond renderings of the same striking coiffure (see figs. I.1 and I.2): one being a shy female waitress in Paris and the other a bold male adventurer in Alaska.

Figures I.1, I.2. Antipodal characters.

Both go a long way to support or protect others whom they perceive as particularly vulnerable or threatened. In so doing, however, one is withdrawing herself into privacy in the middle of a global capital, while the other reaches out for intimacy by isolating himself in a remote corner of the planet. Indeed, their "fabulous destinies," and hence the tones of the films, could hardly lie further apart. Jeunet's feel-good movie ends on such an excessively charming and romantic note—it is, as a *New York Times* critic wrote, such a sweet "cinematic bon-bon"—that "some people are going to insist on spitting it out" (Zalewski 2001). By contrast, Herzog's film, which documents the actual life and death of a man eaten alive by one of the bears he set out to record and protect, reaches a point so gruesome that the filmmaker feels compelled to intervene. Yet what interests me in both Amélie Poulain and Timothy Treadwell is their shared tendency to conflate the fantastic and the real to the point of indiscernibility. I take this as a specific continuation—and variation—of cinematic skepticism, whose significance I will relate to the switch from analogue to digital exploited in both films: *Amélie* invites reflections on analog film in a crucially digital production, whereas *Grizzly Man* takes digital footage to heart in a docufiction shot in analog. Beyond mere material justifications, my analyses of the films serve to explore the political, ethical, and ontological ramifications of cinematic skepticism in light of this digital turn.

In that context, the pun of words in the title of this chapter indicates a dual concern. Both films, I argue, engage (or play with) the digital aesthetics of seamlessness, with a plasticity of the image replacing the cut. I then connect this seamless aesthetic to ideas associated with seeming or appearing. Both *Amélie* and *Grizzly Man* entertain such associations in specific ways. *Amélie*, for example, gives a Cavellian spin on Kant's noumenal-phenomenal distinction when it toys with the idea that a photographic subject is neither a "thing-in-itself" (Amélie in the flesh) nor a mere appearance, which is given an additional spin by comparing the photograph to her appearance on an allegorical digital screen. The film also features the idea of seeming in the sense of make-believe, that is: of simulating, manipulating, directing, and controlling the manifestation of things. I will argue that the more Amélie engages in such efforts, the more she struggles with her sense of being screened from the world.

Herzog approaches such ideas from the opposite direction. The filmmaker is known for his career-long search for "authentic images" that go beyond the world of appearances. In relation to *Grizzly Man* specifically,

I will interpret Timothy Treadwell's effort to transcend the distinction between the animal and human worlds as an instantiation of a more generic desire for seamless border crossing, which is further expressed in efforts to blur lines between the worlds in front of and behind the camera, between a persona and a true self, between the staged world and the world as a stage. Yet Herzog, I further argue, gives Treadwell's efforts another spin and shows how we can interpret them in terms of drawing a skeptical conclusion rather than attempts at defeating the skeptic by transcending the limitations of the human.

Together, then, *Amélie* and *Grizzly Man* display a variety of efforts to tear down barriers that make the world—and our relation to it—seem more seamless.

～

The second case study concerns a comparative analysis of two films, both released in 2008, that start off with a hit-and-run accident. Traffic collisions are, of course, a staple in chase scenes and action films. Yet, for all their spectacular effects, most of these barely impact the lives of the people involved, least of all when interchangeable, numerical entities such as "cops" turn dozens of death-proof cars into heaps of scrap metal (as epitomized in *The Blues Brothers* (USA 1980) and its sequel *Blues Brothers 2000* (USA 2000), both directed by John Landis).

The opposite is the case with the films I single out for discussion, as indeed with so many contemporary films that we might well discover another subgenre of world cinema in what we could call the "collision film." Accidents in these films have been stripped almost entirely of their spectacular value, focusing instead on the long aftermath of the seemingly minor event.[6] I find these accidents emblematic of contemporary experience. Even minor collisions raise questions about individual agents and their personal responsibility within complex networks of traffic systems. Far from being an expected consequence of a heroic escape from the law, the significance of the collision lies rather in the radical unpredictability and high degree of chance and randomness, combined with the sudden loss of control, not only over the car, but—survival permitting—over one's life. It opens up deeper fissures in family ties and touches on profound sociopolitical pressure points. The accidents in such films thus reach well beyond the significance of their own (literal and figurative) impact: they all-but-instantaneously reshuffle the premises and promises of one's quotidian existence against the daunting scale of a global politics, calling for a reevaluation of the moral conditions under which it had been lived.[7]

Such is indeed the case with the films I single out for discussion: Lucrecia Martel's *The Headless Woman* (*La mujer sin cabeza* 2008) and Nuri Bilge Ceylan's *Three Monkeys* (*Üç Maymun* 2008). These films lend themselves particularly well for a comparative case study, as they share interesting formal qualities and unfold according to remarkably analogous plot developments. The respective car accidents themselves take place during the prologue of each film, though their exact nature is in both cases withheld from view. After this initial event, the main characters in both films lose their ability to act purposefully and seem withdrawn from the world. They find themselves caught, moreover, in a claustrophobic atmosphere surrounding their families, especially when their situations get further complicated by adulterous affairs and the mysterious presence of a drowned boy, while potentially incriminating traces are gradually being erased.

Focusing on their ethical implications, I aim to show that the films present *the threat of skepticism* in a specifically cinematographic manner. Both films significantly rely on what I will introduce as the *virtual point of view*, which at once expresses and challenges a sense of distance to the world. Yet *Three Monkeys* and *The Headless Woman* crucially differ in their use of narrative strategies and the ways in which they implicate the viewer (who, like the respective protagonists, becomes subject to manipulation). I will try to distill a new expression of cinematic skepticism from these stories and techniques.

―

A floor plan for this book, then, is as follows: After laying out how my concept of cinematic skepticism emerges from the interaction between Cavell and Deleuze's respective takes on film, and demonstrating how these takes in turn relate to the larger contexts of their philosophical oeuvres (chapter 1), I will present Jean Renoir's *Rules of the Game* (*La règle du jeu*, 1939) as interpreted, respectively, by each of the film philosophers (chapter 2). Taken together, their analyses enable me to posit the film as holding the key to postphotographic developments in cinematic skepticism. Before looking more specifically at those developments through the comparative analysis of *Grizzly Man* and *Amélie* (chapter 4), I will insist that Deleuze's call upon cinema to film *belief in this world* amounts to an embrace of the skeptical impetus rather than its defeat, an argument I will develop in conversation with film scholars claiming the contrary (chapter 3). The reason for my insistence will become apparent when I turn to recent work by Thomas Elsaesser and D. N. Rodowick (chapter 5), as it helps to counter their arguments that the digital and global turns bring about an ontological turn and an acceptance of skepticism. This is where I put forth my basic assumption, namely, that cinematic skepticism is refracted rather than replaced by the digital-global turn. In particular, the digital will to control information, intervene in narratives, and manipulate minds will provide additional turns of the skeptical screw. The digital dominance of culture is so profound that it impacts films that do not necessarily take digital (post)production to heart. In the final chapter (6), my second comparative analysis (of *The Headless Woman* and *Three Monkeys*) aims to show just how deep the digital rabbit hole goes and speculates on and where it leads—or perhaps fails to lead.

Chapter 1

Broken Links

A Cavello-Deleuzian Approach to Film

The concept of cinematic skepticism, as I use it, can be found neither in Cavell's nor in Deleuze's work on film: it rather emerges from their encounter. To draw out that concept (1.7), this chapter will establish a common ground between Cavell and Deleuze's approach to cinema by placing them in the context of some of their broader philosophical interests. I will first outline Cavell's work, which contains the most explicit and extensive investigations into skepticism in relation to the medium of film. While Cavell's engagement with Wittgenstein's later philosophy is generally explicit and pervasive—the *Investigations* inform Cavell's work all the way from the first collected papers published in *Must We Say What We Mean* (1969) through to his autobiographical *Little Did I Know* (2010)—I will attempt to connect the significance of a Wittgensteinian ontology to Cavell's *The World Viewed*, from which Wittgenstein, at least in name, is strikingly absent.

In the chapter's second half, I will turn to Deleuze (1.5–1.6; I will continue elaborating his take on modern film and cinematic skepticism in chapter 3). Almost a mirror image of Cavell's, the impact of Deleuze's career-long embrace of Henri Bergson's philosophy on the two volumes of his *Cinema* book (*1: The Movement-Image* and *2: The Time-Image*) is at once explicit and well established, but it might seem less immediately obvious that these books should have any direct bearing on cinematic skepticism. Indeed, because of the importance of Bergson, whose seminal texts establish a form of *philosophical intuition* that could easily be read as an attempt at foregoing, if not at refuting *philosophical skepticism*, I imagine that my endorsement of Deleuze will appear counterintuitive to various readers. In this chapter, I take up the challenge to argue why Deleuze's cinema books are crucial to cinematic skepticism, not in spite of Bergson's take on intuition (a concept Deleuze rarely discusses directly), but thanks to it.

1.1. Resisting Resistance: Cavell and Film Theory

In the more than five hundred dense pages of his magnum opus, *The Claim of Reason* (1979), Cavell argues that *skepticism of other minds* is a special case of skepticism, and not merely a subcategory of epistemological skepticism. Inquiring whether we can know that a human mind exists inside a body, Cavell argues, requires a different set of criteria than addressing the question of whether we can know that the world (including the body) exists outside of our minds. From this basic distinction, Cavell later develops this "moral perfectionism," which relies on a fundamental difference between moral and epistemological arguments. In that light, the works on film from his middle period—especially *Pursuits of Happiness* (1981) and *Contesting Tears* (1996)—are probably the most relevant to discuss (as I have done elsewhere).[1]

I find that there is an important attempt in recent film-philosophical studies at covering this gap between the two kinds of skepticism, or at any rate at thinking through the relation. Daniele Rugo, for example, argues that Cavell himself sought to reconcile the initial distinction in his later texts, and discusses Cavell's take on romanticism as a way of bridging the two kinds of skepticism (Rugo 2016a). Robert Sinnerbrink makes a similar attempt at linking Cavell's "moving image of skepticism" and his moral perfectionism in *Cinematic Ethics* (2016). In what is to come, I will not engage Cavell's moral perfectionism directly. Indeed, I will focus primarily on Cavell's early "little book on film," as Cavell himself describes *The World Viewed* in its preface (xxv). Yet here it already becomes clear that epistemological, ontological, and ethical questions go hand in hand for Cavell. And when I get to discuss the digital-global turn later on (esp. chapter 5), the question of other minds will re-enter the discussion as well.[2]

While published as a cheap paperback outside academia in 1971, *The World Viewed* originated in a seminar taught at Harvard eight years earlier, in 1963, when Cavell had hoped to draw "pedagogical advantages" from discussing a medium in the absence of an academic discipline and established canon of criticism (Cavell 1979, xx). The time between the book's conception and its publication marks the establishment of film studies in the United States, and the young discipline did not greet the book warmly. For example, Leo Braudy wrote in *Film Quarterly*, mocking Cavell's own qualification: "This little book seems designed to make anyone interested in good film criticism very unhappy" (Braudy 1972, 28).

In many ways, *The World Viewed* is indeed a muddled, convoluted, and "obscure" piece of writing, as Braudy, among many others, complained. But the primary cause for its hostile reception consists in the book's insistence on the importance of reality in the medium of film. Braudy, at any rate, stopped pulling any further pieces from the book after two or three citations to prove that Cavell takes the question of reality seriously—noting that fact alone apparently settled the issue for him.

Given the dominance of the neo-Marxist critique of reality as a social construct emanating from Althusser and the Frankfurt School during the implementation of film theory as an academic discipline, Cavell indeed expected this resistance to what must have seemed an anachronistic, if not retrograde book. In terms of the now commonly accepted differentiation between classical and modern film theory, *The World Viewed* was made to fit squarely into the classical paradigm at a time when the modern paradigm was establishing itself in an attempt to reject the former's preoccupation with questions of art and photographic realism—then re-coined under the header *indexicality*. In his lengthy essay "More of *The World Viewed*," published two years after *The World Viewed* itself and appended to the later editions thereof, Cavell counters the ideological critics with an ironic twist, calling their resistance to the pressure of reality upon art itself a "natural inclination." The inclination here—a "natural" one no less—is to follow a "vague and pervasive intellectual *fashion* according to which we never really, and never really can, see reality as it is" (Cavell 1979, 165, emphasis added). With this objection, Cavell is not defending the opposite view, one according to which we would have an unmediated access to reality in itself (more on that later). Rather, Cavell dismisses the idea that we could "never really" see reality, and that photographic film could never really project it, as a "fake" form of skepticism, one that, under the pretense of a skeptical argument, avoids the actual pressure of skepticism in the context of film by jumping to conclusions. For Cavell, it is *obvious* that photographic film has something to do with reality; it is much less obvious just how that relation is to be understood. The broad ("vague") gesture of denying reality to play any role at all (like the one Braudy was making) is a way of foregoing the discomfort the latter question could cause. In his attempts to resist this resistance to the pressure of reality upon art, Cavell embraces Panofsky and Bazin, despite his own discomfort regarding their "unabashed appeals" to nature and to reality (Cavell 1979, 166).

I shall return to this idea of a fake form of skepticism later on in this chapter. As for now, it is worth noting that Cavell's book has recently undergone a revival, as can be seen from the growing body of scholarship that takes *The World Viewed* to heart, both in the United States and abroad (e.g., D. N. Rodowick, William Rothman in the United States, Stephen Mulhall and Daniele Rugo in the United Kingdom, Robert Sinnerbrink and Mathew Abbott in Australia, Sandra Laugier and Élise Domenach in France, and Josef Früchtl in Germany). To some extent, this revival goes at the expense of his erstwhile critics. Referring to the ideology-dominated period of the 1970s and 1980s by the term "the *October* moment"—a reference to the leading journal in the humanities at the time (and, of course, to its namesake, the Bolshevik revolution)—Robin Kelsey and Blake Stimson wrote in 2008:

> When we entered the professional ranks of the academy, we took up our inherited task of ushering photographic indexicality from promise to myth, of explaining how photography always pointed, both fore and aft of the camera, to its own discursive constructions. But for us recent events have cast the relevance and timelines of this critical project into doubt. (xi)

Retrospectively casting doubt on the ideological critique of indexicality, the "recent events" mentioned by Kelsey and Stimson—they mean the digital turn—by the same token rehabilitate Cavell's insistence on the importance of reality in film. However, Kelsey and Stimson's specific way of phrasing their "inherited task" points out an interesting and, at the time at least, entirely overlooked element of Cavell's take on the movies. As I shall elaborate in the course of this chapter, the indexical quality of analog photographic film stands out to Cavell not merely for its ability to convince us of the (past) existence of its subject matter, but also for the pressure this existence exerts onto human myths lodged deep in philosophical skepticism. And to Cavell, unlike Kelsey and Stimson, this latter ability, this mythological character, is cause for alarm, not for rejection.

At the same time, the capacity for film and photography to tap into human myths (and, with that, into human uncertainties,) relies significantly on the material condition of the analog form. So it is unavoidable to approach Cavell's take on the medium in its current, postfilmic, or postanalog condition with caution, not now for ideological, but for technological reasons.

No longer tied to an automatic kind of causation on the photochemical level, the digital evoked sighs of relief as well as of lament. In *Death 24x a Second*, Laura Mulvey states, for example, that digital film is an "abstract information system . . . *finally* sweeping away the relation with reality" (Mulvey 2006, 18, emphasis added).[3] In an article that appeared around the same time, entitled "The Indexical and the Concept of Medium Specificity," Mary Ann Doane points out how others, on the contrary, bemoan the loss of believability and trust resulting from the manipulability to which digital images lend themselves so well.[4]

Doane addresses an important aspect of this change to the digital by connecting the sense of trust attributed to analog photography to the specific relation indexicality bears to contingency. It may sound surprising to find contingency not opposed, but *wedded* to necessity; we would likely expect anything to occur by chance because it eludes the laws governing necessity. But necessity, in this context, qualifies the indexical relationship that ties a person or object to an analog photograph (whose subject it becomes): whatever occurs in front of the camera at the moment of recording will, ipso facto, find its way into the print. Doane's point is that this form of causality secures a certain believability concerning the subject's (past) existence. "Automatic analogical causation"—to use D. N. Rodowick's term—necessitates that the slightest detail manifests itself in the developed product and may catch the attention of a particular observer (Rodowick 2007, 113). Think not only of the "annoying" details we would now "Photoshop away," but also, say, of the once fashionable but now singularly striking shape of a shirt's design, of a dirty-nailed hand resting on a doorknob, or of any background matter that seems to have escaped the intentional message the photographer or filmmaker had wished to convey.[5]

The link between necessity and contingency, then, consists in the fact that any analog photograph necessarily implies the mutual presence of the photographer (or the camera at least) and whatever he or she (it) takes a picture of; and further that the very desire to arrange and control the setting—if such desire be there—only indicates just how susceptible photographs are to anything exceeding intentionality and artistic concern. In *Death 24x a Second*, Mulvey had called this the *inhuman* aspect of the medium.[6]

This relation between contingency and necessity is implied in Cavell's conception of automatism, which is equally concerned with the supposedly "inhuman" nature of analogue photography and film and forms a crucial aspect of the fundamental relation a film (viewer) bears to skepticism. However, Cavell's appeal to the force of skepticism is not reducible to the (loss of) trust and believability Doane attributes to the digital turn. On the contrary, I want to claim that Cavell's take on skepticism crucially precedes the digital turn and that it is *not* warded off by the necessity that ties an object to its analog representation. This is the reason I think Cavell's "little book" is ultimately relevant today: it intervenes in current debates about the presumed loss of believability in digital photography, not by making a case for trustworthiness of the digital, but by pointing in the opposite direction. The analogue should manage to evoke an even more profound confrontation with skepticism, causing an "ontological restlessness" we ought to take seriously. Far from denying the relevance of the digital turn for my discussion of cinematic skepticism, in the following sections on Cavell, I intend to deepen it.

To grasp Cavell's take on ontology and skepticism in relation to film, we will first need to elaborate on his engagement with ordinary language philosophy, especially the later Wittgenstein.[7]

1.2. Linguistic Confusion and Ontological Restlessness

By subtitling *The World Viewed* as *Reflections on the Ontology of Film*, Cavell does not mean to suggest that he is after the essence of the medium, not, at least, when this is understood as some "fixed, mysterious thing underlying all [its] manifestations" (Cavell 1984, 194–95).[8] And although the subtitle does hint at Bazin's influence on Cavell—Cavell explicitly discusses essays like "The Ontology of the Photographic Image" and the privileged relation photography bears to the existence of its subject matter—the reference to the ontology of film should also be read (despite the sheer absence of his name throughout the book) as Cavell's attempt to bring Wittgenstein's thought to bear on the movies.

It was Wittgenstein, after all, who warned in the *Philosophical Investigations* not to hold on to the idea that "there must be something common" to all instances that fall under a general rubric. Instead, he affirmed that there are likely to be many overlapping and crisscrossing similarities ("family resemblances"), which, like so many threads, form a fabric that holds together even if it is not tightly knotted (Wittgenstein §66 and §67).[9] And he also holds, perhaps more pertinently, that "it is grammar that tells us what kind of object anything is" (§ 373). Wittgenstein uses the term "grammar" not in the conventional sense of an external set of rules for the correct use of language, but in the specific sense of investigating what linguistic moves are (or are not) allowed as making sense. Grammatical investigations involve questions such as the following: In what ways and in what contexts are words actually used in our daily lives? In what circumstances and particular cases do we confidently employ certain expressions, and how do we distinguish or relate them to other expressions? Far from determining the meaning of words once and for all, such investigations often lay bare the conventionality, flexibility, and dynamic nature of language, without, however, reducing linguistic conventions and movements to totally arbitrary decisions. This dynamic aspect, or, if you will, this inexactness of ordinary language is not, for Wittgenstein, an objection against it—it is precisely what keeps languages alive and makes them work. Another implication here, and one relevant to Cavell, is that in cases in which we do not feel comfortable with a certain expression or confident in a specific use of a word, it is not necessarily the case that something is wrong with our (knowledge of a) language. It more likely indicates that we hit on something we do not understand quite as well as we thought we did.

This, Cavell claims, is often the case when we talk and think about the movies. In order to know what *film is*, Cavell investigates its grammar and its grammatically related expressions. Thus, *The World Viewed* examines what we say—or do not tend to say—about photographs, about screens, about projections, about audiences, and so on. I will focus here primarily on the first of these investigations—the one examining our language use regarding photography—as it immediately puts ontology up front and so ties back to the question of reality. What kinds of expressions do we use that should make us reflect upon our knowledge of its nature?

Taking up Erwin Panofsky's claim (from his 1934 essay "Style and Medium in the Moving Pictures") that "the medium of the movies is physical reality as such," as well as Bazin's many declarations along those same lines (as in: "Cinema is committed to communicate only by way of what is real"), Cavell intends to follow their basic assumptions, though he immediately modifies (or moderates) their claims by understanding them to be saying, in his reformulation, that "the basis of the medium of movies is photographic, and that a photograph is *of* reality" (Cavell 1979, 16).[10] Cavell underlines the obvious difference between being taken *of* reality and physical reality *as such* from the very outset of *The World Viewed* by asking: "What *happens to* reality when it is projected and screened?" (ibid.).

Another, yet more obvious, question is then already implied: What does a photographer "take?" Yet Cavell's insistence on the matter soon exposes the fact that obvious answers may well turn out to be so many signs of obliviousness. (This is hardly an accusation, however, given Cavell's view that "the oscillation between obliviousness and obviousness is something Austin and Wittgenstein make philosophy of" [Cavell and Klavan 2005, 206].) It sounds like a truism to answer that the photographer takes a picture of reality. But then the question is not only "What is it a photograph taken *of*?" but also, more pressingly: "What *is* it that a photographer 'takes' of reality?" Cavell then immediately contests answers that come readily to mind, such as a *representation*, or a copy, a reproduction, a recording. In his words: a photograph, as opposed, say, to certain paintings, "does not present us with the 'likeness' of things; it presents us, *we want to say*, with the things themselves" (Cavell 1979, 17, emphasis added). When we look at a photograph of someone we know, we do not say that the picture "looks like" the person it was taken of. We would rather say, probably as we point at it: "That's me, right there in the middle," or, "That's your grandmother just before she got married." Why are we tempted to say that the subject of a photograph *is* me, or generally that we are presented with the things themselves rather than with their images or representations? And yet Cavell warns not to take this inclination for granted either, for "wanting to say *that* [that we are presented with the things themselves] may well make us ontologically restless" (ibid.). That neither of these expressions feels quite right forms the basis for Cavell's assertion that photography and film entertain a privileged relation to (a Wittgensteinian) ontology. He explains:

> "Photographs present us with things themselves" sounds, and ought to sound, false, or paradoxical. Obviously a photograph of an earthquake, or of Garbo, is not an earthquake happening (fortunately), or Garbo in the flesh (unfortunately). But this is not very informative. And, moreover, it is no less paradoxical or false to hold up a picture of Garbo and say, "That is not Garbo," if all you mean is that the object you are holding up is not a human creature. Such problems in notating such an obvious fact suggests that we do not know what a photograph is; we do not know how to place it ontologically. (Cavell 1979, 17–18)

To respond to someone claiming "That is not Garbo" by saying "Of course not; it's a picture of Garbo" is one way of begging (or avoiding) the question just what a picture *is of* Garbo. With another turn of the screw, Cavell asks us to compare a photograph with a sound recording. Whereas we can properly speak of a record of the *sound* of an instrument (which it, ideally, copies and reproduces perfectly), there is no clear equivalent of this in the case of the photograph. We would not with like confidence say that a camera records the *sight* of someone or that a photograph presents us someone's *appearance* or *surface*. This is not a matter of lacking a word (nothing should be easier than the invention of a new one) but of lacking something "to pin the word *on*," since, as Cavell writes, "objects don't *make* sights, or *have* sights" (Cavell 1979, 19–20, emphases in the original). To say that we see light inscribed on photosensitive material does not particularly illuminate the relation between original model and the picture's subject either. I would not say that I am seeing your shadow or light bouncing off of you. The subject of a photograph is neither something emitted (or blocked) by the original, nor is it reproduced of the original; at any rate, assertions of this kind sound no less paradoxical than the statement that the subject itself is present in it.[11]

The discomfort exposed by our ordinary ways of speaking about photography (and, by extension, about cinematography) is ontologically disconcerting on two levels at once. When Cavell points out that "we do not know how to place a photograph ontologically," he not only means that we have trouble comprehending the relationship between a photograph and its subject (its subject being taken of reality), but also that photographic media, far from pointing at a flaw in our language or at being underinformed about the technical nature of photography, point beyond themselves to the fact that we do not quite understand our very ordinary relationship to the world itself. Cavell argues that the pointing finger of photography's indexical nature pokes into vulnerable and sensitive spots on the very tissue of our existence in the exact way the skeptic tends to do. So we need to take a closer look at Cavell's very special take on philosophical skepticism in order to pinpoint the force of film.

1.3. Philosophical Intuition and Skepticism

The paradoxical situation we ended up with in the previous section—the one in which we were comfortable neither to affirm nor to deny the idea that "photographs present us with things themselves"—alludes, of course, to the Kantian distinction between the *noumenal* world and the *phenomenal* world. With this distinction, Kant meant to acknowledge the existence of the thing-in-itself, or generally of the world as it exists in itself—that is, the noumenal world as it would be independently of our experience of it—while simultaneously denying that we can actually get to know it as such. In other words, while we have to postulate its autonomous existence as a logical presupposition, our access to this world is by default mediated through forms or perception and understanding shared by all beings endowed with reason. Kant calls an unmediated form of access to the world, or an immediate apprehension of the sensible, "philosophical intuition"—only to deny its possibility.[12] What is immediate and necessary, to Kant, is the subjection of a manifold of incoherent sense data to the fundamental structures of the mind, which synthesizes them, thus allowing us to make sense of an otherwise incomprehensible sensible realm. Cavell captures this crucial Kantian point by saying that if we cannot know the whole of things intuitively, or the world as it is in itself, it is not because "we are limited in the extent of our experience, but, as we might say, because we are limited *to* experience, however extensive" (Cavell 1981, 75–76). It is not, he adds, "a matter of having more of something we have a little of," but immediate intuition is something "beyond us in principle." For Kant, the a priori forms of the understanding (categories) and of perception (time and space) by definition preclude knowledge based on sensuous experience from being immediate.

In a note in the preface to *The Critique of Pure Reason*, Kant called it a "scandal of philosophy and of universal human reason," that "the existence of the things outside us should have to be assumed merely on faith" to the effect that, "if it occurs to anyone to doubt it, we should be unable to answer him with a satisfactory proof" (Kant 1998, B xxxix). With his division of two worlds and by formulating criteria for what is generally knowable (grounded in the universal forms of perception and understanding), he intended to protect knowledge of the one (phenomenal) world from skeptical threats at the expense of any possible knowledge of the other (noumenal) world. To Cavell, however, Kant exactly formulated *the truth* of skepticism in his attempt to refute it. That is, the very notion of the thing-in-itself stands for the fact that our knowledge is limited in principle (and not just for empirical reasons); for the fact that human capacities for knowing are not finite de facto, but de jure; that we cannot just know that the world or other human beings (and God) exist (the way we may think they do, or at all). This is the vulnerability inherent in the human tissue the skeptic prods his finger in. The skeptic starts from the assumption that we do not normally doubt our conviction that we are actually dealing with, or living in, reality, but then proceeds to inquire just what that conviction is grounded upon. In so doing, she touches on what Cavell calls the truth of skepticism—he also calls it the skeptical impetus—which consists precisely in this recognition of the condition of human subjectivity: the world is not just given to us, and even if we do not continuously doubt its existence in our ordinary lives, we cannot justify our conviction in it either. Yet this acknowledgment of human subjectivity—of our being limited *to* experience—does not necessarily lead to the skeptical *conclusion*, which Cavell is careful to distinguish from its impetus. The skeptical conclusion, arrived at by way of a radical inference, states that the world, or anything in it, may just as well not exist at all: we may turn out to be living in a dream world à la *Inception*, in a *Matrix* style computer simulation, or, in more traditional philosophical terms, we may turn out to be a classical brain in a vat or a victim of a Cartesian evil genius. In his attempt to safeguard us from such a conclusion, Kant posited a world that really does exist "out there"—albeit beyond the reach of our knowledge. In Cavell's words: "Kant . . . really does take the mind as *confined* in what it can know, takes it that there are things beyond what we can know" (Cavell 1981, 78). Kant's safety net of universal forms meshed onto a postulated noumenal world hardly seems to protect against the skeptical threat: our conviction in reality is not ordinarily based on a logical presupposition. The way to really defeat the skeptical conclusion would force one to accept the conditions of human subjectivity—its limitations—as so many shortcomings to be overcome. It requires, in other words, a transcendence of the human condition, a conception that the imperfect forms of knowing have yet to develop into more perfect, ideal states.

Philosophical intuition, in this view, is one way of expressing a desire. To Cavell, however, the demands placed on the radical overcoming of skepticism are no less dangerous than the radical skeptical conclusions themselves: whereas the latter may spark the worst kind of cynicism, leading one to laugh at the vanity of any human ambition and to become desensitized to any impression, the attempt to refute it requires a hyperambitious break with the human condition. (One such attempt inspires my discussion of Herzog's *Grizzly Man* in chapter 4.) Now Cavell asserts that nothing is more human than this desire to overcome the limitations of the human, and he shows his respect to the skeptic for acknowledging the situation of human loss and of being thrown, in the Heideggerian sense, into a world that is withdrawing from us or is perceived at a distance from us. But he also warns against the danger that, in the attempt of either underscoring or refuting the skeptical conclusion, the world may well be sealed off for good, with our isolation being rendered absolute as a consequence. Rather than trying to grasp the world in thought, to demand unity in our judgments (as Kant did) or to build, in Wittgensteinian terms, a "super-order of super-concepts" (Wittgenstein § 97)—an attempt Cavell also coins in the Emersonian terms "thinking as clutching," Cavell calls for an insistence of what Emerson captured by the term *attraction*, a term "naming, the rightful call we have upon one another, and that I and the world make upon one another . . . Heidegger's term for the opposite of grasping the world is that of being *drawn* to things" (Cavell 1989, 86–87). Thus, to Cavell, an acknowledgment of the limitations of the human capacity for knowledge is as important as the acknowledgment that our way of relating to this world is not primarily one of knowing—especially when our models of knowledge are grounded on sense perception.

1.4. Cinema and Skepticism

Cavell finds that photography and (especially) film confront us with these philosophical reflections. In "What Photography Calls Thinking," Cavell specifies this connection as follows:

> The name skepticism speaks, as I use it, of some new, or new realization of, human distance from the world, or some withdrawal of the world; it is what Romantics perceive as our deadness to the world . . . It is perhaps the principle theme of *The World Viewed* that the advent of photography expresses this distance as the modern fate to relate to this world by viewing it, taking views of it, as from behind the self. It is Heidegger who calls it distance; Thoreau rather thinks of it as the oblivion of what he calls our nextness to the world; Emerson preceded Thoreau and Heidegger in calling nextness to the world nearness to it; Kierkegaard and Wittgenstein say, in different contexts, that we are "away"; others speak of alienation. (Cavell 1985, 116)

In a way, photography and film don't need to do anything in particular to express the force of skepticism: it is expressed through the very relation between the viewer and the photographic/cinematic subject. To Cavell, the most accurate way to describe this relation to the projected people and events is the experience of them, not as though they were mere illusions having nothing at all to do with actual people acting out their lives in our world, but as though they were acting or happening *in the past*. It bears mentioning, though, that the notion of the past is used here in a metaphysical and not in an empirical sense. What matters is not that the recoding took place at some specific past moment at a measurable distance from the present viewing, but that the world is right *there*, on the screen right in front of us, *without actually existing*. That is, we cannot intervene in it, act in it, be exposed in it, or relate to it in any other way than by "taking views of it." The experience of film viewing thus releases us of the responsibilities we normally bear for our relation to the world, when we are not, or not automatically, protected by or hidden behind a screen. And that release provided by film may feel, Cavell suggests, like a particular kind of satisfaction. At the same time, while this form of satisfaction is not normally granted to us outside of the film theater, our experience inside it may well be indicative of an anxiety we ordinarily do tend to experience in its place, even if only latently. As Cavell writes:

> Film is a moving image of skepticism: . . . our normal senses are satisfied of reality while reality does not exist—even, alarmingly, *because* it does not exist, because viewing is all it takes . . . [T]o deny, on skeptical grounds, just *this* satisfaction—to deny that it is ever reality which film projects and screens—is a farce of skepticism. It seems to remember that skepticism concludes against our conviction in the existence of the external world, but it seems to forget that skepticism begins in an effort to justify that conviction. The basis of film's drama, or the latent anxiety in viewing its drama, lies in its persistent demonstration that we do not know what our conviction in reality turns upon. To yield here to the familiar wish to speak of film as providing in general an "illusion of reality" would serve to disguise this latent anxiety—as does the conclusion of philosophical skepticism itself. (Cavell 1979, 188–89)

Film, then, is not only a moving image *of skepticism*; it is also a *moving* image of skepticism, as opposed to a farcical image of it that would leave us unmoved (a distinction that will inform my take on *Amélie* in chapter 4). As a moving image it is also a complex one: it alludes to at least three aspects relating to the way we outlined Cavell's take on skepticism in the previous section.

First of all, through the mechanical process of photography's automatism—Cavell's word for its indexical nature—film relates to the idea of philosophical intuition and its claim to defeat the skeptic and to transcend or escape (the limits of) human subjectivity. Cavell indeed argues that photographic media bear within themselves the promise of an immediate relation to this world. They satisfy, in his words, "the human wish . . . to escape subjectivity and metaphysical isolation—a wish for the power to reach this world" (Cavell 1979, 21).[13] Yet this only forms an apparent solution to the skeptical problem, and in fact it achieves quite the opposite of what it aims for. For the film screen that separates (and in that sense "screens") us from the world viewed has the same effect as the skeptical conclusion: it renders this distance absolute. This, then, is the second way in which film relates to skepticism. As Cavell writes in retrospect:

> I described the artistic significance of the motion picture . . . as its apparent and unpredictable solution of the problem of reality at a stroke, by its miraculous neutralizing of the need to connect with reality . . . And I went on to say that this had also not solved the problem of reality but had brought it to some ultimate head, since the connection is established by putting us in the condition of "viewing unseen," which establishes the connection only at the price of establishing our absolute distance and isolation. And this is exactly the price of skepticism. (Cavell 1979, 195)

Thus, film confronts us with the overcoming of skepticism and the skeptical conclusion at once. Cavell himself renders this paradox as follows: "In screening reality, film screens its givenness from us, it holds reality before us, i.e., withholds reality before us" (Cavell 1979, 189).

From this paradoxical situation follows the third way in which film addresses the theme of skepticism. This time, however, it does not do so automatically. It follows, rather, from a perceived break in the history of cinema, which is conventionally perceived as a shift from classical to modern film. Cavell underscores the need for this distinction, granting that it is "sufficiently obvious" that the genres and audiences of classical (Hollywood) film were "drawing to an end" by the time that the world went to war (Cavell 1979, 60), but not without insisting on his impatience for the way in which many postwar, modern films claim to be engaged in some form of "self-reflexivity."[14]

In the post-war period, Cavell holds, traditional genres "no longer naturally establish conviction in our presentness to the world" (Cavell 1979, 60). This, however, does not mean that the world itself is no longer given to us in film. What postwar film foregrounds, to him, is not the world's presence or absence from us, but, more precisely, our presentness to it. An effect of this can be seen in the lost conviction in the originating myths of cinema. If these now seem hard to embrace, it is because "[w]e no longer grant, or take for granted, that men doing the work of the world together are working for the world's good, or that if they are working for the world's harm they can be stopped" (Cavell 1979, 62).

This is not to say that humans have turned into monsters all at once. It suggests, rather, that modern cinema breaks with certain ideas of action, agency, and transparency. In other words, not the world itself is at stake, nor its presence, but rather the conception of our relation to it. This explains Cavell's impatience with a plethora of modern films that feel a need to make the "apparatus" palpable beyond narrative justification, for no other reason than to "reveal" the illusory nature of reality in film. According to Cavell, we really do not need to be reminded that we are watching a film—nothing could be more obvious than that. What is less obvious to him is that, for a camera to acknowledge itself, to *declare*, in a modernist fashion, its necessary conditions and material basis, it must "acknowledge not its being present in the world, but its being outside of its world" (Cavell 1979, 130). Not without a sense of irony, Cavell argues that modern film may just as well turn out to be a form of romanticism, albeit in a new sense: "The faith of this romanticism, overcoming the old, is that we can still be moved to move . . . that nature's absence . . . is only the history of our turnings from it" (Cavell 1979, 114). What the new romanticism of modern film calls for, then, is neither a method for grounding or ungrounding knowledge of the world, nor to foster or undermine belief in the existence of the world (in film), but faith in the human ability to re-establish a connection with it.

1.5. From Cavell to Deleuze

Cavell asserted that, despite our continued *liking* of such classical film genres as the Western or the detective, it had become sufficiently clear in the aftermath of World War II that "certain ways of giving significance to the possibilities of film . . . are drawing to an end" (Cavell 1979, 60). Likewise, according to Deleuze, the movement image may still provide the most secure route to commercial success after the war—it does so today—yet it no longer contained "the soul of the cinema" (Deleuze 1986, 206).[15] In the previous section, I suggested reading Cavell as claiming that modern cinema breaks with certain ideas of action, agency, and transparency, and that traditional genres "no longer naturally establish conviction in our presentness to the world." Deleuze corroborates this idea when he analyzes the "crisis" of the action image: "We hardly believe any longer that a global situation can give rise to an action which is capable of modifying it—no more than we believe that an action can force a situation to disclose itself, even partially" (Deleuze 1986, 206).

Despite this shared perception of a break in cinema's history, Deleuze's take on modern film may seem far removed from Cavell's conceptual and critical concerns. Deleuze makes it clear from the very start of *The Time-Image* that his project (unlike Cavell's) departs from Bazin's preoccupation with realism. Although Deleuze prefers Bazin's *formal* aesthetic approach to neorealism over the more common interpretations of Italian postwar cinema in terms of its social *content*, he claims that both of these approaches tackle the neorealist challenge on the level of reality. To be sure, for Bazin, neorealism presents us with an *ambiguous* reality, which, as Deleuze puts it, "was no longer represented or reproduced but 'aimed at.'" Still, Deleuze adds: "[W]e are not sure that the problem arises at the level of the real . . . Is it not rather at the level of the mental, in terms of thought?" (Deleuze 1989, 1).

The very title of *The Time-Image* (along with its companion volume *The Movement-Image*) must surely be read against Bazin's suggestion that the "fact-image" captures the newness of the neorealist cinema (and, by extension, of the new waves emerging in its wake).[16] Yet I will contest that Deleuze's question ("Is it not rather . . . ?") is merely rhetorical, as it would have been for Baudry: Deleuze's hesitation ("we are not sure") betrays the idea that this first page observation would suffice to settle the issue for him. In the remainder of this chapter I will argue that the unspecified "problem" which Deleuze detects in modern, postwar cinema arises precisely because of a conceived *break with reality*. Indeed, this break with reality *is* the very problem—although the "problem" is here not understood merely in negative terms as something in need of fixing (by way of fact images, say), but a positive condition for thinking *as such*.

Per Deleuze's account, the break manifests initially on the level of the narrative of neorealist films as a sensory-motor break that prevents the protagonist to act or react meaningfully in the diegetic world. As such, neorealism constitutes what Zavattini, to Deleuze's approval, called the "art of encounter" (Deleuze 1989, 1). Deleuze's own theory of the encounter relies on Bergson's theory of perception, memory, and philosophical intuition. While these culminate in Deleuze's concept of the time image, it is not primarily my aim here to explain the time image (and its varieties) itself. I will also bypass Deleuze's deep engagement with Bergson's ontology of the image and with Bergsonian duration; excellent accounts of these are readily available.[17] Instead, I will focus on Deleuze's account of Bergson insofar as the latter provides the groundwork for the possibilities of a renewed form of philosophical intuition, out of which Deleuze's theory of cinema emerges as an art of encounter in direct confrontation with the skeptical dilemmas addressed by Cavell.

1.6. Deleuze's Interpretation of Bergsonian Intuition

In his seminal 1898 book *Matter and Memory*, Bergson provides a theoretical account of the interplay between perception and memory. His concern, however, is metaphysical rather than psychological: the account of the ordinary workings of our sense impressions and remembrance is ultimately meant to argue, against Kant, that the possibility of a direct contact with reality may still be possible. This possibility of a philosophical intuition, however, would require a reversal of the normal direction of thought, so it is in order to explain the latter that Bergson elaborates on the way we perceive and recollect things.

To do so, Bergson positions himself between, or rather beyond, rivaling epistemological theories of *realism* (which conceives perception in terms of mental images directly and automatically caused by external objects) and *idealism* (which states that images have their origin in the human mind and are then projected outward). Bergson's claim that we perceive things where they are—out there—undermines the idea that a percept is a mental image at all. Based on the idea that the perception of living beings is selective (perception being a matter of leaving out everything in which the body does not have an interest, a procedure that prevents the organism from reacting automatically and in causally determined ways to all the influences it receives), he claims that, in its pure state, there is not more, but less in perception than in the autonomously existing world. In principle at least, our perceptions are not automatically filtered or colored through our perceptive and cognitive apparatus.

Bergson makes sure to add that this is the case *in principle* only: *in practice*, our present perceptions tend to become colored through our recollections of previous, similar perceptual experiences.[18] So a second selection procedure is involved here: just as perception, with a view to action, leaves out everything in which the body has no specific interest, so "to act is to induce memory to shrink" (Bergson 1990, 106). Action requires that we actualize only those recollections that can throw light on the present situation. Between perception and reaction, or between received and executed movement, the brain inserts an interval—a gap that Bergson qualifies as a *zone of indetermination*. "Recognition" names the driving force behind the procedure of covering this gap—that is, of relating selected perceptions and relevant recollections. In Bergson's conception, re-cognition is a form of cognition whose function it is to find possible connections between past recollections and present perceptions based on the "intermediate knowledge" of resemblance (Bergson 1990, 158). The brain merely serves a "kind of central telephone exchange": rather than to manufacture representations or to intervene into the communication itself, "its office is to allow communication or to delay it" (Bergson 1990, 30).

For a successful case of recognition, it is necessary that recollection images are not recalled in all their specificity and details; they must be emptied of their distinguishing features if they are to be applied to the present perception. Perceptions and recollections incessantly go back and forth in a kind of circuit, the one coloring the other until they become indistinguishable in a "general idea" of the at once perceived and remembered object. This capacity characterizes what Bergson calls a "man nicely adapted to life" (Bergson 1990, 153). Pure perception would limit one to mechanical movements, whereas pure memory would never allow one to rise above the particular. Yet the adaptation of the real into its practical equivalent amounts to an obliteration of differences, as Bergson points out, since "that which interests us in a given situation, that which we are likely to grasp in it first, is the side by which it can respond to a tendency or a need. But a need goes straight to the resemblance or quality; it cares little for individual differences" (Bergson 1990, 158). As a consequence, Bergson mentions in his most Platonic of moods, "[T]he world into which our senses and consciousness habitually introduce us is no more than the shadow of itself" (Bergson 1992, 128).[19]

This is to say neither that this world in which we act is any less *real* than any other world, nor that anything is wrong with this world in our everyday lives. The shadow world is "only" the real actual peak of an equally real virtual whole: it is what remains when both perception and memory have been shrunk according to the demands of the present. In practice, Bergson argues, "we measure the degree of reality by the degree of utility" (Bergson 1990, 66). But however crucial the function of recognition in our practical lives, it is something else to take it as a *model for thinking* or for knowing reality in general. So, in a sense, Bergson reinforces Kant's claim of a duality of worlds, one "reality as it appears to immediate intuition" and one of "adaptation" (Bergson 1990, 183). But whereas Kant declares the former to be unknowable, Bergson reopens the question concerning the possibility of a philosophical intuition by claiming that the normal workings of the human mind are relative to utility (and hence to our interests and needs). This possibility is premised on the condition, as Bergson formulates it in *Creative Evolution*, that we shall not "import into speculation a procedure made for practice" (Bergson 1998, 273). In *Matter and Memory*, he puts it in the following way:

> The impotence of speculative reason, as Kant had demonstrated it, is perhaps at bottom only the impotence of an intellect enslaved to certain necessities of bodily life and concerned with a matter which man has had to disorganize for the satisfaction of his wants. Our knowledge of things would thus no longer be relative to the fundamental structure of our mind, but only to its superficial and acquired habits, to the contingent form which it derives from our bodily functions and our lower needs. The relativity of knowledge may not, then, be definitive. By unmaking that which these needs have made, we may restore to intuition its original purity and so recover contact with the real. (1990, 184)

Whereas Kant conceives the forms of the understanding (the categories) and of perception (time and space) as conceptually insuperable molds conditioning all possible experience, Bergson argues that Kant's conditions of all possible experience are not absolute, but relative—relative, that is, to the pragmatic concerns of *homo faber* and the utilitarian functions of the intellect within the evolutionary tendencies of the human species in natural history.[20]

Whereas Kant understood time as a faculty of the mind, understanding it in terms of space, that is, as an abstract, empty diagram meant for measuring relative variations, Bergson understands a plurality of different rhythms with different degrees of tension and relaxation to exist in the world. These do not express the relative temporal distance or proximity from privileged centers (according to which "now" can be defined), but, being so many absolutes, they each express duration as a whole in which they partake. Bergson concludes that the possibility of philosophical intuition, and hence of an immediate contact with the real, does not depend on a *suppression* of the influence that the mind exerts over the world, as one might expect, but instead on a *reversal* of the natural direction of thought. For the intellect has a natural affinity with space, which "disarticulates," "parcels" and so "disfigures" true experience, whereas Bergson has it that "intuition is located . . . in duration" (Bergson 2002, 180). We enter into contact with other durations (as well as with duration as a whole) through our own when, being incapable to organize received movements into possible action, we get stuck in the interval, or the zone of indetermination. For time, Bergson writes, is that indetermination itself, or that very hesitation preceding actions that marks our freedom from a purely causal and automatic reaction. In other words, when the function of recognition breaks down or fails to inform our present perception through useful recollections, it translates into our waiting, and Bergson argues that what we feel within ourselves at these moments of being stuck inside the cerebral interval are in fact "the forces which work in all things" (Bergson 2002, 124). The empirical time of the hesitation itself is not the relevant factor; it is enough that the break allows for a glimpse of time beyond the multiplicity of rhythms and movements. In this regard, Deleuze likes to quote Proust speaking of a "little time in the pure state."[21]

It is around these notions that Deleuze's cinema books are developed: the sensory motor break, aberrant movements, the Whole, Time in its pure state. But it was already in *Difference and Repetition* that Deleuze objected to a conception of thought as modeled on recognition, defined there as the "harmonious exercise of all the faculties upon a supposedly same object" (Deleuze 2001, 135). Such an image of thought, Deleuze argues, merely serves to subordinate resemblance in perception to identity in the concept, such that "difference can be no more than a predicate in the comprehension of a concept" (Deleuze 2001, 32). Deleuze suggests that *thinking*, by contrast, requires the ability to grasp difference in itself by apprehending *directly* in the sensible: While representation (the comprehension of the concept) "mediates everything," apprehension in the sensible gives us "the immediate, defined as 'sub-representative'" (Deleuze 2001, 55–56).[22] The immediate, far from being within the reach of the natural exercise of a faculty relating perceptions to memories and concepts, *can only be sensed*, and, as such, it "moves the soul—'perplexes' it" (Deleuze 2001, 140). This perplexity forces one to think, and according to Deleuze one can only ever be *forced* to think. As an activity, thinking understood in this strict sense is always related to the new and must thus be distinguished from mental activities often associated with it, but that are in fact so many functions of recognition, such as (Cartesian-style) meditating, synthesizing, contemplating, recollecting, analyzing, interpreting, and so on. Hence Deleuze's dictum: "Experiment, never interpret" (Deleuze and Carnet 2007, 36).

That which can only be sensed is not a sensible being, although any sensible being can, in principle, reveal it. What it reveals is precisely imperceptible from the point of view of recognition. To recognize an object is to relate it to something already known, to compare it by means of an analytic procedure that Bergson had already distinguished from the process of intuition.[23] The difference between the two compared states is, if not obliterated in perception, measured *between* the object and whatever it is compared to (another similar object; a former state of it, etc.). Hence it is made external to either, and always relative to the prior identification of each. What is imperceptible from the point of view of recognition, then, is difference or change in itself. What Deleuze calls an object of encounter (or an event) is a being we do not manage to relate to anything else. As a result, it breaks our sensory-motor link, deferring our (re-)action as we are stuck in the interval. In an act of attentive recognition, we dive into memory in search of useful recollections, but failing to find such empirical memories, we find ourselves confronted with the limits of the past as a whole, with the being of the past. This "transcendental" memory in turn transmits the force of the object of encounter into thought.

This is to say that we are not thinking by *uniting* all the faculties; on the contrary, we are only forced to think because the faculties are *disjointed*. Thought is, so to speak, left by itself, confronted with itself or with that which can only be thought exactly because it cannot be grasped in perception and memory—it cannot be recognized. "In recognition," Deleuze writes, "the sensible is not at all that which can only be sensed, but that which bears directly upon the senses in an object which can be recalled, imagined or conceived" (Deleuze 2001, 139), whereas in an encounter, the "pragmatic view" gives way to "a vision which is purely optical" (Deleuze 1989, 101). This pure optical vision thus forms one side of the Möbius strip, which folds into thought as its outside.

1.7. A Cavello-Deleuzian Cinematic Skepticism

With this excursus through Bergson and *Difference and Repetition*, it should now be evident why Deleuze cites Zavattini approvingly when he defines neorealism as the "art of encounter" while distancing himself from Bazin's "fact-image." If a "fact" reduces the sensible to an established recognition, the encounter precisely names that kind of sense experience that jams our sensory-motor system and prevents our cognitive faculties from corroborating in an effort of recognition, thereby ultimately forcing us to think. Italian neorealist films are indeed littered with characters that no longer manage to perform a function as center of action: they are wanderers who turn into "pure seers." Consider the children in Vittorio De Sica's *Bicycle Thief* or in Roberto Rossellini's *Germany Year Zero*, or the women incarnated by Ingrid Bergman in the other films of Rossellini's quartet (*Stromboli*, *Europe 51*, *Journey to Italy*) or by Monica Vitti in Michelangelo Antonioni's quartet (*L'Avventura*, *La Notte*, *L'Eclisse*, *Red Desert*): all experience a break of sensory-motor connections.[24] In Deleuze's reading, this is not a merely negative response. As opposed to "the old realism," in which reality was first and foremost a "functional reality" determined by the demands of the situation and provoking the actions of its protagonist (whom Bergson would call a "man nicely adapted to life"), neorealism—and the modern cinema emerging in its wake—liberates the sense organs of its protagonists (and hence of the spectator), who are stuck in what Bergson had called the interval between received and executed movement and are thus confronting what Deleuze calls *purely optical and sound situations*.

Crucially, Deleuze finds this sensory-motor break to be conditioned by a break that Cavell had identified as the pivotal axis around which the skeptical questions revolve. As Deleuze writes: "Now this sensory-motor break finds its condition at a higher level and itself comes back to a break in a link between man and the world. The sensory-motor break makes man a seer who finds himself struck by something intolerable in the world, and confronted by something unthinkable in thought" (Deleuze 1989, 169). Just as Cavell saw the cinema as an expression of what he called our "modern fate" of relating to the world merely by taking views of it, Deleuze calls it a "modern fact" that "we no longer believe in this world," meaning not the sheer existence of the world as such but the link that connects us to it (Deleuze 1989, 171). Deleuze practically defines cinematic skepticism when he claims that if the modern cinema is to live up to its own power, it "must film, not the world, but belief in this world, our only link."

This is not to say that Cavell and Deleuze are simply speaking in one voice, and it can be important to insist on differences. What matters to me, however, is that a concept of cinematic skepticism emerges from the interaction of their respective film philosophies. This concept, in turn, enables me to interpret recent developments of film within a larger context, seeing them as constituting a variation rather than a break with ontological and skeptical concerns in film history and theory. Better yet, it continues by way of a broken, refracted line.

More concretely, with Cavell we saw that the two radical positions on skepticism—its final conclusion and its ultimate defeat—are intrinsic to the medium of analog film by virtue (or vice) of its screen and of its photographic automatism respectively. However, what I call cinematic skepticism proper concerns the continuous oscillation between or struggle with these positions as it is played out on the level of the film's narrative and in the use of specific cinematic techniques. Such films thus take the skeptical impetus to heart, positing that the world is not simply given to or known by us, that a perceived break or distance continues to stand in need of being overcome. But lest we overcome human finitude as such, a final solution to the threat of skepticism, Cavell warned, is not to be found once and for all. So, if we are to avoid the disillusion or disappointment resulting from the failure to meet that demand, while equally avoiding the standing danger of falling prey to the moral nihilism of the skeptical conclusion itself, every one of us stands in need of finding our specific ways to recover each time we peer into the abyss.

At the same time, Deleuze argues that this gap also has the force to open us up to an Outside, to a world more external than the external world, thereby forcing us to think beyond the parameters of the given as well as beyond the conditions of our quotidian lives. The films that take cinematic skepticism seriously thus engage with struggles to find specific recoveries from the fall into the abyss, with protagonists hovering between the embrace of a potential for ethical discovery and an effort to ignore the crisis and recover the sensory-motor link. In the following chapter, I discuss Cavell's and Deleuze's respective interpretations of Jean Renoir's *Rules of the Game* (*La règle du jeu*, 1939). Reading them together enables me to argue how the film forms a specific rendering of cinematic skepticism, a rendering, moreover, that foreshadows the refraction of cinematic skepticism through the digital and global turns.

Chapter 2

Renoir's Key to Cinematic Skepticism

If cinematic skepticism plays itself out as a struggle between the extreme poles of the skeptical conclusion and its ultimate defeat, Jean Renoir's *Rules of the Game* (*Règle du jeu*, 1939) leans heavily toward the former pole. Indeed, it plays out the condition of film (as opposed to theater) as drawing the skeptical conclusion automatically, presenting a world past that fails to lead to a "clarified reality" by finding *new* connections. Combining Deleuze and Cavell's respective readings of the film will cast a remarkable shadow not only on the war that was about to erupt at the time of the film's release, but also on the digital-global turn that would still take half a century to come into full force.

2.1. Film Responds to Theater

Cavell and Deleuze are certainly not alone in observing *Rules of the Game*'s engagement with theater, or more specifically, with "the point at which theater and society are absorbing one another" (Cavell 1979, 225), "putting into circuit the actual image and the virtual image, and absorbing the real into a generalized theater" (Deleuze 1989, 86).[1] Indeed, "that *Rules of the Game* is interested in theater," Cavell writes, "is about as obvious as that Marx is interested in money" (1979, 225). But just as we won't take Marx as having an interest in *making* money, so the power of Renoir's film is not to be found in its ability to *make* theater. Indeed, this film's interest in theater rather serves to explore the possibilities of a specifically cinematic expression by marking its difference from theater. This interest, or that expression, is tied to what Cavell calls "our sense of reality" (ibid.); Deleuze speaks of "a new Real" or "clarified reality."

As has often been pointed out, theater—French comedy of manners specifically—enters Renoir's script by way of explicit borrowings or obvious allusions, from Pierre Beaumarchais' *The Marriage of Figaro* (*La Folle Journée, ou Le Mariage de Figaro*, 1778) for example (which was conceived as foreshadowing the French revolution with its satirical portrayal of the aristocracy just as *Rules of the Game* foreshadowed the impending World War), and especially Alfred de Musset's *The Moods of Marianne* (*Les caprices de Marianne*, 1833), from which Renoir took the model of matched opposing pairs of characters (Bazin 1974, 73; Sesonskse 2011). In the film as in the play, we find types among the *haute bourgeoisie* corresponding to those among their servants: a jealous husband (in the film this would be the pair Robert, Marquis de la Chesnaye—his gamekeeper Schumacher); a faithful wife (the marquise, Christine de la Chesnaye—the gamekeeper's wife Lisette, who serves as Christine's room maid); the despairing lover coming from outside (the aviator André Jurieux—the little poacher Marceau), and the intervening friend (Octave in both cases, a character played by Renoir himself). The stereotypical mannerism and conformism of these types gives "ordinary" interactions a deeply theatrical flavor: actions and expressions appear everywhere bound by social norms and class-based conventions. The sense of theatricality is only deepened when servants and masters mimic one another's actions, gestures, and opinions, and this commingling ("absorption") culminates in the celebrated scene of the *danse macabre*, in which performers of a sketch staged inside the chateau, "spill from the stage into the audience, entangling them in the performance," as Cavell puts it (Cavell 1979, 225).

Cavell, however, focuses his discussion of *Rules of the Game* on another scene: the film's finale, which he reads as an epilogue of sorts. Three crucial events lead up to this conclusion: 1) Christine (the marquise) had spotted her husband embracing a lover (whom he was ironically bidding farewell) and is now hoping to leave with Jurieux (the aviator); 2) The poacher, Marceau, having been hired by the marquis as lackey, chases the gamekeeper's wife, Lisette; when the gamekeeper bursts into the chateau (where he is not permitted to go) to take his revenge on the poacher, both are dismissed from their service; 3) After the danse macabre "spilled over" from the stage and continued an elaborate exchange of clothes and appearances, the gamekeeper (Schumacher) mistakes Christine for Lisette. Fearing that an approaching man is going to take his leave with her, he fires at him before learning his identity—Jurieux—now shot dead.

In the final scene, the marquis tells the gathered crowd of the "deplorable accident:" "My keeper Schumacher thought he saw a poacher, and he fired, since that is his duty. Chance had it that André Jurieux should be the victim of this error" (as quoted in Cavell 1979, 222).[2]

In Cavell's reading of this excuse, the marquis tells the crowd a truth by lying—which, Cavell adds, defines fiction. After all, the marquis had fired (*laid off*) Schumacher earlier that day for having fired (shot) at the guests. To say it was the duty of "my keeper" to shoot a poacher is thus a lie. Moreover, even if we assume Schumacher *mistook* Jurieux for a (the) poacher—which we are not to know—he still did not shoot him "by accident" (a turn of phrase with such obvious Austinian implications that Cavell apparently feels no need to make the point explicitly).[3] But then again, since the marquis was not only aware of Jurieux and the marquise's plan to take off together but had, having lost the fight for her, respected her wish to leave, Jurieux, in his mind, really was a poacher of sorts (indeed, the aviator had been the double of the little poacher Marceau all along). Cavell concludes: "The poacher-rabbit [Jurieux] was expelled, if by mistake, according to the rules of Schumacher's game—not his game as the marquis' gamekeeper but his own game of honor" (Cavell 1979, 224).[4]

Yet, for the most revealing truth of the lie, Cavell pries into the question of why the marquis would accept and even protect such a "foreign rule of honor." Here Cavell posits that the marquis had been afraid of Schumacher from the outset, and had therefore entered into a conspiracy with the little poacher to spite the keeper (hiring him as lackey being part of the deal). He owes Marceau as a result, which the poacher will exploit later on, when he asks the marquis for a return of favors in his pursuit of Lisette. "The Marquis," Cavell observes, "thus becomes the servant of his servant"—a line of thought Cavell pursues with an Escher-twist: "The final result is that the Marquis, as if confessing this conspiracy [with Marceau], enters into a conspiracy with Schumacher, and so becomes the accessory against his own authority" (ibid.). The new conspiracy involves a retroactive cancellation or reversion of the Marquis' earlier decision to fire Schumacher—taking him back into service—in order to cover the accident. That way of *doing things with words* at least makes part of the lie come true. Yet, in so doing, the marquis makes himself vulnerable to the gamekeeper's rule.

With this Escher twist, we finally arrive at Cavell's understanding of the power of Renoir's film. When the marquis addresses the audience with his account of the "deplorable accident," Cavell not only draws our attention to the theatrical angle on the scene (the frontality of the view) and the stagelike situatedness of the speaker (standing on the terrace with the chateau almost as a backdrop behind him); he also notes that such a direct address to the audience was a conventional practice in the tradition of eighteenth-century comedy. In that tradition, so abundantly referenced throughout the film, the epilogue following the dramatic finale was used to beg the audience pardon for any offenses or to invite it to applaud a fortunate ending together. Theater productions, as Cavell puts it, "permit the cast jointly to ask the blessings" of the audience. He then notes that the marquis, acting in the style of a theater director in the final scene of *Rules of the Game*, "speaks alone, in confusion, to, not for the cast; they face him, their backs to us" (Cavell 1979, 220).

Just as the marquis had allowed himself to become "the servant of his servant," "the accessory against his own authority," the society he speaks for (or to) had itself become fully theatricalized. This society, as Cavell writes, is "conscious of its rules but inaccessible to their backing, the fool of its own artifice." When the social role of theater reaches this critical point, he adds, "[C]inema reestablishes our sense of reality by asserting its own powers of drama" (Cavell 1979, 225).

Renoir's final tableau breaches the rules of theater, asserting its own cinematic power in a doubling manner. First it places Schumacher halfway up the stairs, hovering between the (diegetic) audience (i.e., the film's cast) and the marquis. Slightly bent over, his strapped-on gun (with its powerful eyepiece) points directly at the marquis' face (fig. 2.1). The implication is clear: outside the chateau, the photographic rifle rules. Cavell parenthetically remarks that this also explains the absence of the little poacher from this final scene. The marquis is no longer able to protect him against Schumacher.

Figure 2.1. Schumacher halfway up the stairs.

2.2. A Skeptical Conclusion

Even more significant to Cavell is the absence of another character from this scene: Octave/Renoir. In the preceding scene, the poacher and Octave had walked away from the chateau together. Bidding farewell, the latter offers up the conventional comment that they may see one another again some day, to which Octave dryly responds that he doubts it. The response, however, is rather appropriate if read against Cavell's suggestion that Octave/Renoir does not subsequently leave the chateau for another place in the diegetic world (he claims to leave for Paris); he "has taken place behind the camera"—that is, behind the *actual* camera situated *behind* the marquis' audience (hence behind Schumacher's allegorical camera), and indeed outside of the world in which the poacher roams off-screen.

By my count, Cavell offers three (interrelated) interpretations of that move. First, Renoir's taking place behind the camera is a way of declaring his responsibility for what had been going on before it (rendered fictionally by Octave introducing Jurieux to the marquis and his wife in the first place and by having him orchestrate the exchange of clothes that leads to Schumacher's mistake/accident). Second, it marks what Cavell calls an *ontological difference* between theater and cinema: whereas the theater director tends to continue to exert influence from one performance to the next, a movie director has no choice but to "step absolutely aside" once his or her work occurs on screen: "[T]wo screenings of the same film bear a relation to one another absolutely different from the relation borne to one another by two performances of the same play" (Cavell 1979, 229). Third, by taking place behind the camera, Renoir, perhaps most importantly, declares not only his, but also our absence from the world it presents, thereby unwittingly providing us with what Cavell calls "a sense of reality." Cavell explains this sense as follows:

> Films' presenting of the world by absenting us from it appears as a confirmation of something already true of our stage of existence. Its displacement of the world confirms, even explains, our prior estrangement from it. The "sense of reality" provided on film is the sense of *that* reality, one from which we already sense a distance. (Cavell 1979, 226)

Octave/Renoir's dis/placement behind the camera so happens to coincide with the marquis's confusion: rather than turning to an audience with his crew, he turns his crew into an audience, "[a]s if to declare: this production has from the beginning had no audience, none it has not depicted" (Cavell 1979, 220.) Such a declaration is not, of course, to deny that *Rules of the Game* drew a public at all (although it surely was a box office disaster); it rather affirms that, once the film occurs on the screen, its audience will be screened from its world; will not be present at it.[5] That we already sensed this distance to the world before film automatically displaced it for us is once again to say, as Cavell does in his discussion of *Rules of the Game*, that the emergence of cinema did not so much change the way we see as that "cinema entered a world whose ways of looking at itself—its *Weltanschauungen*—had already changed, as if in preparation for the screening and viewing of film" (Cavell 1979, 226). This preparation notwithstanding, Octave/Renoir's final words in the film ("I doubt it") would hardly help us to anticipate his surprise move (in Cavell's surprise reading) by stepping outside of the world of the film altogether—drawing a skeptical conclusion indeed.

2.3. Cracks in the Crystal: Depth of Field

The mise-en-scène in the final tableau, with its foreground (the spectators/crew), middle ground (Schumacher/camera), and background (the marquis/theater director), is a great example of the use of depth of field, Renoir's signature technique, which Cavell curiously leaves unaddressed. It is all the more curious given that this was André Bazin's main reason for championing Renoir's realism. As Bazin argues in "The Evolution of the Language of Cinema," the use of deep focus allows for simultaneous actions to take place within a single take, thus reducing the need to cut from one scene to the next. Whereas montage, in Bazin's words, *analyzes* reality by "chopping up the world into little fragments," depth of focus "reveals the hidden meaning in people and things without disturbing the unity natural to them" (Bazin 1971, 38).[6] André Bazin thus adopts Henri Bergson's critique of analysis (discussed in the previous chapter) and adapts it for film theory, claiming that, by analyzing reality, montage seeks to dictate what we see and how we are to understand the sequence of images. In so doing, it drains as much ambiguity from the images as possible so as to generate a unity of meaning of the dramatic event. In that regard, the Bergsonian perspective becomes all the more striking, as we are now to understand Bazin's claim about the revelation of "the hidden meaning in people and things" in contradistinction from a meaning imposed on them. In Renoir's films, writes Bazin, the "search for composition in depth is . . . based on a respect for the continuity of dramatic space and, of course, of its duration;" indeed it is, before all else, "a temporal realism" (Bazin 1971, 34, 37). In addition, depth of focus goes beyond the long take by allowing a co-existence of durations, each having a unity and continuity of its own, to generate an ambiguity of meaning even within a single shot. This further contributes to Renoir's realism. For as Bazin argues, the viewer is (again: in principle) at liberty to derive meaning based on a selection of coexisting actions and events. By reintroducing ambiguity into the image, the depth-of-field technique not only restores the temporal realism of people and things; it also affects the relation between viewer and screen because "its structure is more realistic" (Bazin 1971, 35).

Unlike Cavell, Deleuze makes much of Renoir's use of depth of field. Indeed, his analysis of *Rules of the Game* hinges on it. Like Cavell, however, Deleuze starts from two observations we marked above: first, the mutual absorption of theater and reality in the film (like Max Ophüls, Renoir creates what Deleuze calls a "properly cinematographic theatricality . . . that only cinema can give to theater" [Deleuze 1989, 84]); and, second, the use of matched opposing pairs of characters. In fact, Deleuze expands the latter idea, writing that *Rules of the Game* "produces a coexistence . . . of the actual image of characters and the virtual image of their roles during the party [the *danse macabre*], the actual image of the masters and their virtual image in the servants, the actual image of the servants and their virtual image in the masters." Then he adds: "Everything is mirror-images, distributed in depth. But depth of field always arranges a background in the circuit through which something can flee: the crack" (Deleuze 1989, 85).

With its nesting of frames, its system of rhymes, its mirroring images of masters and servants, of reality and theater, of the actual and virtual, *Rules of the Game* is a clear example of what Deleuze calls a crystal image, itself a specific type of time image of which Renoir, however, created a special instantiation. We should observe in passing that with this image of the crystal, Deleuze distances himself from Bazin's reading of the use of depth of field as "a pure function of reality." Deleuze counters: "The function of depth is rather to constitute the image in crystal, and to absorb the real which thus passes as much into the virtual as into the actual" (Deleuze 1989, 85).

Deleuze uses the metaphor of the crystal or the circuit (the two are interchangeable) in cinema generally for any film that grows by splitting and doubling into asymmetrical jets—a fundamental operation of time itself, which divides the present into the past and the future.[7] Yet because the real in this film becomes *absorbed* by the theater, because the actual and the virtual form *closed* circuits, Deleuze finds *Rules of the Game*'s crystal to be merely a negative one, a crystal that represents only one side of this operation. "Everything that has happened falls back into the crystal and stays there: this is all the frozen, fixed, finished-with and over-conforming roles that the characters have tried in turn." As a crystal, in other words, *Rules of the Game* marks *the past as such*, which Bergson would equate with pure being in itself and can only be entered by way of a "leap into ontology," as Deleuze calls it in *Bergsonism* (Deleuze 1991, 57).[8] What is missing in the crystal is the asymmetrical jet, the one that "launches itself towards a future as a bursting forth of life": the jet of pure becoming (Deleuze 1989, 88). In *Rules of the Game*, the primary question is not how to enter into the crystal, but how to get out of it.

If Renoir's crystal is merely a negative one, it is also an imperfect one. And this imperfection, this "flaw" in (and by) design, may still allow for a line of flight to lead out of the crystal, for "theater to open into life," for the jet of becoming to split off (Deleuze 1989, 87). This, then, is the crack, "and this is what depth of field reveals: there is not simply a rolling-up of a round in the crystal; something is going to slip away in the background, in depth, through the third side or the third dimension" (Deleuze 1989, 85). During the masquerade in particular, unexpected exits constantly occur in the background, be it for Marceau, Lisette or a variety of other characters (figs. 2.2, 2.3).

Nevertheless, Deleuze remains ambivalent about *Rules of the Game*. Although "one of Renoir's finest films," Deleuze writes, "it does not give us the key to the others. For it is pessimistic, and proceeds by violence" (Deleuze 1989, 85). This ambivalence comes out most forcefully in the crucial role attributed to the gamekeeper for it is he, according to Deleuze, who does not play by the rules of the game. This is another way of saying what Cavell had claimed, namely, that Jurieux's "accident" followed from the imposition of Schumacher's "foreign rule." Following an argument by Jean-Pierre Bamberger, Deleuze explains:

> [T]he only character who is out of line (*hors règle*), not allowed in the chateau and yet belonging to it, neither outside nor inside, but always in the background, is the gamekeeper, the only person who does not have a double or reflection. Bursting in, despite the prohibition, in pursuit of the poaching valet, mistakenly killing the airman, he is the one who breaks the circuit, who shatters the cracked crystal with rifle shots and causes its contents to escape. (Deleuze 1989, 85)

Figures 2.2, 2.3. Marceau (left) and Lisette (right) fleeing through a crack in the crystal.

Various slippages entered this assessment of the keeper's function. As the husband of Lisette (who was chased by a poacher), Schumacher surely has a double in the marquis himself. Moreover, Cavell's discussion of the position which Schumacher quite literally occupies in the final tableau does not support the claim that he is always in the background (nor does fig. 2.2, in which Schumacher again occupies the middle ground). Furthermore, after Schumacher (mistakenly) killed his double's poacher and the marquis spoke of an accident, the latter directs the guests back into the chateau (the realm of theater). Rather than "causing its contents to escape," then, it would seem more convincing to argue that Schumacher had either shot them dead or forced them back in line, leaving it to the marquis to cover the breach of rule—to seal the crack.

In "A Deleuzian Imaginary: The Films of Jean Renoir," Richard Rushton calls Deleuze "quite simply wrong" for arguing "that it is Schumacher who shatters the crystal and opens up the crack" (Rushton 249). He calls it wrong, however, not because the crystal remains intact, but because it was *another* character—the marquise—who opened it up. Intriguingly, Rushton argues that her imagination of alternative, clarified realities (leaving with Octave, leaving with Jurieux) offers concrete lines of flight, which could only be cut off by having a recourse to violence. Even so, the lines of flight fail to lead out of the crystal, and Christine finally falls back in line when she re-enters the chateau at her husband's invitation.

The film, in my view, appears unwilling to follow Deleuze's call that "from the indiscernibility of the actual and the virtual, a new distinction must emerge, like a new reality which was not pre-existent" (Deleuze 1989, 85). Despite the slippages in Deleuze's assessment of the film, he is quite right in calling it pessimistic for that very reason. Deleuze adds that, in proceeding by violence, the film also does violence to what he calls "Renoir's complete idea." He explains:

> This complete idea is that the crystal or the scene is not restricted to putting into circuit the actual image and the virtual image, and absorbing the real into a generalized theater. Without recourse to violence, and through the development of an experimentation, something will come out of the crystal, a new Real will come out beyond the actual and the virtual. Everything happens as if the circuit served to try out roles, as if roles were being tried in it until the right one were found,

the one with which we escape to enter a clarified reality. (Deleuze 1989, 85–86)

Rules of the Game stops short of Renoir's complete idea, which is itself an instantiation or variation of Deleuze's complete idea of modern cinema. The latter idea, discussed in the previous chapter and to be revisited in the next, starts from the same fundamental assumption as *Rules of the Game*, namely, that we no longer manage to relate to the world, which strikes us as frozen (call it a "world past"). But it ends with the programmatic claim that if cinema wishes to restore our link to the world without taking a recourse to violence, it ought to film *belief* in this intolerable world as harboring the promise of newness, of possessing the potential for emergence. To do so, modern film will have to rely on experimentation, exploring new kinds of connections. This, to my mind, explains Deleuze's ambiguity viz-à-viz *Rules of the Game*. It is a film in which characters keep redistributing worn-out roles rather than trying out new ones. But is also features deep-focus scenes that rank high among the most celebrated experiments in cinema history. Then again, the cracks it reveals in the depth of the crystal only appear to provide temporary escapes rather than genuine lines of flight, failing as they do to lead to "a clarified reality."

We could also make that point by saying that the cracks in the depth of field only lead its characters to a relative outside—to the out of frame. Although outside the actual shooting range, they remain inside the crystal, without invoking the absolute Outside—that externality "more external than the external world," which would provoke thought (rather than the imagination). To say that, however, is also to invoke Cavell's reading of Octave/Renoir's disappearance, his absence from the final scene. With his step outside of the diegetic world altogether (the director's work being done), the narrative definitively closes down on itself, marking its world as a world *forever* past. Beyond its own willing, however, the film launches itself to the future by suggesting the refracting of cinematic skepticism caused by the digital-global turn—a point I revisit and address in the conclusion of this book.

Chapter 3

What Cinema Calls Believing, or: Deleuze beyond Skepticism?

I rounded up my discussion of *Rules of the Game* with an opposition between Cavell's notion of a "sense of reality"—that is, our distance to the world (a distance that bears the name of skepticism)—and the Deleuzian notion of a "clarified reality." In calling for the latter, Deleuze may sound as though he seeks to overcome skepticism. Numerous scholars and commentators do in fact interpret Deleuze's work on cinema in just that way. I apologize if, so far, I have given the impression that I do too. In this chapter, I make a point of understanding Deleuze as taking the skeptical impetus to heart, a point that gains pertinence in light of the digital and global turns in cinema. I single out three interlocutors for my discussion: Malcolm Turvey, Philipp Schmerheim, and D. N. Rodowick, each of whom recently argued, albeit it for very different reasons, that Deleuze's work on cinema seeks to defeat the skeptic.

3.1. The "Revelationist Tradition": Epstein between Bergson and Deleuze

To be sure, Deleuze is not the primary target of Turvey's *Doubting Vision: Film and the Revelationist Tradition* (2008). In this study, Malcolm Turvey rather criticizes (and ultimately dismisses) early film theorists who claim, in Turvey's reading, that film has the power to overcome a "visual skepticism" by uncovering features of reality invisible to human vision. Turvey specifically discusses texts and/or films by Epstein, Vertov, Balázs, and Kracauer, all of whom share "near-religious extremes of euphoria about [cinema's] revelatory capacity." (In the previous chapter, we saw that Bazin developed his own version of revelationism, too.) Turvey dismisses this position for being "rife with the sort of logical and empirical errors that philosophers and theorists have exposed and criticized in recent years, such as adherence to the doctrine of medium specificity" (Turvey 2008, 7–8).[1] He aligns Cavell with these early film theorists as well, claiming that he "is only able to renew skepticism about human vision and the revelationist conception of the cinema by taking considerable liberties with the meanings of the concept of seeing and related concepts such as being invisible, being present, and sights" (Turvey 2008, 89). Turvey thus presses Cavell to provide a logical answer to a question like "how can something that is past be present to me?" and he objects to a "similar confusion" resulting from Cavell's apparent ignorance of the fact that "it only makes sense to say that something is unseen or invisible if it could be seen or visible," whereas "by definition . . . we can neither be seen nor not be seen by those in a film . . . For what direction would they have looked in?" (Turvey 2008, 88–89). Whereas Cavell takes paradoxes, aporias, or discomforts in the use of our language as symptoms of underlying philosophical uncertainties, Turvey takes them to be self-refuting arguments that disqualify the inquiry: having put the demands of logic on the table, Turvey foregoes rather than engages an account of Cavellian skepticism.

This difference in philosophical demeanor comes out more pressingly still in Turvey's discussion of Deleuze. Since he arrives at a conclusion far from my own, I will take a closer look at this discussion, which connects Bergson to Epstein before it links up to Deleuze.

Turvey takes his point of departure from Bergson's view that a pure perception is not ordinarily available to human beings: even if we were able to suppress memory's interference, the sensible input would still not amount to an immediate perception of the material universe since we tend to reduce its spatiotemporal interconnectedness to a set of relatively isolated representations. Yet Bergson uses this subtractive (rather than additive and associative) idea to make a case for the possibility of a reversal of the ordinary direction of the intellect. Relating this to Epstein's writings on film, Turvey captures this as follows:

What Cinema Calls Believing, or: Deleuze beyond Skepticism? / 55

> Epstein . . . like Bergson, believed that even though the naked human eye fails to see the true nature of reality people are not forever unable to access reality. Both drew on the Romantic tradition to argue that artists, in particular, possess a special mental power that enables them to overcome the limitations of the senses. Bergson tended to refer to this power as "intuition," while Epstein, drawing on the language of associationist psychology popular in his day, called it the "subconscious" . . . In his film theory, Epstein attributes this power to the movie camera, calling it "photogénie," the revelation of the inner "personality" of objects. (Turvey 2008, 25–26)

The idea that the camera eye could surpass certain physical limitations of the human eye already inspired protocinematic developments. The celebrated case of Muybridge's mid-nineteenth-century serial photographs of the galloping horse settled the question of whether the horse ever had all legs off the ground in the course of this specific movement by taking twelve snapshots in the course of a second. But this case, of course, runs counter to Bergson's claim about perception and temporality: serial photography and the cinematic mechanism generally may possess the power to settle the issue about the galloping horse, but in analyzing movement, they reinforce the human habits of reducing a qualitative inner duration to a quantitatively measured abstract time. Our conditions as *homo faber*, Bergson argued, confine us to the present, which ordinarily determines what aspects of the past will be "called up" to inform us about the present perception.

Although Turvey points out that Epstein (like Deleuze) does not follow Bergson's analogy with the cinematograph, he does insist that Epstein shares Bergson's idea that perception is ordinarily confined to the present. Unlike Bergson, on the other hand, Epstein "tends to blame the *weakness* of our perceptual and cognitive faculties for this, rather than practical necessity," as Turvey writes. Hence Epstein reverts to (nonnarrative) cinema for its presumed ability to "capture a continuous event in four dimensions" (Turvey 2008, 50).

If narrative cinema assumes chronology and sequential events, Epstein prefers an "art of incidences," which centers on "encounters" or "events" in which past and future become visible in the present. Turvey explains per Epstein's own account that his film *The Three-Sided Mirror*

(1927—an early collision film, perchance) features such a crystallization when the protagonist ("Him") crashes his sports car on a country road after being struck on the forehead by a bird in flight. Up to this event, Epstein had intercut a variety of seemingly disconnected scenes, which, in Turvey's reading, now fall in place as a four-part structure consisting of apparent flashforwards and -backs, all folded into a present. While I leave the more detailed account and discussion of this crystal of time to Turvey, I do want to single out his conclusion here:

> That events of past, present, and future are connected and that the film medium can represent these connections through flash-backs and flash-forwards are hardly controversial ideas. But does this mean that humans are confined to the present due to the weakness of our perceptual and mental faculties? Is time really something that we could see or experience more of if our eyes were only stronger, as Epstein claims? (Turvey 2008, 52)

Perhaps redundantly, Turvey responds to his rhetorical questions: "[N]o matter how strong our eyes are, we cannot point to where events in the past or future are or adjust our position to see them as we should be able to if the past and future did coexist with the present" (Turvey 2008, 54). According to Turvey's grammatical investigation, then, Epstein misuses concepts by finding "surface grammatical analogies in our language between spatial and temporal expressions," which, in fact, "mask profound logical differences." Who, after all, would contest that to think of time "like a spatial whole we can see more or less of" amounts to what Gilbert Ryle would call a category mistake (Turvey 2008, 52)?[2]

This is not the occasion to defend Epstein's account of his crystalline "art of incidences," to contest that he embraces "hardly controversial ideas" of flashbacks and -forwards, or to challenge the idea that he "is only able to make his claim about the limitations of human vision and the revelatory power of the cinema through a misuse of perceptual concepts." If I did bring up these questions in the first place, it is because Turvey extends his objections from Epstein to Deleuze, which leads him to conclude that Deleuze, like Epstein, embraces a "skepticism about sight," which the cinema manages to "overcome" (Turvey 2008, 69, 93). Although I will ultimately contest that conclusion, I do think Turvey puts pressure on two interesting questions in the course of his argument. The first is whether time, according to Deleuze, is actually visible in the image; the second concerns the status of human perception (or more generally human forms of cognition, knowledge, and thinking) in comparison to the cinema. These questions are relevant for any Deleuzian-inflected take on cinematic skepticism, as will become evident. But let us first see how Turvey connects Deleuze to Epstein.

3.2. Deleuze as Visual Skeptic? or: Do We See Time in the Image?

Observing that both connect their concept of cinematic temporality to the figure of the crystal (and referring in particular to Deleuze's discussion of Resnais' *Last Year at Marienbad* in that respect), Turvey finds that Epstein and Deleuze share the idea that cinema is able to "grasp and reveal time as duration" only when films employ "nonchronological temporal relations" (Turvey 2008, 95). However, he objects that such relations cannot be perceived in an image and that "the cinema does not . . . reveal time which the human eye cannot see" (Turvey 2008, 97).

In noting that time, for Deleuze, is not something visible within the image, Turvey effectively confirms rather than refutes Deleuze's argument. So how does he arrive at his dismissive conclusion? I think the following passage contains the crux of Turvey's argument:

> For Deleuze, the post–WWII modern cinema directly reveals time as duration, which the naked eye is incapable of seeing. But as I noted when examining Epstein's work . . . the dimension of time is not something that, logically speaking, can be seen, and thus the eye cannot intelligibly be accused of failing to see it . . .
>
> It is not surprising, therefore, that when Deleuze gives examples of what he means by an image of time, it is not something in the cinematic image that he points to, because there is nothing he could point to. Instead, he refers to the temporal relations between things in films. As he puts it, "What is specific to the [cinematic] image . . . is to make perceptible, to make visible relationships of time which cannot be seen in the represented object." But . . . a relation between object A and object B is not an invisible property of object A (or

B) that our eyes are too weak to see and that needs to be revealed by a visual technology in order to be seen. (Turvey 2008, 96; Deleuze 1989, xii)

Among the many nuts and bolts to pick up on here, I want to single out Turvey's significant series of slips in his interpretation of the brief quotation he pulls from the preface to the English edition of *Cinema 2*: where Deleuze speaks of "relationships of time" (which cannot be seen in the represented object), Turvey rather speaks of "temporal relations *between things* in films," which he then further reduces to "a relation between object A and object B." Turvey then makes the rather tautological point that a relation between objects is not a property of one object. I am not sure whether he believes Deleuze mistakes relations for properties (surely an odd mistake to make for a philosopher who embraced Hume's dictum "relations are external to their terms" throughout his career).[3] It would surely not do justice to Deleuze, in any event, to interpret him as saying that such a relational "property" is normally "invisible" because our eyes are too weak to see it—only to hold it against Deleuze that he is making a logical error.

The comment Turvey picked from the prefatory pages of *The Time-Image*—that the image makes visible relationships of time not perceptible in the represented object—is meant to elaborate on Deleuze's claim that "[i]t is not quite right to say that the cinematographic image is always in the present" (Deleuze 1989, xi). With that statement, Deleuze may seem to challenge Robbe-Grillet, Resnais' collaborator on and writer of *Last Year at Marienbad* (1961), who wrote in his 1963 essay "Time and Description in Fiction Today" that its "perpetual present" constitutes cinema's primary quality (Robbe-Grillet 1963, 152). Yet from the context, it should be clear that Deleuze in fact takes issue with a surface reading of this statement only, while embracing Robbe-Grillet's more profound point that a film like *Last Year in Marienbad* presents the spectator with incompatible durations. Indeed, Robbe-Grillet's provocative declaration of film's perpetual present is meant to undermine the very idea of chronology, that is, of a present as the center in relation to which a past and a future can clearly be distinguished. In film, Robbe-Grillet writes, "flashbacks and -forwards are still determinations of a present in relation to which they are determinable as past or future presents" (ibid). *Last Year in Marienbad* undermines such determinations by equating storytime and discourse time (to use Seymour Chatman's terminology).[4] Despite the title's reference to "last year," Robbe-Grillet explains:

> The duration of the modern work is in no way a summary, a condensed version, of a more extended and more 'real' duration which would be that of the anecdote, of the narrated story. There is, on the contrary, an absolute identity between the two durations. The entire story of *Marienbad* happens neither in two years nor in three days, but exactly in an hour and a half." (Robbe-Grillet 1963, 152–53)

It would be impossible for the mutually exclusive images and events in *Last Year* to co-exist in a logically and chronologically ordered story world. One image does not continue to build on a previous one; it rather cancels it out and starts over. As a result, the past and future cease to be distinguishable from the present, and the film does not possess an underlying logic or key whose discovery would allow us to re-arrange events so as to make them fall in place. Rather, in the absence of conventional indications of flash-forwards and flashbacks, all images in *Last Year* are arranged on the same temporal plane, to which Robbe-Grillet attributes the grammatical mode of the present indicative tense. At stake in the image thus treated, Robbe-Grillet writes, is that it "keeps us from believing at the same time what it affirms" (Robbe-Grillet 1963, 151). What we can say about *Last Year*, so far, is that, far from overcoming skepticism, it confronts us with the very force of its impetus.

With that in mind, let us return to the main argument. When he challenges the idea that the cinematographic image is always in the present, Deleuze distinguishes the image itself from what it "represents," claiming that only the representation may be said to be in the present. If the image is not itself in the present, it is because it always already consists of a "system of relationships between its elements, that is, a set of relationships of time from which the present only flows" (Deleuze 1989, xii). The temporal relations are thus no longer organized around a present that would itself be determined by a logically and chronologically organized narrative and its representations. This, of course, marks the main difference between the movement-image and the time-image: instead of inferring the order of chronological time from the movements and logical connections within the film, aberrant movements and irrational cuts bring about an absolute image of nonchronological time.

But although Deleuze speaks of a direct image of time, this time is not anything we could perceive directly in the image, as Turvey correctly mentioned. It is not anything we could "point at," as Turvey wrote in the block quote above, or any-thing that is itself represented in the image (as though it were a spatial entity). Turvey thus aims at the wrong target when he objects against Deleuze with Wittgenstein's comment that we should not mistake time for an "entity of some kind" just because we refer to it with a noun (Turvey 2008, 96). Indeed, far from making a category mistake by understanding time in terms of space, Deleuze takes the specificity of the time-image to consist in time's incommensurability with space.

D. N. Rodowick's recent *Philosophy's Artful Conversation* provides a convincing account for the fact that Deleuze still speaks of a direct time-image *even though* it cannot be perceived (or pointed at) *in* the image.[5] "Time's direct image," D. N. Rodowick writes here, "is not time in itself, but rather the force or virtuality of its becoming, or what remains both outside of, yet in reserve and immanent to, our temporal modes of existence" (Rodowick 2015, 155).

Moreover, D. N. Rodowick not only argues that we do we not perceive *time itself* as much as its force; he further claims that we do not quite see it *in the image* either. It is not even quite correct to situate it *between* the images, or between images and sounds, although such irrational cuts (or "aberrant movements") crucially contribute to the production of incommensurable relations, of "holes in appearances," of the interstices (rather than intervals) of the time-image. D. N. Rodowick indeed uses scare quotes to alert us to this when he writes: "There is movement in the image, of course, which is given as an actual perception in space. But the differential relations 'between' images and sounds are furrowed by a pure virtuality—the force of time. *Time is always outside the image*" (Rodowick 2015, 148, emphasis added).

In the movement-image, Rodowick explains, the outside is the *referent*, that is, the pre-diegetic people and objects in the world, with which the image entertains at once iconic and indexical relations. But in the time-image, the Outside lies beyond the world that pre-exists the image: its fractures point to a world and a people that are yet to come or in the process of be/coming. Time is thus not anything that can be seen *in* the image, but we do perceive its dissociative force at work in, or between, or through the irrational cuts and interstices. For lest we reduce the force of becoming and the return of difference to a simple flow between pregiven states or identities, the impersonal form of time *is* this very "splitting [of] the present in dissymmetrical jets between the past and future" (Rodowick 2015, 153).

3.3. Spiritual Automata and "Properly Human Experience"

Deleuze, then, far from pointing at time as a recognizable object represented in the image, takes the force of the time-image as undoing subjective perception grounded in the recognition of such objects. This, then, raises the second question I announced above: To what extent does this imply that cinema seeks to go beyond the conditions of human perception? For Turvey rightly insists on the important observation—which he, despite his antagonism, shares with Cavell—namely, that the limitations of human knowledge and perceptions are not failures of it. Deleuze seems to take modern cinema as participating in the Bergsonian "enterprise," formulated in *Matter and Memory*, "to seek experience at its source, or rather above that decisive *turn* where, taking a bias in the direction of utility, it becomes properly *human* experience" (Bergson 1988, 184, emphases in the original). In the course of his oeuvre, Bergson develops the idea of a philosophical intuition that would open up to an alternative mode of experience.

In *Gilles Deleuze: Cinema and Philosophy*, Paola Marrati explicates this link between the Bergsonian turn away from "properly human experience" through a reversal of the ordinary workings of the intellect and Deleuze's rendering of modern cinema's enterprise. The cinema's engagement with the decisive turn, she writes, can take on two different directions:

> It can undo the sensorimotor link of human perception both in order to go back toward the acentered universe of movement-images—toward matter not yet incurved by the human gaze—and to go beyond it toward dimensions of time, spirit, or thought freed from the demands of action and pragmatic perception. (Marrati 2008, 40)

The first of these directions, the one going "back," concerns a move from the action-image to the perception-image, which deprives the subject of its function as a stable center of action and perception around which images are organized, putting these images in universal variation instead. Deleuze describes this re-turn to a pre-subjective perception in *The Movement-Image*, with Vertov as the exemplary (though also quite exceptional) case.[6] But if Deleuze takes cinema to engage rather than to overcome skepticism, as I claim, we will rather need to follow the second of the two directions Marrati indicated above, which is not leading us from one modality of the movement-image to another (from the sensory-motor links of the action-image back to the universal variation of the perception-image), but from the movement-image to the time-image.

Deleuze brings up the Spinozist "spiritual automaton" in relation to this second turn. This spiritual automaton is a figure the modern cinema seeks to awaken in its protagonists and viewers alike, yet we do not need to take it for an in- or superhuman being at all; Deleuze uses the term to describe what Schefer called "the ordinary man of cinema" (Deleuze 1989, 169).[7] But just as the "decisive turn" of experience for Bergson primarily involved a reversal rather than the overcoming of the ordinary workings of the intellect, the figure of the spiritual automaton invites us to rethink (and indeed reverse) our concept of the subject and of human agency. Automatism combines with the spiritual in this figure, not because a self-identical form of interiority follows laws of thought and rules of logical reasoning (as though thinking consisted of a set of algorithmic functions), or because our faculties automatically conjoin in an act of recognition, but because the opposite is taking place: like the form of time itself, the subject (with its dissociated faculties) is split, divided from itself by the very form of time.[8]

Through its incompossibilities, aberrant movements, and irrational cuts, the modern cinema taps into this internally divided and fractured subject, awakening, as Deleuze writes, "the presence to infinity of another thinker in the thinker, who shatters every monologue of the thinking self" (Deleuze 1989, 168). The sensory-motor connections and rational cuts characteristic of the movement-image correspond to a mode of thinking that takes informed reactions to recognizable situations, people, and objects as its model. But Deleuze writes with reference to Schefer that as soon as the time-image "takes on its aberrant movement, [it] carries out a *suspension of the world* or affects the visible with a *disturbance*." These severed or disturbed links with the world, Deleuze continues, are "directed to what does not let itself be thought in thought, and equally to what does not let itself be seen in vision" (ibid.).

The spiritual automaton, then, does not help us to overcome a visual skepticism through cinematic images that can somehow show us what ordinary vision does not allow us to see. Instead, modern cinema's suspension of the world "gives the visible to thought, not as an object, but *as an act* which is constantly arising and being *revealed* in thought" (Deleuze 1989,

169, emphasis added). So there is a revelatory aspect here indeed, but this does not involve some "invisible property of objects," as Turvey took Deleuze to claim. It is precisely because of our inability to reveal, grasp, recognize, or relate to an object or situation that the *being of the sensible*, or *vision as an act* is transmitted to thought as a shock. And what cinema reveals there, in thought, "is not the power of thought but its 'impower'" (Deleuze 1989, 168). "To think is not to have thoughts," as Blanchot said of Artaud, on whose concept of *impouvoir* Deleuze is drawing here; it is rather "to touch . . . the point at which thinking is always unable to think: it 'uncan' (*impouvoir*)."[9] Since the concept of power [*pouvoir*] is conceived as a *possession* of a *subject*, it is rendered inoperable when the spiritual automaton takes over. Yet for Deleuze, *impouvoir* does not merely mark an absence, lack, or weakness of power, nor even a counterforce or resistance against power. Rather, it concerns a force of thought to think "its dispossession of itself *and of the world*" (Deleuze 1989, 169). Only on the condition of such *dispossession* can the modern cinema start exploring new types of relations to foster belief in the world.

Thinking the unthought in thought: this is not a likely formula for the overcoming of visual skepticism. If Deleuze indeed sees modern cinema as partaking in the Bergsonian "enterprise to seek experience above that decisive *turn* where it becomes properly *human* experience," as I believe he does, then it does not follow that cinema provides us with a superhuman (audio-) visual experience. Rather, by passing the visible on to thought, and by having thought confronted with the fact that we are not yet thinking, modern cinema bypasses or impasses the very idea that a visual skepticism is to be overcome by superior forms of perception (if at all). Rather than calling on the cinema to grasp an otherwise invisible reality or to provide a form of ocular proof, Deleuze, we saw in the first chapter, responds to the broken link with the world by calling for a replacement of the model of knowledge by a model of belief.

This, then, raises the question to another level: if belief is the opposite of doubt, and a model of belief is meant to restore our link to the world, is Deleuze's call still meant to *overcome* skepticism? While such a question exceeds the scope of Turvey's study of revelationist theorists, it features prominently in another recent study in cinematic skepticism: Philipp Schmerheim's 2016 *Skepticism Films: Knowing and Doubting the World in Contemporary Cinema*.

3.4. What Cinema Calls Believing

In *Skepticism Films*, Schmerheim mainly focuses on recent mainstream films that explicitly (and quite literally) entertain the possibility that the world inhabited by its protagonists is but a simulation, dream, or deception. "Skepticism films," Schmerheim writes in his introduction, "update and fictionalize philosophical doubts about the external world, and therefore can be functionally similar to, for instance, Descartes' evil deceiver hypothesis, Hilary Putnam's brains in a vat . . . or Robert Nozick's experience machine" (Schmerheim 2016, 4).

Based on this general description of his own work, we might situate Schmerheim's *Skepticism Films* at the other end of the skeptical spectrum as Turvey's *Doubting Vision*. If Turvey takes on (or takes down) the revelationist tradition of early film theorists that celebrate cinema's overcoming of skepticism, Schmerheim rather engages the more recent tendency in cinema that "puts into doubt the ontological status of their character's environments by *revealing* the manipulative potential of modern technology" (Schmerheim 2016, 3, emphasis added). From Turvey to Schmerheim we thus shift 1) from theoretical accounts that doubt the capabilities of human vision to films that fictionalize doubt about the very existence of the external world, 2) from an attack on the idea that cinema (as opposed to human vision) can reveal reality to a discussion of films revealing the unreality of the world inhabited by its protagonists, and 3) from accounts of overcoming skepticism to films that draw the skeptical conclusion.

Schmerheim extensively draws on Cavell and Deleuze in his theoretical account of skepticism films, primarily following Josef Früchtl in this respect. But although Schmerheim notes that Früchtl "aspires to a symbiosis" between the two, Schmerheim insists to such an extent on the differences Früchtl nevertheless finds between them that he ends up pitching Cavell against Deleuze, with the latter taking on a position similar to the one Turvey assigned to him (Schmerheim 2016, 147). Along with Früchtl, Schmerheim takes Deleuze's call for a model of belief to be a "call for salvation," an ambivalent call that they ultimately reject: "With the help of Cavell and all the other pragmatists one is able to dismiss this grand gesture" (Schmerheim 2016, 150, quote Früchtl 2013, 37, Schmerheim's transl.).[10] While I will argue against this conclusion, I do want to pick up on Schmerheim's sense of ambivalence regarding Deleuze's call for belief, even if I will take it in a different sense or direction.

I quoted Turvey earlier as saying that he detected "near-religious extremes of euphoria about [cinema's] revelatory capacity" in the early film theorists, which he saw reflected in Deleuze's take on modern cinema. Schmerheim likewise finds that Deleuze's "heavily metaphysics-infested account" of cinema "explicitly carries religious undertones" (Schmerheim 2016, 147). The rather unsympathetic ("infested") and oxymoronic ("explicit undertones") expressions aside, Deleuze indeed explicitly states: "It is clear from the outset that cinema had a special relationship with belief. There is a Catholic quality to the cinema (there are many explicitly Catholic auteurs, even in America, and those who are not have a complex relationship with Catholicism)" (Deleuze 1989, 171, translation modified). He adds, however, that "the crucial point" here concerns a "whole transformation of belief," no matter "whether we are Christians or atheists" (Deleuze 1989, 171–22). Since Schmerheim, like Turvey, ends up claiming that Deleuze overcomes skepticism through belief (a position that sets Deleuze apart from the contemporary skepticism films Schmerheim discusses later), I want to take a closer look at the nature and function of belief and its relation to thought.

When Deleuze speaks of the importance in modern cinema of a broken link with the world that must henceforth become an object of belief, he does not think of cinema as an absorptive medium that entrances its spectators by *suspending their disbelief*, as Schmerheim assumes on several occasions. In his case study of *Cinema Paradiso* (dir. Tornatore, 1988), for example, he approvingly cites the "lesson" of one of its protagonists: "Life is not what you see in films. Life is much harder," adding that a "life lived in and with the movies has the bittersweet taste of escapism" (Schmerheim 2016, 134). And upon describing what he calls the "primal scene" of the film—a child in the cinema seat staring at the screen with open mouth and eyes—he notes that cinema history is full of "such images of spectators lost in reverie." Listing examples ranging from *Sherlock Jr* to *Hugo*, he continues:

> All these scenes reveal ... the ambivalence of a cinematically mediated belief in the world: The cinema as a belief procurement location is always also cut off from the rest of the world, from the rest of life, at least during the film screening in a darkened room behind closed doors that keep out the noises and lights of everyday life. (Schmerheim 2016, 151)

Seemingly contradicting (or paradoxically deepening) such ambivalence of a cinematically mediated belief in the world, Schmerheim finds in the course of his account of Deleuze that being affixed to the dream world on screen is still "a way of discovering the world (and thereby temporarily 'heals' the broken link between subject and world)" (Schmerheim 2016, 152). He quotes Michael Wedel to say that "for Deleuze, cinema is a grand belief restoration machine, the only place where 'the world as an ontological certainty becomes evident'" (Schmerheim 2016, 153, quote Wedel 2011, 403, Schmerheim's translation). Schmerheim affirms as much when he claims that "for Deleuze the shock elicited in the spectator by the cinema reassures us in our belief *that* there is a world" (Schmerheim 2016, 162).

This paradoxical situation, in which cinema's "belief restoration" relies simultaneously on its difference from reality (providing escapist relief from it only for the duration of the screening) and on the ontological certainty it supposedly provides (because we discover *that* there is a world, or that *that* is evident), can be resolved, at least in part, by adjusting our understanding of the function and nature of belief in Deleuze. In particular, even if we were to accept, with Schmerheim, that *Cinema Paradiso* is indeed "an aesthetically authoritative film on the power of cinema as a dream factory" (ibid.), we would not grant that Deleuze takes this power to be the "essence of cinema." Indeed, Deleuze explicitly refutes the idea when he writes:

> It is true that bad cinema (and sometimes good) limits itself to a dream state induced in the viewer, or—as has been the subject of frequent analysis—to an imaginary participation. But the essence of cinema—which is not the majority of films—has thought as its higher purpose, nothing but thought and its functioning. (Deleuze 1989, 168)

There is little ambivalence, then, in the sense that the cinema's ability to restore belief does not depend, for Deleuze, on its power invoke a dream state, depriving the spectator "lost in reverie" (in Schmerheim's qualification) of her (im)power to think.[11] Modern cinema is not *ambivalent*, as Schmerheim claims, because it stands out for its sheer difference from ordinary life, presenting us with time-images as "anomalies" we cannot ordinarily experience. It is true that we do not perceive time-images outside the cinema, but these are the cinema's way of expressing a mode (or "image") of thought we may very well adopt outside of the theater. So cinema certainly is not "*also* ambivalent because whatever it restores belief in is a state of (or at least perception of) the world to which the spectator is not able to return after leaving the movie theater" (Schmerheim 2016, 137). In other words, when Deleuze, in his discussion of Renoir, called for a "clarified reality" to emerge, he did not expect the filmmaker to create a film about a fictional utopia. Far from asking us to believe in a fictional world on screen, Deleuze insists that cinema is to provide reasons to believe in *this* world—reasons that, again, are no different inside the theater than they are outside of it.

3.5. One or Many Crises?

On the other end of the paradoxical equation, statements that seek to link belief to ontological certainty, evidence, and reassurance go to show that, to Schmerheim, Deleuze ultimately takes cinema to *defeat* skepticism, as though belief were to have the same effect as absolute knowledge. Deleuze, to be sure, does call "restoring our belief in the world" the "power of modern cinema (when it stops being bad)," claiming moreover that "only belief in the world can reconnect man to what he hears and sees" (Deleuze 1989, 172). But if the model of belief is to *replace* the model of knowledge, questions of certainty, evidence, and reassurance are no longer the most relevant or pressing ones to ask. As various scholars have pointed out, Deleuze's call for belief marks a turn from epistemological to moral or ethical concerns—a crucial connection, indeed, between Deleuze and Cavell.[12] D. N. Rodowick again puts it succinctly when he writes in *Philosophy's Artful Conversation*:

> The impower of thought may be considered a positive and creative force, but it also initiates moments of profound ethical crisis that potentially shatter our adherence to habitual modes of existence . . . [H]ow do we negotiate these crises, which are less epistemological than ethical? (Rodowick 2015, 159)

If belief replaces knowledge as a model, it is because, as I discussed above, the latter's assumption about the subject and the nature of thinking is under erasure: we no longer believe in an indubitable cogito as the Archimedes point from which all other knowledge could be derived.

Thought on the contrary confronts us with its own impower: far from the idea of knowledge as possessing the world in thought, it confronts us with its dispossession of itself and of the world, that is, with itself as its intrinsic Other and with this world opening up to its own Outside. Thought's impower faces this world in its immanent state of becoming, whose qualities and directions cannot be known and do not follow in any causal or linear way from its past trajectories. Scattering stable identities, recognizable situations, and indeed the very ground of our quotidian lives, the force of time may strike us as grotesque or disturbing; thought's impower, it's "uncan," thus has an uncanny quality to it. It is "terrifying because unknown and unexpected," as D. N. Rodowick writes (ibid.), not only because it unhinges a stable, recognizable picture of the world, but also because the dazzling possibilities to which it opens up have a vertiginous effect: "Between each measure of time there is an infinite movement, so many possible worlds and immanent modes of existence, that we must recover from time's passing" (Rodowick 2015, 155).

This, to me, comes as close as it gets to a description of cinematic skepticism. It is the name I reserve for films that deal with a recovery from time's passing, from a crisis initiated by a break experienced between the world and ourselves, from the wound, opened up by the encounter, that manifests the latent anxieties that we do not or cannot know what our convictions in the world are grounded upon or whether its immanent becoming is to better our future. Belief is therefore ungrounded: it is precisely because nothing in history could convince us any longer to have faith in progress and because the actual state of the world may well strike us as atrocious and unbearable, inspiring cynicism rather than soliciting love, that we are asked to believe in it "as in the impossible, the unthinkable" (Deleuze 1989, 170).

Any reason to believe in it will not be universally valid, nor will our recoveries, which can take on various directions, restore the link once and for all. The transformation of belief brings it closer to a Nietzschean form of affirmation or the faith associated with Pascal's wager than to the "grand gesture" of "salvation" Schmerheim and Früchtl take it to be. Rather than for the overcoming or defeat of skepticism, Deleuze, in my reading, calls for recoveries of crises, which are also so many opportunities for self-renewal and ethical experimentation. A specific recovery will be required each time a crisis occurs, as D. N. Rodowick suggested, and based on the new model of belief, a successful recovery or productive ethical experiment cannot be granted.

Schmerheim appears to acknowledge as much by the end of his chapter on Deleuze, when he writes, despite previous assertions to the contrary: "Even though one might decide to believe instead of to doubt, there always remains the possibility that this belief is illusory or in another sense a fabrication of the imagination" (Schmerheim 2016, 161).[13] Schmerheim seems sensitive here to the idea that a model of belief is a response to, yet not a defeat of, the skeptical threat. Even so, a convolution between the models of knowledge and belief still surfaces through his expressions: belief will "turn out" to be illusory only if it can be verified and judged from a position of knowledge. But the problem of epistemological (knowledge-based) skepticism is that it imagines a stable or static mind-world relationship. This excludes the notion of becoming as self-differentiation and radical newness; at best, it exists as an extrinsic movement running between present and future states of actuality. But as Deleuze writes, "belief is no longer addressed to a different or transformed world" (Deleuze 1989, 172). Just as "this world, as it is," is not limited to its actual state, but includes its immanent power of becoming, so the latter is not to be pinned down to a possible future state, whose future actualization would allow us to measure the "correctness" of any particular belief. The "New Real" or "clarified reality" Deleuze spoke of regarding Renoir must therefore not be understood as a possible future state of the real, nor is it a version of the current one that is known with more clarity, or certainty. Deleuze rather calls for a worldview, or mode of thinking, in which the jet of Being (the pure past) does not quell the jet of becoming—the emergence of the New—which is not yet and cannot be known as such.

Since I found support in D. N. Rodowick's assessment of Deleuze in countering some of his critics, it is perhaps all the more striking that he too occasionally suggests that Deleuze (and even Cavell) is aiming at a defeat or overcoming of skepticism. Rodowick writes, for example:

> Skepticism is the sign of a thought disconnected from Life that consists of a single substance and time of constant becoming. But Being and thought are in Life; they speak with a single voice and become in the same time, such that skepticism must be overcome with another will to power, which draws its energy from Life's potential and self-differentiation, and moralism must be overcome by choosing to believe in the ever-renewable possibility of beginning again—eternal recurrence. (Rodowick 2015, 179)

D. N. Rodowick thus addresses the Deleuzian dictum that "Life will no longer be made to appear before the categories of thought; thought will be thrown into the categories of Life," whereby Life is understood precisely as standing reserve, potential energy, and difference in itself (Deleuze 1989, 189). Yet despite this imperative "that skepticism must be overcome," D. N. Rodowick affirms that such overcoming involves a belief in "the ever-renewable possibility of beginning again," which is not only affirmed as a force of Life, but also as an ethical attitude. So when he confirms that "Cavell and Deleuze share a conception of philosophy that seeks to recover itself from Cartesian skeptical dilemmas," he adds:

> Our responsiveness to the world will not be rekindled only by believing again in Life and our connection to the world; it also requires that we find strategies for reanimating our deadened or alienated relations with the world and with others, and to do so as a daily practice. (Rodowick 2015, 203)

The implication here is that a reestablished connection with the world, if achieved, will require continuous attention through daily practice, as the "ever-renewable possibility of beginning again" is accompanied by the eternal recurrence of the skeptical threat, that is, with the impending danger of breaking that fragile link again. This much I would assert: if we were to manage to believe in the world again, we would at least have avoided falling prey to the skeptical conclusion. But if this requires a daily practice indeed, it is precisely because the skeptical threat—its impetus, which is inherent in our groundless and limited mode of existence—has not been defeated or overcome, but rather embraced.

For the same reason, modern cinema has not simply come to an end by showing us how to reestablish our connection to the world. Indeed, we may wonder whether there is still some lingering ambiguity here, which troubled Schmerheim and which we already found in Deleuze himself viz-à-viz *Rules of the Game*. For it remains an unresolved question just how the modern cinema would "film belief" such that it could help to restore our link to the world. And how are we to translate (or transform) cinematic strategies, such as the use of deep focus, irrational cuts, or incommensurable relations between sound and image, back to strategies for our daily lives?

Surely, the cinema is not to provide a manual for Life—we do not need (cinema for) that. Nor does it simply solve a connectivity problem, so to speak, as though the skeptical threat were the spiritual equivalent of a mere technical issue for a solution must exist. Again, I take those films to be "moving images of skepticism" that, through their stories and the use of specific cinematic techniques, deal with struggles to recover from a broken link and its subsequent ethical crisis. Skepticism films share the premise that the world will be dead to us once we turn away from it, yet each features a specific encounter with it and tries out specific recoveries from it.

Not all films (or even the majority of films) engage skepticism in just this way. Indeed, films that perhaps most explicitly seem to deal with skepticism are in my view not the most likely candidates to be listed. This is the case, for example, with the ones that feature in Schmerheim's case studies on "external world skepticism films"—*The Matrix*, *The Thirteenth Floor*, and *The Truman Show*. Of these, Schmerheim writes:

> Even though all three films are built on a multi-layered diegesis, they rely on different diegetic ontologies: While *The Matrix* and *The Thirteenth Floor* at least initially contrast one or more simulated worlds with one outer layer or level of physical reality, *The Truman Show* contrasts an isolated part of physical reality (the TV studio) with the rest of the physical world as we know it. (Schmerheim 2016, 229)

Despite these differences, each of the three films stages an encounter with "the outer layer," with physical reality "as we know it," or with the "real world" (which is pointedly indicated as capital "R" in Schmerheim's diagramed representations of the films' diegetic structures). These films do not actually stage the skeptical conclusion but a trapped way of defeating it. The true epistemological skeptic does not care to disclose the unreality of the world (or disclose its reality *as* simulation or TV show) as much as doubt the reality of any outer layer. Moreover, the films under discussion stage skepticism primarily as a problem of knowledge rather than of ethics or belief. As such, they imply a stable mind-world relationship; call it a static rather than a moving image of skepticism. Since the criteria for knowledge in these films, furthermore, are not ones that apply anywhere outside of their diegetic worlds, "external world skepticism films" appear to me subject to the fault Schmerheim (inaccurately) finds with Deleuze.[14]

The concept of cinematic skepticism as I use it is not meant to classify or organize film history. Rather than forming a (sub-)genre of films representing a (pre-existing) philosophical idea, cinematic skepticism emerges as a problematic that is at once pervasive in its scope and often surprising in its manifestation. It runs deep and wide throughout film history, yet it would often go unnoticed were it not for criticism to draw it out. Rather than limiting itself to the epistemological concern with certainty of knowledge, cinematic skepticism premises that any relation to the world, if it is to be had, is not primarily going to be based on knowledge or grounded in ocular truth. It rather posits that films are called upon to create new links to the world despite their supposed material grounding in reality.

That a catch-all solution for restoring a broken link to the world is not to be expected is evident from the impressive scope and unexpected choice of films Cavell discusses in this context, which range from *The Wizard of Oz* (Victor Fleming and George Cukor, 1939) to Dusan Makavejev's *Sweet Movie* (1973), and from Carl Theodor Dreyer's *The Passion of Joan of Arc* (1928) or *Gertrud* (1964) to entire (self-invented) genres within the classical Hollywood tradition—to say nothing of Deleuze's enormous arsenal and complex classification of films cited. It is not my aim here to generate a map of skepticism films, but to claim that its sheer pervasiveness and ongoing prevalence underscores the idea that the threat of skepticism requires a continuous practice rather than an encompassing solution. In this I am led by my intuition that cinematic skepticism does not result from the mutually implied digital and global turns in the 1990s, yet tends to respond to it, refracting (and only in that sense "breaking") its course at the interface of old and new media.

In the next chapter, I take a start at marking this refraction by way of a comparative analysis of two films situated at this interface: Jean-Pierre Jeunet's *Amélie* (*Le fabuleux destin d'Amélie Poulain*, 2001) and Werner Herzog's *Grizzly Man* (2005). If that pairing sounds surprising, as I hope it does, we may well come across a characteristic of cinematic skepticism.

Chapter 4

A Seem-less Digital Skepticism in *Grizzly Man* and *Amélie*

Jean Renoir's crystal threw a shadow onto the interface of old and new media, I postulated, by forming circuits between the actual and the virtual and by commenting on reality's absorption into theater. Renoir did not seem to allow for a way out of the crystal, despite its various cracks. The films I will discuss in this chapter form circuits of similar structure, albeit of a different substance.

4.1. Herzog's Docufiction

Although not a new phenomenon as such, the genre of the docufiction film has grown spectacularly since the global and digital turns in the 1990s. Retrospectively attributed to the practices of such diverse filmmakers as Robert Flaherty, Jean Rouch, or Abbas Kiarostami, the genre, as the name suggests, applies to hybrid films that cross the traditional division of films between fiction and documentary. This may happen in a variety of ways, for example, because fictional stories spill over into real life or because staged performances are introduced into documentaries, though its most fascinating instances combine several of these broad tendencies. The docufiction genre generally, and Werner Herzog's recent films in particular, form crystals of a special kind.[1]

Herzog himself, as is well known, has long resisted the division of his oeuvre into fictional and nonfictional films ("it's all just movies").[2] He proudly denied his films officially labeled as documentaries their very documentary status because of his refusal to avoid what Brad Prager straightforwardly calls "deliberate fabrication." Herzog, he writes, "stages, invents and scripts dialogue for them" (Prager 7), just as he often actively participates or intervenes in his films. This conflation of the fictional and the documentary also works the other way around: in Herzog's fiction features, conditions of production inform the story itself. Thus, in *Aguirre, the Wrath of God* (1972), the literal exhaustion of and fights among members of crew and cast spell the energetic draining and spiritual deflation of a fictional group of gold diggers in the Amazonian rain forest. This invasion of the real in the fictional reaches a point of indiscernibility in *Fitzcarraldo* (1982), in which the failure to haul a 320-ton steamship over a steep hill is both part of film production and the central action within the film itself. At its best moments, it is all but impossible for the viewer to tell whether any given incident or accident took place in the diegetic world, on the set, or both at once. As Alan Singer pointed out, Herzog himself made sure to add another turn of the screw by boasting about *Aguirre's* strenuous efforts of real people in a real jungle, "not because it is real, but, in his own words, because it *looks like* the exorbitant Hollywood spectacle" (Singer 1986, 204, emphasis in the original).³

In short, Herzog has long contaminated the separation between the fictional and nonfictional and the thereby implied distinctions between the rehearsed and the improvised, the deliberate and the accidental, the controlled and the contingent, and so on. Commenting on his recent films in his 1999 "Minnesota Declaration: On Truth and Fact in Documentary Cinema," Herzog appears to take Deleuze's dictum to heart by privileging the "mysterious and elusive" "poetic truth" of performative documentary, which emerges through formal experimentation, over the "truth of accountants" conveyed by supposedly objective, observational documentaries recording anterior truths (Herzog 1999).⁴

With his 2008 film *Grizzly Man*, officially labeled as documentary, we can connect such contaminating strategies to the dichotomy between opposite tendencies ushered in by the digital turn. One of these tendencies is to move in the direction of the fantastic: the big-budget cinema of simulation with its computer-generated special effects. Later in this chapter, I will discuss *Amélie* as providing a twist to this tendency. The other tendency, enabled by affordable and manageable digital equipment, goes in the opposite direction, towards a new realism, which was so

A Seem-less Digital Skepticism in *Grizzly Man* and *Amélie* / 75

"eloquently illustrated," I already quoted Lúcia Nagib in my introduction as saying, "by the Inuit film *Atanarjuat, the Fast Runner*."

Timothy Treadwell's more than one hundred hours of footage taken with his digital video cameras in a remote Alaskan peninsula over the course of five summers might well form another illustration of this tendency. But this case is complicated by the fact that the "eloquence" of his material in *Grizzly Man* was provided by Werner Herzog, who adapted these raw materials for his own purposes. He not only selected and edited Treadwell's unorganized database of footage (with the help of a four-headed team); he also accompanies the footage with his own voice-over and intersperses it with interviews of people commenting on the life and death of its maker. To turn the tables, we could put it with Seung-hoon Jeong and Dudley Andrew as follows:

> [L]et us not pretend otherwise: *Grizzly Man* is a commercial feature film, a fully cultural enterprise . . . but with a difference. The indigestible footage in its belly gives *Grizzly Man* the nightmare of losing control . . . At the center of Herzog's professional film lies Treadwell's wild video. (Jeong and Andrew 4)

With *Grizzly Man*, then, the contamination of the fictional and nonfictional lines up with the dynamic between commercial professionalism and amateur filmmaking, a distinction expressed in the fact that Treadwell's footage was shot on a DVCAM, whereas the final product was printed on 35mm.

In the next section, I will center my discussion on *Grizzly Man* and what Jeong and Andrew call its "nightmare of losing control"—a fear I relate to the digital turn and to contemporary cinematic skepticism. To establish this, I will explain how *Grizzly Man*, in spite of Treadwell's use of the digital video camera, is entirely premised on the "good old" notions of photographic indexicality and automatism.

4.2. *Grizzly Man*'s Invisible Lines

From the very first scene, it is clear that the raw video footage of wild nature—impressive as that may be—does not of itself generate the disturbing force of the film, nor even can Treadwell's shocking proximity to the grizzlies account for it. During the film's long first take, Treadwell, having secured the camera on its tripod, kneels down in front of it while a giant grizzly roams not too far behind him. Treadwell talks directly into the camera to tell the implied viewer how the bear could easily tear him to pieces if he were to show weakness (theatrically pointing at the lens to stress *weakness*). While that might ordinarily be taken as a statement of fact, here it should be clear that the force of the scene is entirely and morbidly ironic, premised as it is on the viewer's knowledge of Treadwell's fate in relation to such statements as these. Jeong and Andrew bring Roland Barthes's paradoxical definition of the punctum to bear on the scene to bring the point home: To the viewer of *Grizzly Man*, Treadwell "is dead and he is going to die" (Jeong and Andrew 2008, 9; Barthes 1981, 95).[5] And he is going to die—has died—in pretty much the exact way described here. Treadwell indeed comes to impersonate Barthes's dictum as his fiery monologue slips from one grammatical tense to another: "For once there *is* weakness, they *will* exploit it, they *will* take me out, they *will* decapitate me, they *will* cut me into bits and pieces . . . *I'm* dead." And a little later: "No one *knew* that. No one ever freakin' *knew* that there *are* times when my life is *on the precipice* of death." Treadwell ends his monologue saying, "I will die for *them*, but I will *not* die at their claws and paws," only to add when he walks out of the frame to lift the camera off its tripod, "I can smell death all over my fingers." Although Herzog refrains from imposing his voice-over onto the scene, he does momentarily insert a discrete text with Treadwell's name, and his year of birth and year of death, to ensure that a potentially uninformed first-time viewer won't miss out on the morbid irony intended here (fig. 4.1).

Herzog's voice-over *does* occur in the subsequent edited sequence of closeups of bears—shots that are further accompanied by the relaxed (if subdued) guitar riffs delivered by Richard Thompson and Henry Kaiser, but in which Treadwell himself is not present. As narrator, Herzog introduces Treadwell and his footage, in which, he says, he discovered beyond a wildlife film "a story of human ecstasies and darkest inner turmoil, as if there was a desire in [Treadwell] to leave the confinements of his humanness and bond with the bears." Meanwhile, one of the younger bears is seen sniffing and poking at the camera. Herzog continues: "Treadwell reached out, seeking a primordial encounter." Suddenly, and quite shockingly, Treadwell's hand now appears from underneath the camera, his finger touching the bear's nose (fig. 4.2).

A Seem-less Digital Skepticism in *Grizzly Man* and *Amélie* / 77

Figure 4.1. Herzog's text over Treadwell's footage.

With an invisible transition, the finger then turns from a physical point of contact to an indexical sign pointing beyond the bear to a place where it should (and soon will) be. "Go back and play," we hear Treadwell's child-imitation voice say. Herzog takes over to contrast it with his own, more serious tone, which continues where it broke off:

Figure 4.2. "Treadwell reached out . . ."

"But in doing so, he crossed an invisible borderline." The guitar riffs, having grown discordant, suddenly stop when the scene cuts to a bear growling and snapping threateningly at the camera. The bear backs off at the sound of Treadwell's command: "Go back!"

These two opening scenes perfectly set the stage for the film as a whole. The dynamic interaction between the images and the voices, including the sheer difference between Treadwell's voice-off and Herzog's voice-over, invites us to read the film as a commentary on filmmaking generally, and on cinematic skepticism in particular.

Most relevant in the latter regard, so far, is Treadwell's attempt at reaching out "to seek a primordial encounter," leaving "the confinements of his humanness" behind, as Herzog called it. To seek to cross an invisible borderline between the animal and human worlds, overcoming our distance to the natural, is one way of expressing the desire to defeat skepticism. Moreover, the crossing of that invisible borderline is given cinematic significance by coinciding with the finger crossing from the world behind the camera to the one in front of it—linking the world to the world screened, say. On one level, the appearance of Treadwell's hand, pointing to touch the bear's nose, *declares* his physical presence (already *suggested* by the handheld camera). But on another, it reveals the presence of the screen, of the metaphysical abyss that prevents the viewer from touching that nose (unfortunately) or from its snout to touch us (fortunately), whereas Treadwell needs to rely on his voice and the force of the index to ward off the latter.

Herzog made clear from the outset of *Grizzly Man* that he values Treadwell's material beyond its quality as a wildlife film—an important reason to find a parallel between Treadwell and himself ("Having myself filmed in the wilderness of jungle . . ."). Indeed, in his next film, *The Cave of Forgotten Dreams* (2010), Herzog continued this identification by "reaching out" himself, hanging his 3D camera on a stick in his attempt to reveal the hidden side of a rock pendant that contained a painting of a half-animal/half-human creature. In so doing, he said, he hoped to get closer to the mysterious dawn of the human mind—the "familiar yet distant universe" of Chauvet's cave painters—thus offering an expression of his own desire to overcome skepticism. Back in *Grizzly Man*, however, Herzog gradually comes to distance himself from Treadwell's heroic attempts at closing the distance to nature. While Treadwell may not be protected from the bears by a metaphysical abyss, Herzog does find allegorical significance in a glacier ("a gigantic complexity of tumbling ice and abysses") that separates Treadwell in his grizzly sanctuary from "the world out there." Herzog, to be sure, primarily understands this physical barrier in psychological terms, finding in this "landscape in turmoil" a "metaphor of [Treadwell's] soul" (which, presumably, is equally rugged, multifaceted, and difficult to navigate).[6] But in suggesting that it separates him from "the world out there," we can surely find metaphysical significance in the physical barrier as well. Herzog indeed suggests in the course of his film that Treadwell, being on the verge of breaking his link to a world shared with others, was not so much trying to defeat the skeptic as he was struggling against the skeptical conclusion. In the remainder of this section I will discuss three scenes that support this view of Treadwell's switch between the radical positions of skepticism.

4.3. Scenes of the Switch

Scene 1: Michelle Pfeiffer of the Bears

About halfway through the film, Herzog starts adding footage in which Treadwell slips from reporting on the bears' situation to confessing his own. When a male bear suffers defeat in a showdown with another over a female, for example, Treadwell records himself talking to the humiliated grizzly. Admitting that the female no doubt is the "Michelle Pfeiffer of the Bears," Treadwell makes sure to add that the defeated bear need not fear his rivalry: "Don't beat me up over it, I'm cool, I'm respectful." And then: "Things are bad for me with the *human* women, but not so bad I have been hitting on bears yet." Treadwell directs his gaze in a by now familiar gesture from the bear to the camera to stress the adjective *human*, assuming his audience relates to that.

On the one hand, we find here a tendency in Treadwell to treat animals like humans, drawing comparisons between some outstanding specimens on both sides. We should also note Treadwell's self-ascribed respect for the animals, which slips into things being "bad for me with the *human* women." Yet perhaps his nod at the camera is most striking here: it is a gesture not merely in acknowledgment of his audience, but of his camera providing the last connection with it—a point to which

I shall return shortly. For now, it bears noting (to wit) that Herzog uses the occasion to account for Treadwell's down-spiraling life before he adopted his grizzly man persona. Through interviews with Treadwell's parents and old friends, Herzog sketches a portrait of a troubled man who reached the point of a near-overdose drug addiction and who had been playing with various other identities before sticking to the grizzly man persona. As the latter, we further learn, Treadwell returns to the social world during winter seasons to visit schools on the US mainland, telling children with the support of his footage about his life among the grizzlies and the bears' need for protection. This audience in turn impacts the grizzly man's persona, his tone of voice, and the kinds of conversations he has with the bears. Yet, increasingly, other personae slip through, addressing other audiences.

SCENE 2: A SAD BUT REAL TURN

A hint of such slippage occurs in a scene in which Treadwell finds the dead body of a young fox, which he had adored as though it were a pet. "This expedition 2001 is taking a sad turn" he tells the camera, "but it is a real turn, and I mourn the death of this baby fox." Within the same breath, he suddenly undergoes a sad but real turn himself. Wiping a fly away from the corpse, he addresses it aggressively: "Get out of his eye, freakin' fly, don't do that when I'm around. Have some respect, f***er."

Beyond the apparent contradiction of finding fault with an anthropomorphized fly for acting inhumanly, Treadwell displays an interesting ambiguity as to whether he is asking the fly to show some respect to the dead fox or to himself. After all, the request not to start feasting on the fox's eye "when I'm around" is one way of expressing a felt lack of respect to his very presence.

At this point in the film, Herzog's voice-over takes a turn as well by explicitly opposing his own view of nature to Treadwell's. To Herzog, Treadwell's disbelief and shock at being confronted with nature's cruel indifference—its basic feature in Herzog's conception of it—implies a "sentimentalized view that everything out there was good, and the universe in balance and in harmony." Human society and culture, by contrast, with their exploitation, double moral standards, and hypocritical cruelty, fail to respect and protect that natural order.

Scene 3. Drawing a Line

Treadwell's privileging of nature over culture (as well as Herzog's disagreement with this view) comes to the surface in a later scene, consisting of a single long take, in which Treadwell concludes this same "expedition 2001." Here it turns out that he is indeed deeply insulted by the idea that both nature and his presence in the grizzly sanctuary are met with disrespect. When Treadwell, impersonating his friendly and uplifted grizzly man imago, records his conclusion of the expedition, he inadvertently aborts his role to mock, curse, and insult the park rangers, who had dared to "challenge" him for violating park rules. In Treadwell's view, they do nothing to protect the bears, tormenting him instead with their petty rules (keep distance from the bears, don't camp too long on the same location). His rage culminates in a violent burst of "f*** you's" punctuated by middle fingers obscenely directed at the camera—until he suddenly interrupts himself, fixes his hair and his bandana, and restarts his rehearsed lines to address his audience of school children, only to slip right back into the next tirade. Herzog dryly turns down the diegetic sound to interject with his voice-over narration: "Now Treadwell crosses a line with the park service which we will not cross." Herzog, however, does not merely *refuse to cross* a line, either because Treadwell attacks the very institution that has tolerated him for too long or for reasons of decency. To be sure, Herzog does side with the park rangers, suggesting that Treadwell's proximity to the bears in fact endangers rather than protects them: grizzlies may not on the face of it be able to tell the difference between respectful and disrespectful human beings. On the other hand, Herzog is fascinated by Treadwell's outbursts. In awe of his rage, calling it "almost incandescent, artistic," and alluding to Klaus Kinski in so doing, he comments: "I have seen this madness before on a film set, but Treadwell is not an actor in opposition to a director or a producer, he's fighting civilization itself." Indeed, Treadwell is not in opposition to a director; he is *his own* director even while he is also his own actor whose performance, like Kinski's, excels when he loses control and who appears most authentic when he identifies with his self-fabricated persona. But while Treadwell is becoming the "poetic truth" incarnate by crossing lines between director and actor, authenticity and performance, self and other, freedom and control, improvisation and rehearsal, he is also drawing a line (or Herzog does it for him). His desire to cross the boundary between humans and nature may well appeal to the romantic transcendence of the limitations of human subjectivity; this, again, would amount to the defeat of skepticism. In the process, however, Herzog suggests that Treadwell rather turned his back onto the world shared with others, rendering his isolation complete. Perhaps we could argue for a third option here for it now seems that the camera forms Treadwell's last connection to the world out there or is offering a new way of establishing one. At the point of the digital turn, when the camera breaks or attenuates its ontological connection with the world it records, Treadwell's incarnation of poetic truth thus takes on metaphysical significance. How does *Amélie* work in comparison?

4.4. *Amélie*'s Surface Effects

A good fifteen years after its release, Jeunet's *Amélie* still sits uneasily within the larger history of cinema and its global and digital turns. On the one hand, it creates a fantasy world through digitally animated visual effects, as is the case with the high-budget blockbusters epitomized by films such as *The Matrix* (dir. Wachowski brothers, 1999) and *Avatar* (dir. Cameron, 2009), or *Amélie*'s predecessor, Jeunet's own Hollywood production *Alien: Resurrection* (1997). On the other hand, in *Amélie*, Jeunet does not employ his digital tools to allow a chosen one to act in bullet time, a futuristic tribal warrior to plug into a flying horse or an alien to turn on a scientist by showcasing its dark blind force. They rather serve sentimental and mostly quite redundant purposes, for example through literal visualizations of figures of speech. Thus, Amélie's heart can be seen glowing in her chest, or she literally melts by morphing into a pool of water. Likewise, she arouses a blind man to a state of digital bliss by helping him across a busy street, relating to him all the goods displayed in the shop windows. Instances such as these bring the film closer to the visual language of cartoons than to the special effects of the blockbuster action movie.

The relevant point in relation to cinematic skepticism is not, however, that cartoon effects as such challenge the idea of film's relation to reality—that argument predates digital intervention.[7] I am rather interested in their overall function within a larger framework of *Amélie*'s flirtation with the skeptical conclusion, that is, with her withdrawal from the world at large into an increasingly smaller and more private retreat.

With *Amélie*, Jeunet himself indeed meant to take a step back from the global scene he had just entered with his installment of the *Alien* series by playfully embracing the local. This not only concerned a significantly downsized budget and target audience (even though *Amélie* actually ended up grossing more than its predecessor); the setting of the film itself was pitched at a radically different scale as well. If the Betty crew in *Alien: Resurrection* returned from the universe to that "shithole" planet called earth (as one crew member has it), the vast majority of the action in *Amélie* is safely contained within the Parisian neighborhood of Montmartre, portrayed as a village organized around its local café, its greengrocer's shop, and its newspaper stand. Within this small cobblestone world, Amélie Poulain enjoys small pleasures of daily life that offer instantaneous gratification, such as sliding her hand in a sack of grains, cracking the crust of her *crème brûlée*, and skimming stones on the Canal St. Martin.

Dudley Andrew objects that the film's skyrocketing adorability-factor relies heavily on such (quite literal) "surface effects" and similar "infantile pleasures" (Andrew 2004, 43). He contrasts Jeunet's Montmartre with the way Jean-Pierre Melville portrayed the same neighborhood in his 1956 film *Bob le flambeur*. In that *nouvelle vague* gem, Andrew writes, the "jaded hero winds his way from Montmartre down through Clichy after a long night, sidestepping the debris being washed down the sewers at dawn" (ibid., 37). Jeunet, by contrast, made sure to wash down the debris before the shooting, as his aim was precisely for Amélie *not* to have to mind her steps. That is, to create his picture postcard version of Paris, the director not only had trash, cars, and graffiti physically removed from the Parisian streets before sending out his camera crew; he also, more pertinently, used extensive postproduction to digitally paintbrush the neighborhood in romantic hues and to clean up any remaining traces of audio-visual noise. Critics in France—Serge Kaganski and Philippe Lançon up front—were quick to object that this effort at beautification did not stop short from erasing signs of cultural and racial diversity, of poverty, and of crime as well. Some therefore denounced *Amélie* as a digitally cleansed fantasy of the extreme Right.

Borrowing from the French sociologist Gérard Mermet, Michelle Scatton-Tessier captures Amélie's retreat to the local, to the immediate, and to small pleasures collectively under the umbrella term *le pétisme*, a neologism that could be translated as "smallism." The phenomenon of *pétisme*, she argues, should precisely be read as a reaction against (and hence cannot but imply) "everything that is gigantic or growing, that is, globalization, crime, ordinary violence, unemployment, and the loss of individual identity in the technological age" (Scatton-Tessier 2004, 197).

Scatton-Tessier suggests that *Amélie* does not primarily differ thematically from the films of the New Social Cinema (of such directors as Noé, Ozon, Dardenne, Breillat, or Kassovitz), but formally. Over and against their "sordid naturalism," she writes, "Jeunet weaves the human condition into a (false) sentimentalist story of a heroine out to provoke happiness, out to fix things" (Scatton-Tessier 2004, 199). In her reading, then, *Amélie*—the film—reveals the "human condition," only for Amélie—the protagonist who senses that she cannot cope with it—to withdraw from the threatening world writ large in order to direct whatever benevolent agency she has left at fixing small problems in her small world.

In his reading of Jeunet's work, Stephen Mulhall goes a step further by denying Amélie what little is left of her benevolence:

> Amelie's [sic] attempts as an adult to do good to others should not be seen as the attempts of a rightly oriented heart to correct the world's tendency to frustrate desire, but rather as the attempts of a child in an adult's body to remake her world in the image of her fantasies of it—fantasies whose pursuit leads her to manipulate others, to inflict potentially traumatic experiences of pain and pleasure upon them (at least once by forcibly returning them to the scenes of their own childhood) and centrally to find indefinitely various ways of deferring any definitive revelation of herself to the man of her dreams, and so her own access to adult sexual life. (Mulhall 2008, 115)

Mulhall thus points out that Amélie's intention to "fix things" (to use Scatton-Tessier's expression), no matter how small the scale, is not necessarily benevolent. This, to Mulhall, is interrelated with the idea that Amélie does not merely withdraw into a small world to match the size of her agency; she withdraws into a *fantasy world*, or, more precisely, she redraws the world in the image of fantasy. So it is not merely that some experiences can be distinguished as fantasmatic over and against others marked as real (though the film does stage those as well, for example in the sequences styled after black-and-white news reels); rather, the film *as a whole* displays a world viewed from Amélie's childlike perspective, which Mulhall finds "absurdly misaligned."

Mulhall's ideas on film (especially the ones published in *On Film*, such as the above) are frequently filtered through a Cavellian lens. This may seem the case with the idea that *Amélie* does not present clearly distinguishable scenes of fantasy as well, which resonates, for example, with Cavell's statement from *The World Viewed*: "It is a poor idea of fantasy which takes it to be a world apart from reality, a world clearly showing its unreality" (Cavell 1979, 85.). Statements such as these should alert the critic ready to dismiss Cavell's ontological reflections on film as merely another instance of realist film theory. Yet this particular passage does not quite align with Mulhall's view either, and this difference leads me to an alternative take on *Amélie* as well. Consider the full paragraph from *The World Viewed* from which I just pulled the quote:

> It is a poor idea of fantasy which takes it to be a world apart from reality, a world clearly showing its unreality. Fantasy is precisely what reality can be confused with. It is through fantasy that out conviction of the worth of reality is established; to forego our fantasies would be to forego our touch with the world. And does someone claim to know the specific balance sanity must sustain between the elaborating demands of self and world, some neat way of keeping soul and body together? What was Freud's advice? To retrieve stifled fantasy so that its annihilating power can commend the self's self-esteem, the admiration of men, and the love of women—to insist upon a world with room in it for fruitful work and love. Merely that. (Cavell 1979, 85)

Freud's advice, as evoked in this passage, may be *merely that*—that one wake up dormant or abandoned fantasies allowing one to (re-) turn towards the world—but to Cavell, such a trite suggestion is far from trivial, especially considering fantasy's immanent "annihilating power." Cavell indeed continues to point out the dangers of a politics that advocates a radical separation between fantasy and reality rather than to acknowledge the fantasy inherent in its own ideology. The "realities of politics so brutalized and specialized," Cavell writes, cause the individual to withdraw her fantasies into privacy, with the effect that "fantasy and politics [now] each try to devour each other." *Ergo*: "Here are two directions of nihilism" (Cavell 1979, 86).

It can readily be seen that these two directions of nihilism coincide with the two extreme positions of skepticism discussed in a previous chapter. One direction aspires to establishing an objectively known reality unmediated by fantasies (or by any form of subjective intervention), that is, to the overcoming of skepticism. The other direction, which leads to a withdrawal from the world back into privacy, amounts to a drawing of the skeptical conclusion by positing that there is no way of knowing whether anything exists at all outside of our own minds. Cavell's mediated position between these two extremes—a position that asks us to acknowledge human separation and finitude and hence to accept the skeptical impetus, but which still holds us accountable for establishing or severing our connections to the world—is here expressed through the warning: "to forego our fantasies would be to forego our touch with the world."

In my Cavellian reading of *Amélie*, then, I would adjust Mulhall's argument by casting Amélie's problem not primarily as her "absurdly misaligned" inflection of the world through her fantasies (be they malicious or beneficial); if anything, her fantasies keep her in touch with the world (as well as with "everything that is big" in that world). However, by failing *to emerge from* her own fantasies, she remains on the verge of rendering her own isolation complete. I am arguing, in other words, that what Mulhall aptly captured in the quotation above as Amélie's "indefinitely various ways of deferring any definitive revelation of herself" marks Amélie's struggle with the skeptical conclusion. This is to say, Amélie finds herself in a condition which film, according to Cavell, renders automatically.

Whereas Scatton-Tessier and Mulhall agree on the significance of Amélie's isolation, other critics have pointed out that *Amélie* can be read as an allegory of film as such (e.g., Moore 2006; Andrew 2004; Ezra 2004). That Jeunet is interested in the concept of the analog in this digital production of *Amélie* is indeed as obvious as that Renoir is interested in theater in his analog production of *Rules of the Game* (or that Marx, for that matter, is interested in money). The concept of cinematic skepticism enables me to connect the themes of analog film and isolation, as I will demonstrate in my discussing the "stratagem" Amélie invents for Nino, the man she pursues without wanting to reveal herself to him. But in so doing, I will also consider how the film allows us to re-examine that concept as it gets refracted through the digital. To put this discussion in perspective, I offer a brief interlude of Cavell's reading of Frank Capra's *It Happened One Night* (1934), which will set the stage for a crucial scene in *Amélie*.

Interlude. Holding the Trumpet in *It Happened One Night*

In this Hollywood classic, Clark Gable plays a recently fired journalist named Peter, who recognizes a woman sitting on a bus as the young heiress Ellie (Claudette Colbert). Ellie, he knows, is on the run from her wealthy father, who disapproves of her desire to marry (what happens to be) a bounty-hunting pilot (I take the coincidence with Jurieux's profession in *Rules of the Game* to be just that—coincidental). Peter half-blackmails her into journeying together, and gradually a romantic attraction develops between the fellow travelers. During this time, they register as a married couple for motel rooms, but Peter makes sure to hang a blanket on a rope between their separate beds, explaining to Ellie that he likes his privacy and that prying eyes annoy him. "The woman," writes Cavell, "is understandably skeptical: 'That, I suppose, makes everything all right'" (Cavell 1981, 81). The man responds to her by rendering the blanket allegorical: "Behold the walls of Jericho. Maybe not as thick as the ones Joshua blew down with his trumpet, but a lot safer. You see, I have no trumpet" (ibid.). Rather than descending into the allegorical nature of trumpets, which might in turn render the blanket a membrane of virginity, Cavell provides yet another allegorical rendering of blanket. He points out that Peter, unable to see Ellie directly as she undresses behind the blanket, stares as if mesmerized at the ripples and waves in the blanket itself, which are caused by (read: indexical signs of) her body's movements. In this tale of automatism, then, the walls of Jericho function as a screen. The question now becomes: how will the lovers tear down a wall of that nature, and who will be holding the trumpet?

Towards the end of their journey, Ellie finally appears on Peter's side of the room, casually shoving the blanket aside. To mark the moment,

Figures 4.3, 4.4, 4.5. Capra's shift of focus in *It Happened One Night*.

Capra reframes the image of Ellie crossing the border (fig. 4.3) by cutting to a shot that shows her in a tighter close-up and in soft focus (fig. 4.4). When Ellie throws herself at Peter to declare her love, the image returns to "normal" hard focus again (fig. 4.5). "Here," Cavell comments, "is Capra taking on responsibility for the Hollywood device of soft focus" (Cavell 1981, 99). That is: whereas soft focus is commonly used to indicate a romanticized or imaginary vision in contrast to the hard focus indicating ordinary or objective perception, Cavell reads Capra's use of the foci in reverse: it is the turn back to seemingly ordinary focus that stands in need of being interpreted as Peter's shift of mood: it is not so much a shift from dreamy to objective, but from soft to hard. "Why," Cavell ponders, "can he not allow the woman of his dreams to enter his dream? But just that must be the answer. What surprises him is her reality" (Cavell 1981, 100). In Cavell's reading of this scene, then, what normally counts as the default, objective focal lens is rendered here as a subjective expression of Peter's stubborn, unaccepting, or unreceptive mindset. Failing to acknowledge the existence of Ellie's reality (and the reality of his dream), he plays out the condition of film by placing himself outside of her world. Instead of embracing his own fantasy (as she throws herself into his arms), he sternly sends her back behind the screen.

4.5. Amélie's Stratagem

Peter and Ellie's metaphorical game resonates with the dynamic between Amélie and the object of her love, Nino Quincampoix. (The Nino character is played by Mathieu Kassovitz, who had previously directed *La Haine* [1995], a film referenced throughout *Amélie*, if mostly obliquely; we will discuss an occasion later on.) We should note from the outset that the analogy is imperfect: the latter pair does not share motel rooms—Nino and Amélie will not in fact travel together until the very last shot of the film—and the gender roles are mostly reversed. Whereas Capra's film primarily centers on the question of who will be holding the trumpet, Jeunet's story rather revolves around the question of whether Amélie will ultimately reveal herself. Still, Cavell's rhetorical question addressed to Peter equally applies to Amélie: why, that is, can't she embrace the reality of her fantasy? The films can thus be meaningfully related as both tie together issues of fantasy and privacy, of isolation and emergence, which are woven into an allegory of the cinema and the screen. In the remainder of this chapter, I will discuss *Amélie*'s rendering of cinematic skepticism by analyzing the heroine's stratagem, which for convenience's sake I have subdivided into five sections.

SCENE 1: DIGITAL HEART BEATS AND AN EYELINE MISMATCH

I take as my point of departure a scene that occurs about halfway through the film, but let me first set the stage properly. It has been clear from the outset that the film is obsessed with automatic analog causation: in the prologue, we saw how Amélie got reprimanded as a child for "causing" a car accident by taking a picture of it with her camera; whereas her current adventures got started with Amélie's discovery of an old analog photograph, a discovery itself "caused" by a chain of events starting from another car accident—Lady Di's—reported on the TV news. It eventually leads to a "chance encounter" with Nino at the Gare de Lyon, which is where I am picking up. Noting that Amélie had already spotted Nino once before, sitting on his hands and knees in a deserted subway station, she now she finds him in similar position at the train station, where Nino appears to be collecting debris from underneath the photo booth of the otherwise impeccably clean train station (figs. 4.6–4.7). At this point, Jeunet follows the conventions of the eyeline match, intercutting close ups of Nino and Amélie who intensify their looks as they appear to exchange glances in a traditional scene of love at first sight (figs. 4.8–4.9). A quick pan down Amélie's body reveals a digitally animated heart beating and glowing underneath her jacket, next to a "real" garden gnome statuette she is holding against her chest (fig. 4.10).[8] But Amélie, like the viewer, had apparently misaligned the looks: when Nino gets up and seeks to draw the attention of the object of his look, he continues to rush past Amélie—in fact heedlessly bumping into her without paying the slightest attention—only to chase down a man leaving the station in the distance. By pursuing the man, Nino unwittingly initiates Amélie's pursuit of *him* (fig. 4.11). The scene makes

Figures 4.6–4.9. At the Gare de Lyon.

Figures 4.10–4.11. At the Gare de Lyon.

clear that Amélie's fantasy of being the object of the Nino's attention, rather than his actual actions, determines the beating of her heart. What is more: Amélie's heart (and her subsequent stratagem) get animated digitally by a mismatch of classical cinema's continuity editing. This sets the parameters of the stratagem she is about to invent for Nino (and, in parallel, for the gnome).

In his pursuit of the unknown man, Nino loses a bag containing a photo album—another classic item from the analog age—which Amélie picks up after him. The album contains torn-up and discarded passport pictures, collected by Nino from underneath the numerous photo booths throughout Paris and reassembled into what the voice-over narrator dubs "some family album!"[9] The "phantom man" whom Nino pursues appears twelve times in the album, each time photographed at a different location and marked as "*toujours lui!!*" (him again!)—the text being written on a missing part of the picture, in place of a part of his skull (fig. 4.12 on page 92).

92 / Cinematic Skepticism

Figure 4.12. *"Toujours lui!!"*

SCENE 2: FROM SEX SHOP TO GHOST TRAIN

Unwittingly, Nino makes the first move in the game by putting up signs (posted on the photomaton in the Gare de Lyon), asking the finder of his lost album to dial the provided number. Amélie actually does call it and continues to trace Nino's steps, but instead of facing him directly to return the album, she turns the tables and evokes a desire on his part to pursue his mysterious benefactor. Amélie first gathers information about Nino in the sex shop where he works. There she learns that he used to take photos—not of nudes, but of prototypical indexical signs: foot- and handprints left in wet cement. She then goes looking for him by taking a ride in the ghost train at the fun fair, where he works a second job as a living phantom to scare the visitors.

The phantom train, Dudley Andrew points out, functions as an allegory for the cinema: "A paying spectator, Amélie is transported into a world constructed to amuse, frighten, and astonish her. A tenuous narrative literally motivates the wax or plastic figures . . . [to] reach toward her threateningly in a precisely timed sequence of special effects."[10] Whether or not Amélie's initial tension during the ride is caused by the automated movements of the plastic figures or by the prospect of (not) finding Nino, her body language radically changes—Amélie eventually crossing her eyes in orgasmic excitement—when one of the phantom figures, possessing autonomous movements, breaks loose from the rigid sequence and climbs onto her wagon to "woo" in her ear and fondle her neck (fig. 4.13).

A Seem-less Digital Skepticism in *Grizzly Man* and *Amélie* / 93

Figure 4.13. Going "woo" in the ghost train.

This, to my mind, provides an important additional element to Andrew's allegorical reading: if the train-ride stands for the cinema as such, the Nino-phantom could be read as the digitization of the moving image or its liberation from cinema's "automatic analogue causation" and its mechanical reproducibility. In the language of new media, we could say (with Lev Manovich) that he symbolizes the transition from the continuous to the discrete, which accounts for the manipulability of (parts of) the digital image (see Manovich 2001, esp. pp. 28ff.). The notion of the discrete, in this context, refers to the discrete picture elements (pixels) whose values can be changed individually or in clusters without affecting other parts of elements of the picture. So, whereas the manipulation of analog photographs or film frames, for example through the use of color filters or chemicals in the development process, necessarily affects the image as a whole, digital images are no longer subject to the same physical laws underpinning the unity and continuity of old, thus allowing digital editors to remove, add, or change parts of images while keeping the rest in place. What I am suggesting, then, is that Nino's quasi-autonomous movements in the phantom train are as arousing on the allegorical level as they are in Amélie's erotic fantasy because of their relative independence from the mechanical, purely causal movements around him. And this in turn provokes questions of control and manipulability Mulhall already brought up in the context of Amélie's fantasy. On the one hand, Nino stands for the "liberation" from the mechanical (photochemical) universe of analog photography, thus leaving behind what I quoted Laura Mulvey as calling the *inhuman* aspect of the medium. Yet, despite his "human" intervention, Nino's actions within the ghost train are prescribed as well as confined—his threat is calculated and contained—and have no bearing on any reality outside of it. Indeed, once outside the phantom train, Amélie takes control of their interactions.[11]

Scene 3: Dense Signs at the Sacré Coeur

This allegorical rendering of the digital turn comes to a climax at the next day's *rendezvous* on Square Louise Michel, which Amélie had set up by attaching an anonymous note to Nino's moped (written on the back of a set of passport photos randomly picked from the album) after her phantom train ride. Once Nino arrives on the exact location (at a carousel—yet another automated structure following a predetermined path), Amélie instructs him through a public phone to follow the blue arrows chalked on the pavement, leading up the seemingly endless stairs towards the Sacré Coeur. At the foot of Montmartre's famous white basilica, a living statue points further upwards, and a young boy appears to be part of the intrigue as well when he tells Nino proverbially: "*Monsieur*, when the finger points at the sky, only a fool looks at the finger" (translation modified). The cryptically coded message—cast in the *symbolic* signs of language—is not lost on Nino: this public statue—an *iconic* sign of a historical public figure—provides an *indexical* sign with a private message: its index finger points out something specifically for him, here and now. Nino figures too that not the sky (that vast expanse of empty space receding indefinitely into the distance), but the telescope behind him (a tool to bring a specific distant object into focus), is the object of this sign. Moving with ease in this dense amalgam of Peircian signs (fig. 4.14), Nino takes out the five-franc coin that Amélie's note had urged him to bring along, and, through the telescope, he witnesses how a disguised Amélie takes the stage, waiving the album theatrically at him before putting it in the bag on his moped, which is parked all the way back down the stairs (fig. 4.15).

When Nino tears himself away from this cinematic spectacle and hurtles back down the stairs to retrieve his treasure, Amélie calls him again on the public phone to tell him about her new theory of the man whose pictures keep recurring in the album. That man is an invisible phantom, she tells him, which only appears once the filmstrip has been developed—on the "*pellicule photographique*": "When a girl has her photo taken he goes 'woooo' in her ear while he fondles her neck."

Figures 4.14, 4.15. Allegories of cinema at the Square Louise Michel.

Along with this game of amalgamated signs, then, Amélie is developing an amalgamated fantasy, blending the man she is pursuing with the man Nino is pursuing into a private tale of spooky sensuality. In the process, she blends in ideas of analog film (the celluloid strip and its overdetermined association with ghosts as real appearances without substantial existence) along with those of digital postproduction (which actually can make things appear after shooting). Thus, as the game progresses to combine all the signs of the Peircian triptych, the strong sense of causality associated with the indexicality of analog photography (Cavell's automatism; D. N. Rodowick's "automatic analogical causation") merges with a painterly, *ex-nihilo* creative value associated with the digital image (re)production. Amélie's intrigue employs what Mary Ann Doane conceived as a power of analog photography by folding contingency and randomness into the necessity of her scheme (for example, a random bystander who picks up the public phone is asked to hand over the receiver to the man holding a plastic bag), even as she renders a public

96 / Cinematic Skepticism

space (with its public phones, public statues, and public telescopes) into a private playground for a coded game—an augmented or virtual reality that remains inaccessible to nonparticipants.[12]

Because of its breaks or attenuation of the indexical "correspondence in fact" (as Peirce would have it), it is commonplace to associate digital imagery with painting, insofar as they share the fact of creating (often iconic) images from scratch. Yet, in another way, the transformation into pixels brings the digital image closer to a symbolic sign, as the relation between the imputed values (encrypted as 0s and 1s) of picture elements and their corresponding object is an arbitrary one. Nature, in a word, does not intrinsically determine the coding. In that sense, digital images are more closely related to language than to painting.

In *Amélie*, Jeunet imbues specific significance to this latter relation by fostering connections between photography/film and handwritten texts. Having already combined texts and photos in Amélie's messages and indeed in some of the photographs in the album, Jeunet takes this connection a step further when, by the end of the game I just described, he has Amélie refer Nino to page 51 of his newly retrieved album. Here Nino finds four (unrecognizable) black-and-white pictures of Amélie with the text "Souhaitez vous me rencontrer? ("Do You Want to Meet Me?") written within and distributed across the image spaces. The last of the photographs displays the question mark painted on her revealed belly, using the belly button for its dot as if to connect the texts through an umbilical cord to the body that "caused" the photograph by bouncing and blocking off light (fig. 4.16).

Now determined to pursue his pursuer, Nino photocopies the latter picture on colored paper, which he distributes throughout the stations in Paris, using the question mark to punctuate his handwritten words "where & when" (fig. 4.17). Amélie responds with a picture of herself in Zorro costume, holding up a written message saying that she is frequently to be found at the café Deux Moulins after 4:00 p.m. (when Amélie starts her shift as a waitress); she leaves it torn up underneath a random photomaton for Nino to discover, which of course he does.

SCENE 4. THROUGH THE CAFÉ'S SCREEN

In this crucial scene at the café, Nino takes a seat in a booth backed by a glass partition and has a cup of coffee while he awaits Amélie's move. She stands right behind him, shielded only by the transparent screen—Jeunet's equivalent of Capra's blanket (fig. 4.18).

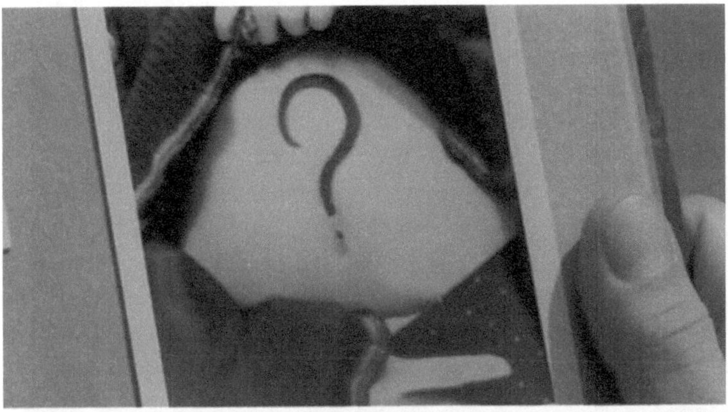

Figures 4.16, 4.17. Body, text, and photo-copy-graph.

Figure 4.18. Through the transparent screen.

When Nino, sensing her presence, turns around to look at her, Amélie attempts to "hide" away by turning the screen into a writing surface: she quickly pens "today's menu" on the glass (in reverse, for him to read). As Nino returns his attention to his coffee, and the point of view switches to Amélie's, we hear her mind's voice (for the first and only time during this film) saying: "Now he has understood." Her voice-over continues to predict, or rather direct, his every action, followed by the camera showing the described action in slow motion and extreme close-up: "He's going to put down his spoon, dip his finger in the sugar, turn around slowly, and speak to me." Amélie continues to write down the menu as Nino turns around; knocks on the glass; and, looking straight through the text while pointing at the Zorro picture he holds up to her, asks, "Is this you?" Nino insists when Amélie initially shakes her head in denial: "Yes it's you" (*C'est vous ça*). With a shrug of the shoulders, Amélie turns away from the screen, scribbles a next appointment on a note, which her colleague Gina slips into Nino's pocket on her behalf. Nino finishes his coffee, pays Gina, and leaves the café. Amélie expresses her relief at having so narrowly—and quite incredibly—escaped a direct confrontation with the object of her love by splashing onto the tiled floor as she melts into a formless pool of water.

This, then, is Jeunet's digital response to Capra's way of giving new significance to "hard focus": whereas Ellie's indexical ripples in the blanket are matched by Amélie's symbolic scribbles on the glass partition, the shift from Peter's soft view to his hard view (expressing his inability to accept the reality of fantasy) is rendered by Jeunet's software as Amélie's morphing into metaphor. It marks a shift, in other words, from lens to language, from index to symbol.

This shift helps explain a notable difference between the respective scenes from *It Happened* and *Amélie* as well, yet I will postpone this explanation until the next chapter (5.3) For now, what matters is that the missed encounter forms a turning point in the narrative as a whole: from this moment onwards, Amélie is losing control over the plot she had set up for Nino.

Scene 5: "Je Reviendrai": Proliferating Screens in the Film's Finale

The resolution of that plot begins when Amélie learns that the discarded photos of the mystery man recurring in Nino's album are simple test results of a mechanic repairing photomata throughout Paris. As

A Seem-less Digital Skepticism in *Grizzly Man* and *Amélie* / 99

the final twist of her intrigue, Amélie purposely jams a photo booth at another of Paris' major stations, the Gare de l'Est, in order to stage an encounter between Nino and the mystery man cum mechanic, with the clear intent of revealing herself as his mystery woman in the process. Amélie, who watches from behind a café window how Nino makes the same discovery as she did, waits for the mechanic to leave, and then she appears from behind her screen to walk resolutely toward Nino, who scrambles around the photo booth, perplexed at "his" discovery of the riddle's solution. Out of nowhere, another screen is pulled up between the two: an electric luggage transfer train crosses the station, momentarily blocking Amélie's path and view (fig. 4.19). The intervention lasts but a few seconds, but Amélie, who closes her eyes and turns away from the scene in disbelief, knows it is long enough: when she faces the photo booth again, Nino, as she feared, is gone.

The way this is revealed to the viewer is itself revealing. Once the luggage train has passed, Amélie, facing the camera, gathers courage, her eyes still closed (fig. 4.20 on page 100). She then opens them and turns around to look in Nino's direction. The camera, however, rather than offering a subjective view by way of an over-the-shoulder shot, merely provides an objective shot of the back of Amélie's head, which in fact blocks the spectator's view of Nino (fig. 4.21 on page 100). Instead of aligning with Amélie's view (thus identifying with her by sharing her perspective), the viewer is forced to dissociate from her. This dissociation is given significance by the camera, which reveals what Amélie already knows through an unnatural, theatrical upward movement, allowing the viewer to look over her head only to find that there is nothing to see (fig. 4.22 on page 100).

Figure 4.19. Nino squats down at the photomaton as the luggage train arrives.

Figures 4.20–4.22. Amélie and Saïd: different turns.

In the final chapter, I will provide a Deleuzian interpretation of this kind of shift between subjective and objective shots in the context of cinematic skepticism, along with an elaboration of the idea of revealing nothingness. For now, I will draw a comparison between this scene of Nino's (Mathieu Kassovitz's) sudden disappearance and Kassovitz's own film *La haine* (1995), alluded to before, whose opening it mimics in remarkable detail. After *La haine*'s opening credits, in which a *third cinema*-style montage of a violent clash between demonstrators and the riot police is accompanied by Bob Marley's *Burnin' and Lootin'*, the film settles in the diegetic world by zooming in on a young *beur* man, soon to be known as Saïd (Saïd Taghmaoui), who faces the camera, inaudibly murmuring to himself with closed eyes (fig. 4.23). The camera suddenly switches 180 degrees to repeat its zoom, this time coming to rest on the back of the young man's head (fig. 4.24). It then makes the same theatrical lateral gesture as we saw in *Amélie*, rising above Saïd's head. The camera, suddenly shifting its focal length, reveals what the protagonist himself initially blocked from view: a fully armed military police squad lined up right in front him (fig. 4.25).

Figures 4.23–4.25. Amélie and Saïd: different turns.

Because the camera's movements in both scenes would seem all but identical, the difference looms large. Kassovitz's scene implies that adjusting the focus of our attention would reveal the reality of a young man like Saïd, whose path is blocked by the force of law. By contrast, Amélie's revelation occurs when her path is no longer blocked: the reality of her fantasy has vanished—perhaps there had never been a reality behind the figment of her imagination. As though to deny the option that Nino's disappearance may again be interpreted as her own wish fulfillment, the point of view, which had already been dissociated from Amélie's, suddenly rises to the empty station's ceiling: a perspective that shows Nino really has nowhere to hide or flee within this diegetic world.

Nino's disappearance marks the end of Amélie's stratagem. Having ultimately failed to blow the trumpet, Amélie, rather than authoring her own plot and directing Nino's actions accordingly, is now being subjected to a script authored and directed for her. The final sequence of events brings out the indiscernibility between fantasy and reality and, along with it, between ideas of automatic causation (associated with the analogue) and painterly manipulation (associated with the digital) in full force, although it actually starts off with a scene in which Amélie's fantasies about Nino are now clearly marked *as* fantasies. That is, when Amélie, sad about her failure, takes to baking a plum cake and discovers that she has run out of yeast, she imagines Nino going out in the rain to buy a pack for her from the greengrocer. Rather than replacing the actual image of her baking, the daydream is inserted into it: to the viewer, it appears to Amélie's left, projected over the space of an open kitchen window; the space to her right is occupied by a beaded door curtain (fig. 4.26). Upon his return, the imaginary Nino, still playing his role of phantom, gently moves the beaded curtain (in the projected image on the left) to produce a trickling sound, while he himself (still in the projected world) hides behind the kitchen wall (fig. 4.27). The imaginary trickling sound turns out to be actual, however, as we see the beaded curtain to Amélie's right move in a magical resonance that cannot be explained away by the heroine's disappointing discovery that her cat just entered the kitchen through that door.

The coincidental magic continues when, at this very moment, the doorbell rings. Approaching the door, Amélie hears Nino's voice calling her name from outside. Rather than opening the door, she lays her ear against it; a gesture mimicked by Nino on the other side, as a slow, ghostlike pan straight through the door reveals (fig. 4.28 on page

A Seem-less Digital Skepticism in *Grizzly Man* and *Amélie* / 103

Figures 4.26, 4.27. Magical resonance.

104). Nino quickly pens down the note "Je reviendrai"—which may equally be read as a casual "I'll be back" or as the uncannier statement "I shall return"—shoves it underneath this screen of fantasy, and leaves again. With a check from behind the curtain at her living room window, Amélie sees him leave her apartment complex; with a familiar gesture, she ducks away when he turns to look up at her window.

Continuing this perfectly timed orchestration, the telephone rings: an anonymous caller directs Amélie to go to her bedroom. Here, Amélie finds a TV set surrounded by lit candles, with a videotape ready to be played. The tape shows her neighbor Dufayel—a "glass man" with a brittle bone disease who is named after the department store that housed the largest film theater in Paris at the turn of the century (fig. 4.29 on page 104).[13] By hobby or profession, however, he is a painter who, for twenty years in a row, has been duplicating the same painting by

104 / Cinematic Skepticism

Figures 4.28, 4.29. Proliferating screens.

Pierre-Auguste Renoir—*The Luncheon of the Boating Party* (*Le déjeuner des canotiers*, Renoir's original, is from 1880–81) over and over again with photographic precision. Throughout the film, Dufayel had been soliciting Amélie to generate a narrative around one of the women in the painting, "the girl with the glass." Dufayel, describing her as being "in the center and yet outside," conveyed that he had long had difficulties capturing her absent-minded look. Seeing that her imaginative force separates her from the lively crowd around her, Amélie obviously takes the girl as a proxy for herself (as the isolated waitress in the center of Paris). It should be worth noting, then, that Ellen Andrée, the real-life girl who, seated as the actual model for Renoir (the real-life painter—the real-life filmmaker's father), was in fact a professional theater actress with a strong preference for performing in naturalist plays. Dufayel, in other words, is a dense figure who brings together ideas of cinema and painting, theater and narration, naturalism and imagination, reproduction and manipulation, isolation and capture, and who now speaks to Amélie through the video recording displayed on her TV screen as though he were addressing her in person and in real time.[14] Apparently in the know about what happened just seconds ago at Amélie's door, he warns her not to let "this chance" go by. Amélie, taking his words to heart, rushes out after Nino only to run into him right at her doorstep. (Perhaps he has returned, or perhaps her glimpse from the window marked yet another fantasmatic image and Nino was still waiting at the door.)

This, then, is the allegory of the screen coming full circle: on a TV screen, the personification of repetition arranges from the past (of the recording) for Amélie to overcome her inhibitions, allowing her to embrace the reality of her returned ("repressed") fantasy in the present. This is celebrated in the film's final montage of the future, in which, it turns out, all of Amélie's schemes will have worked out, leaving the film with an aftertaste of "bonbon sweetness."

4.6. Ironic Turns

In *Grizzly Man* and *Amélie*, the global and the digital enter into an ironic embrace. Jeunet uses digital technology not to create a fantastic future world full of special effects, but instead to take a step back in terms of time and scale, setting the fantasies of an anonymous waitress in a more local and romantic past; perhaps that scaled down realm just *is* an expression of her fantasy. In *Grizzly Man*, Timothy Treadwell takes to digital filmmaking to record his own step back from civilization to bond with the bears in a remote natural environment. Irony then takes another turn of the screw as his digital recordings derive their force primarily from their indexicality.

In *Amélie*, irony deepens too, as the heroine relies on analog tools and tropes to manipulate the people around her into conforming to her digitized fantasy world. Examples (beyond luring Nino into her stratagem with a photo album) include the release of her father and of her landlady from their lethargic states of being through analog forms of fakery. In the first case, she does so by generating a fictional travel narrative of her father's garden gnome, using real-world projections (polaroids taken by a flight attendant friend who carries this fantasy-cum-commodity creature around the globe) rather than simply relying on fake backdrops (not to mention Photoshop). In the other case, she helps her landlady recover from her numbness to the world by creating a fake letter of her late husband, going through the laborious process of physically cutting and pasting his actual letters, using a photocopier and a tea bath to cover the forgery.

By thus "helping" people around her to reverse their withdrawal from the world with the aid of analog tools, Amélie's actions turn the tables on (or give a spin to) Cavell's basic assumption of analog film as automatically drawing the skeptical conclusion by rendering our isolation from the projected world complete. Treadwell could be said to turn the tables as well, albeit in a different direction: despite its alleged break with analog causation, the digital camera might well form Treadwell's last connections to the *human* world—even if that connection is meant to offend. To reach that conclusion, we moved from an account of the Grizzly Man persona seeking to overcome skepticism (crossing the line delineating the human condition) to one in which Treadwell's rage all but draws the skeptical conclusion (crossing a line with the park services). We drew that arch graphically through two corresponding fingers: one, an index finger crossing the line separating the human behind the camera to point-touch into the world of the bears in front of it; the other an obscene middle finger directed straight at the camera—which is still an address, hence a connection. It turns the table on Cavell, who has little patience for such direct confrontations with the camera. As the flipside of the viewer always being outside of the world on screen, Cavell argues, the camera is always outside of the subject it records: even when filming itself in the mirror, the camera cannot help but draw the skeptical conclusion automatically by rendering the distance between the image and itself absolute. In Treadwell's case, the absoluteness of his distance to the world is rendered horrifically rather than automatically at the paws of a bear—when even the camera fails to record to provide a final connection.

Amélie could be said to take the opposite trajectory: having been on the verge of complete isolation all along, she develops a stratagem for Nino that allows her to stay connected to the world without having to (or being able to) emerge from behind her allegorical screen(s). When she finally does emerge, we are offered an image (a montage of images) of such complete satisfaction that we are left to ponder whether this is not rather an expression of wish to defeat any skeptical doubt once and for all.

Despite their various ironic turns (including the turns of the tables against Cavell), we can thus see that the films are inverted, if equally moving images of a skepticism turning digital, playing out their struggles between the extreme poles of the spectrum.

Chapter 5

Digital, Global, Ontological Turns

Having argued that *Grizzly Man* and *Amélie* present inverted images of skepticism, the current chapter looks at recent scholarship, mostly by D. N. Rodowick and Thomas Elsaesser, that enables me at once to place the two films in a more general interpretative framework and to draw out the stakes of my own specific take on cinematic skepticism in the context of the digital and global turns. In the process, it will become evident why I insist on countering interpretations of Deleuze's work on cinema (or Cavell's for that matter) as overcoming skepticism.

5.1. Skepticism and the Digital Turn

I start by picking up a line of thought I had left at the end of chapter 3. There I argued that my conception of cinematic skepticism is not likely to include films explicitly staging what Philipp Schmerheim called "external world skepticism." When Cavell defines film *as such* as a moving image of skepticism, he does not mean that certain films are *about* skepticism, much less so if these films somehow reveal the unreality of a diegetic world by contrasting it with another (equally diegetic, but now "real") one. I argued that such films in fact bypass the very force of the skeptic: in positing a reality behind the illusory world, they stop short of provoking anxiety about the fact that we do not know what our ordinary conviction in reality is grounded upon. At the same time, my own take on cinematic skepticism, even while crucially relying on his differentiation of skeptical positions, took a different turn from Cavell's as well. For what seems most interesting is not primarily that film *as such* provokes an ontological anxiety by automatically rendering our distance to the world (screened) absolute (no matter what film we in fact see on that screen), but that specific films invoke *that* provocation on the level of their narrative and in their use of specific techniques. While this is perfectly on a par with Cavell's own film-critical practice (as I hope my discussion of his readings of *Rules of the Game* or *It Happened One Night* have shown), it follows that not just any film will do so, much less that it does so convincingly. Cinematic skepticism, in short, is neither inherent in the medium of film as such, nor narrowly applicable to films that explicitly stage external world skepticism.

Here I want to add that Schmerheim in fact subdivides skepticism films into two main categories, of which external world skepticism is only one; the other consists of what he calls "self-knowledge skepticism films."[1] It is not my intention to measure the distance between my own conception and this expanded version of Schmerheim's (an expansion that follows the one Cavell made in philosophy). In fact, I will leave Schmerheim's account of the self-knowledge subcategory of skepticism films for what it is. Yet I bring it up because the distinction is further inspired by what Schmerheim calls D. N. Rodowick's "update" of Cavell. It is this update that will lead our discussion of cinematic skepticism beyond the digital turn. Let me therefore repeat here a passage Schmerheim quotes from *The Virtual Life of Film* (2007):

> In the world of computers and the Internet, we have little doubt about the presence of other minds and, perhaps, other worlds. And we believe, justifiably or not, . . . in our ability to control, manage, or communicate with other minds and worlds, but at a price: matter and minds have become "information." In this sense, the cultural dominance of the digital may indicate a philosophical retreat from the problem of skepticism to an acceptance of skepticism. For the highly mutable communities forged by computer-mediated communications, the desire to know the world has lost its provocation and its uncertainty. Rather, one seeks new ways of acknowledging other minds, without knowing whether other selves are behind them. (Rodowick 2007, 175, quoted in Schmerheim 2016, 128)

This is D. N. Rodowick's "guess at the riddle" concerning "the most difficult question," namely, how our ontology has changed in our interactions with computer screens and what kinds of epistemological and ethical relations to the world and to others may be expected to result from this change (Rodowick 2007, 174). His tentative answer (or guess) is based on the mutually reinforcing implications of digital recording and screening or, more specifically, of the break of what he calls "automatic analogical causation" and of the DVD/internet-enabled "ability to control the image interactively (Rodowick 2007, 49, 163).

I take it to be sufficiently known (even if it remains hard to understand) that digital capture turns light reflected from the subject into symbolic (i.e., numerical) machine-readable notation representing color values of discrete pixels. "This is the primary automatism and source of the creative powers of digital computing," Rodowick writes, though not without adding that the gap resulting from the conversion (or "quantizing") of light into code also attenuates the causal relation between inputs and outputs (Rodowick 2007, 49, 116). This "primary automatism" of digital conversion thus replaces the automatism Cavell attributed to the analogue, which was anchored, technically speaking, in the direct, physical inscription of light into photosensitive celluloid. Whereas the distinguishing feature of automatic analogical causation is that "the process of transcription is continuous in space and time, producing an isomorphic record that is indivisible and counterfactually dependent on its source" (Rodowick 2007, 49, 113), the discontinuity of digital conversion enables a host of subsequent automatisms, that is: the algorithmic, programmable transformations of the image, thus opening up the ability to control or manipulate the image in postproduction through digital synthesis and compositing (hence the "creative powers of digital computing").

For D. N. Rodowick, the digitally enabled power to control or manipulate the image in postproduction expresses "another will to power in relation to the world":

> No doubt, [digital information] attenuates or even blocks an earlier photographic relation to past worlds, for the digital will wants to change the world, to make it yield to other forms, or to create different worlds. Before the digital screen, we do not feel a powerlessness, but rather express a will to control

information and to shape ourselves and the world through the medium of information. (Rodowick 2007, 118, 174)

While this sense of increased control over the image is not necessarily put in the hands of film viewers (in the way it could be asserted of gaming), the latter do gain a perhaps more "remote control" over the image, so to speak, in the sense that they can pause, rewind, review, slow down, skip, or randomly access the film released on DVD or on the web.[2] This increased sense of interactivity is not to be taken too far or too literally: despite their cult status, experiments with hypermedia films such as David Blair's *WAXWEB* (1993) or cinematic "choose your own adventure" stories like Bob Gale's *Mr. Payback* (1995) failed to inspire promising new tendencies in cinema. Yet the effect of digital screens, interactivity and a networked world on film is nevertheless not to be underestimated either. As Thomas Elsaesser pointed out, the "geniuses of hypertext architecture and cyberspace" in a way did foresee the kinds of concepts (such as the rhizome, the archive, the database) that now challenge linear narrative as "a universally prevailing basic ordering principle" with its "causally motivated chains of events, propelled by identifiable agents, usually human beings" (Elsaesser 2009a, 23). Under the pressure of this challenge, a new type of film has emerged since the 1990s, as various theorists and critics have noted. Janet Staiger, Jason Mittell, and Jan Simons speak of "complex narratives" in this context, and Elliot Panek and Warren Buckland call the films that employ these narratives "puzzle films." Allan Cameron and Lev Manovich use the terms "modular cinema" and "database cinema" respectively, while Kristen Daly proposed to call for "Cinema 3.0: The Interactive-Image" to complement Deleuze's *Cinema 1* and *Cinema 2*, as did Patricia Pisters with her suggestions to introduce the neuro-image in addition to the movement- and time-image.[3]

Thomas Elsaesser himself names the new type of movie "the mind-game film," a genre (or rather a "mode that transcends genre") he discusses in the 2009 namesake essay as well as its 2018 "complement," "Contingency, Causality, Complexity: Distributed Agency in the Mind-Game Film." In the initial essay, Elsaesser explains that mind-game films are marked by a level of complexity that invites multiple viewings, ideally with the remote control in hand. A theatrical release is, so to speak, but the advertisement for the "economically more profitable afterlife in another aggregate form," meaning most notably the DVD or online streaming services (Elsaesser 2009a, 39).[4] The internet may provide additional layers of complexity as well by allowing films to extend to websites for "cross-media interaction." I think of *The Blair Witch Project* (dir. Daniel Myrick and Eduardo Sánchez, 1999) as perhaps still the paradigmatic case in point. The film itself, marketed as presenting the actual, rediscovered footage of three film students who had disappeared in the woods of Maryland while documenting the legend of the Blair Witch, meant to provoke a discussion over its veracity—a discussion that the official website of the film intended to extend by offering police reports, documentary interviews, and additional found footage. Whether intentionally or not, *Grizzly Man* likewise invites such cross-media interaction and provokes a similar discussion over authenticity through the online circulating of the infamous audiotape of Treadwell's death, which Herzog himself had been listening to in the film, only to withhold its content and push the tape back into collective repression ("You should never listen to this"; "I think you should destroy it").

But even if it is not "interactive" in this strong sense of the word (let alone in the sense that it enables viewers to participate in or influence the direction of the story of the film itself), the new type of narrative is still premised on the idea that viewers can now control the relentless forward movement of film. Viewers may watch it interruptedly or elliptically (perhaps after a first linear viewing), pausing scenes in order to analyze images that seem to contain crucial but understated or downplayed information or skipping back and forth between scenes to find new connections that may not have been evident on first viewing. I will provide examples of this in the next chapter.

The mind-game films' complex cinematic narratives tend to feature characters whose minds are either subject to often perverse or otherwise disturbing games without necessarily being aware of it. Alternately, they often represent a pathological mode of being in the world despite being presented as "normal"—even if the situations the characters are involved in are confusing or disorienting to themselves and to viewers alike. Frequently featured pathologies include paranoia, amnesia, and schizophrenia. But such "dis-ordering" and "dis-associating" affective states, Elsaesser points out, are also "appropriate" for our contemporary network society; where Herzog found an artistic, "incandescent" madness in Treadwell's rage, Elsaesser considers pathologies in contemporary films as productive forces with a creative potential, enabling us "to discover new connections" (Elsaesser 2009a, 26):

> On the one hand, thus, we are dealing with pathologies (of subjectivity, of consciousness, of memory and identity): indications of crisis and uncertainty in relation of the self with itself and with the world (and by extension: of the spectator with the screen). On the other hand . . . these apparently damaged minds and bodies . . . [function] as empowerment, and their minds, by seemingly losing control, gain a different kind of relation to the man-made, routinized, or automated surroundings. (Elsaesser 2009a, 31)

Although Elsaesser does not himself (like to) lay claim to it, we could argue that he interprets the mind-game film as an extension or variation of modern cinema in the Deleuzian conception.[5] Like the postwar modern cinema, in which a crisis of the movement-image involving a break of the sensory-motor link formed the condition for thinking and for the potential development of new relations to the world (expressed through the cinema's nonchronological development, incommensurable situations, irrational cuts), the mind-game film develops a sense of empowerment from a crisis of subjectivity. Indeed, many of the descriptions of the mind-game films could be applied to the time-image just the same. For example, mind-game films "break one set of rules (realism, transparency, linearity) in order to make room for a new set." They concentrate on "unreliable narrators, multiple time-lines, unusual point-of view structures" and challenge "the concept of 'identity' or ask what it means to be human." They raise "matters of *ontology* and parallel worlds, while skepticism and doubt, but also their obverse: belief and trust, are often epistemological issues at stake." As a result, "the question becomes: do the films 'lie,' or is it the very opposition of truth and lie, between the actual and the virtual, the subjective and objective, that is at stake?" (Elsaesser 2009a, 18–19, 20, 38.) So far, then, mind-game films hardly offer anything that should strike us as new in comparison to the time-image.

5.2. The Ontological and Global Turn

By foregrounding matters of ontology and skepticism, mind-game films participate in what Elsaesser (along with others) calls an "ontological turn" in cinema. This turn transcends not only genre, but national cinemas as well—as does the mind-game film itself. Indeed, the ontological turn all but defines or characterizes the global turn to a transnationally produced, distributed, and exhibited world cinema as such, as Elsaesser suggests in an essay entitled "World Cinema: Realism, Evidence, Presence," which was published in the same year as the mind-game film essay and which can in many ways be seen as a companion piece.[6] In the essay Elsaesser actually flirts with what he calls the popular, attractive, and "almost irresistible" idea that "the Deleuzian intervention in film studies" perfectly captures the "ontological turn" in cinema, only to add that he "shall resist the temptation of 'becoming Deleuzian'" (Elsaesser 2009b, 7). While I have no stake in anyone's conversion, I do want to mimic Cavell's gesture of *resisting resistance*, applied here against the pressure of a Cavello-Deleuzian take on cinematic skepticism. Such counterresistance is called for when the ontological turn it involves is understood in the way Elsaesser does in this essay:

> Ontology mark one . . . can give us trust in the world and liberate us from the anxiety of scepticism, thanks either to the presence of the contingently real through photographic indexicality (Cavell) or by redefining cinema as "mind and matter" (Deleuze). My own argument—ontology mark two— would be that such trust has to be a function of scepticism, has to involve a leap across an abyss. (Elsaesser 2009b, 11)

I am insisting throughout this study that a Cavello-Deleuzian cinematic skepticism already implies "ontology mark two": the "post-epistemogical" or "post-photographic" turn, as Elsaesser also calls it, has already been undertaken and involves the kind of leap which Elsaesser, like Deleuze, compares to a "Pascalian definition of faith" (Elsaesser 2009b, 6, 11). I crucially argue that Cavell and Deleuze's shared call for belief or faith in the world is *not* intended to (nor does it in fact) "liberate us from the anxiety of skepticism." On the contrary: their call already *is* a function of the skeptical impetus, even if it seeks to avert or avoid the skeptical conclusion.

Far from claiming that cinematic skepticism is either new or behind us, then, I suggest that the mind-game film, if not indeed contemporary world cinema generally, expresses a variation and intensification of a Cavello-Deleuzian–inflected cinematic skepticism. To find a variation, of course, is not to move on with "business as usual," as though the digital and global turns have not had any impact at all. I did not mean to deny *any* difference when I said that there is *hardly* anything new going on in contemporary film. I think three interrelated points in Elsaesser's essays may account for this new expression of cinematic skepticism.

The first concerns a somewhat downplayed (because parenthesized) comment in a previously quoted passage, which states that the crisis in the relation of self to world extends to a crisis *of the spectator with the screen*. By this, Elsaesser means that the mind-game film no longer seems convinced by the classical ocular-centrist, distance-provoking spectatorship, which positions the viewer as witness, voyeur, or observer—with Cavell we might say as outsider—and the same goes for the appropriate cinematic techniques (identifiable subjective or objective shots, fly on the wall transparency, etc.).[7]

The second point of difference—one that I have not touched upon as yet—concerns a boon Elsaesser took back from his visits to Internet fan sites, namely, that "mind-fuck film" enthusiasts (as they themselves prefer to call this new type of movie) "take for granted the ability to live in fictional or rather virtual worlds" (Elsaesser 2009a, 30). Contemporary films are like puzzles that need to be figured out, so the question as to whether anything happening in the diegetic world is *real* is much less pertinent than the question of whether it provides any clues. Hence Elsaesser: "[R]ather than 'reflecting' reality, or oscillating and alternating between illusionism/realism, these films create their own referentiality, but what they refer to, above all, are 'the rules of the game'" (Elsaesser 2009a, 39). The two points thus mutually imply one another: viewers, as Elsaesser puts it in the World Cinema essay, are "neither master nor dupe" (that is, they are neither positioned as transcendental or absolute subjects, as Baudry would argue, nor as powerless outsiders in the Cavellian sense), but "partners in negotiated conventions" (Elsaesser 2009b, 8).[8]

In *Cinematic Interfaces: Film Theory after New Media* (2013), Seunghoon Jeong elaborates on this point. He argues against the idea that cinema is an "ideological apparatus," meaning that he denies it to be an "illusion mechanism" all but forcing us to suspend our disbelief about its presentation of "reality," but that, as its flipside, posits the viewer as transcendental subject, the implied center and synthesizer of all images. Jeong equally denies the medium the status of what he then by analogy calls the "indexical apparatus," since film's medium-specific materiality and its automatic analogical causation (which accounts for the radical distance of the "duped" spectator) does not, in his view, explain "concrete cinematic experience." Rather than doing away with the notion of indexicality altogether, however, he proposes a reconceptualization of it along two axes:

> first, *para-index* by which to suggest an epistemological concern about the ontological state or place of the diegetic object instead of the non-diegetic medium-specific nature of its image; second, *indexivity* by which to suggest an epistemological concern about the phenomenological activity of the subject coping with the image. (Jeong 2013, 186)

Both terms, *para-index* and *indexivity*, foreground an "epistemological concern," by which Jeong means that "what we want to know from an index is primarily what it refers to, its referent, whether ontologically present or absent, or whether phenomenologically clear or obscure—within the given diegesis that may be documentary or fictional" (ibid.). This is to say, in other words, what Elsaesser had already stated by saying that films do not so much refer to an extradiegetic reality as much as they create *their own referentiality* (which I already quoted in yet other terms as "what they refer to, above all, are 'the rules of the game' "). The term "para-index" thus concerns the status of the object and indicates that what is at stake or called into question is its ontological status *within the film itself*, independently of its status outside of it. In that context, the question whether any fiction (or documentary) was built up out of "automatic world projections" is considered irrelevant. "Indexivity," in turn, concerns the activity of the subject—the viewer—and assumes that, in watching film, this activity does not primarily concern believing or doubting whether what the image shows on screen actually and truthfully corresponds to its existence outside of the film. What matters to the viewer, rather, is to figure out what any given image indicates *within the diegetic world*.[9]

Just as Jeong reconceptualizes rather than discards the notion of indexicality, the crisis of ocular-centrist, distance-provoking spectatorship and the new cinematic "partnership" emerging with the ontological turn bring Elsaesser to propose a reconceptualized realism. This marks the third difference: it entails a "new materiality" or "a new concern and respect for reference in the visual media" (Elsaesser 2009b, 5). This new realism is different from the traditional kind in at least two respects. It involves, on the one hand, a reinvestment in the body, especially in its non- or other-than-visual perceptual qualities (tactility, touch, and the haptic; Elsaesser sees a corresponding investment, in philosophy and evolutionary neuroscience, in the concept of the "embodied mind"). On the other hand, the new realism goes beyond the presence of the body or centrality of the human agent by foregrounding a sense of "ubiquity" defined as "the presence of pure space":

> What is typical of these films is that objects, spaces, houses take on a particular sense presence of agency . . . to produce at first perceptual insecurity but then develop a more directly ontological doubt, as we are obliged to make a kind of cognitive switch or radical retroactive readjustment of our most fundamental assumptions about the diegetic world as a coherent time-space continuum. (Elsaesser 2009b, 12)

This sense of felt presence amounts to a "neo-realism 'virtualized,'" as Elsaesser calls it, and it is epitomized in Kim Ki-Duk's home-invasion film *3-Iron*. In this film, a speech- and nameless young man gains access to the homes of people who have temporarily left. Far from squatting in their places, let alone from entering as burglar or murderer, the young man inhabits the homes to continue the daily business of the legal but absent owners and to help out where he can. Thus, he takes care of their dirty laundry or fixes broken equipment, making sure to leave each house before the owners return. When he gets caught, however, he is convicted for trespassing and his actions are perceived as having criminal intent. In prison, the protagonist trains himself to become practically "invisible" by always staying 180 degrees behind the wardens who enter his cell. He successfully tests his new skill upon his release by revisiting the returned homeowners, who clearly sense or feel his presence, yet are unable to see him.

To Elsaesser, this sense of ubiquity, in the absence of ocular verification, "signifies the very absence of ground" (Elsaesser 2009b, 16–17). The force of the new cinema, then, is all but a reversal of what its early theorists, in Turvey's account, attributed to the medium: far from overcoming a visual skepticism, "nowadays . . . in the cinema, we can no longer trust our eyes . . . 'world cinema,' in my sense, shares the general skepticism toward ontological versions of photographic realism: ontology mark one, if you like" (Elsaesser 2009b, 5).[10]

Having thus arrived at the idea that contemporary world cinema takes skepticism to heart, let us relate Elsaesser's views back to D.N.

Rodowick's "update" of Cavell (and of Deleuze as well), which, as we saw, is equally based on the idea that we have moved "to an acceptance of skepticism." Wondering whether cinema in the age of the digital expresses (or calls for) changing ontological, epistemological, and ethical positions, Elsaesser and Rodowick both look for an answer at the spectator-screen relationship. They share the view, in that context, that "the desire to know the world" on the part of the viewer (Rodowick) or the need for film to "'reflect' reality" (Elsaesser) has lost its urgency. I already quoted D. N. Rodowick as saying that "in the world of computers and the Internet we have little doubt about the presence of other minds and, perhaps, *other* worlds," and that "the digital will wants . . . to create *different* worlds" (emphases added). These statements resonate with the point I brought up from Elsaesser, namely that we "take for granted the ability to live in fictional or rather virtual worlds." Rodowick updates Cavell in relation to this change by suggesting that skepticism of other minds takes on a prevalence over epistemological skepticism—a shift Elsaesser underscores when he writes:

> [T]here is no way back to assuming that "evidence" can be based on ocular verification ("to see is to know"). Not so much because the physical world is per se unknowable, but because people are opaque to each other, and thus intersubjectivity poses special epistemic challenges. Watching characters in the "new realism" mode is like watching other people have a headache: there is no way I can have positive evidence, other than reading signs for minds. (Elsaesser 2009b, 10)

The challenge of reading signs for minds is to pay what Rodowick calls the new "price" of skepticism: in his words, minds have become information, and we cannot know whether there are selves behind it.

I assume that these changed relations to the screen are more readily taken as challenges to Cavell than to Deleuze. After all, Cavell's concept of film as a moving image of skepticism was premised on the viewer's relation to the screen world as one marked by an outsideness: the succession of automatic world projections consists of a sequence of shots taken of *our* world, he claimed, yet we relate to this now inaccessible (because projected) world as though it were a world past. D. N. Rodowick responds to this by writing that digital information "attenuates or even blocks an earlier photographic relation to past worlds," adding that we no longer experience a sense of "powerlessness" in front of our digital screen.

Yet Deleuze also calls upon cinema to foster belief in *this* world, and explicitly *not* in "a different or transformed world" (Deleuze 1989, 172), as the digital will wants (according to D. N. Rodowick). Even more important, perhaps, is that the Deleuzian *impower* of thought finds its productivity or creativity in the cinema through the very *dispossession* of itself and of the world—which resonates to some extent with the powerlessness of the Cavellian viewer—whereas the digital screens, per the accounts of Rodowick and Elsaesser, foreground questions of *control*. D. N. Rodowick wrote: "[W]e believe, justifiably or not, . . . in our ability to control, manage, or communicate with other minds and world." Protagonists in mind-game films, by "seemingly losing control of their mind," also challenge viewers to control theirs. As Elsaesser has it:

> [O]ne overriding common feature of mind-game films is a delight in disorienting or misleading spectators (besides carefully hidden or altogether withheld information, there are frequent plot twists and trick endings). Another feature is that spectators on the whole do not mind being "played with": on the contrary, they rise to the challenge. (Elsaesser 2009a, 15)

Whether or not spectators rise to the challenge indeed, and whether this prepares them to adapt to or participate in our contemporary "societies of control," as Elsaesser suggests, I find this question of control over and manipulation of information and minds (of others as much as our own) strikingly pervasive in contemporary cinema.[11]

5.3. Nino as Interactive Spectator

Given the importance of the relation between viewer and screen in conceptualizing the impact of the digital/global turn on contemporary film, *Amélie*'s crucial scene at the café is worth revisiting, as it fictionalizes that relation by staging it in the film itself. Elsaesser argues that the relevant question for viewers of contemporary films is not so much whether anything happening in the diegetic world is *real*, but whether it offers clues aiding to solve a narrative riddle, to figure out "the rules of the game." As I argued previously, in *Amélie*, the eponymous heroine is playing the tricky game of cinematic skepticism, which involves plenty of role-playing and role-switching (as did Renoir's). Most notably, she seeks to reverse the roles of pursuer and the object of pursuit. While she starts off as pursuer of a mysterious man (Nino) who is himself already in pursuit of a third mysterious "object" (ultimately revealed as the mechanic/filmmaker), she aims to turn the tables by having the pursuer follow her lead to this third object, hoping to become his mystery woman in the process. Jamming a photomaton, she mediates between pursuer and his object of pursuit, directing both of them towards herself. Yet as the revelator of the pursuer's mystery, she nevertheless fails to reveal herself to him. That ends her game.

In the process, Amélie also trades places with Nino in her role as spectator, a position she occupies in the phantom train. Now caught up in Amélie's stratagem, which has plenty of enigmatic clues to offer, he surely does not seem to mind being "played with." Nino had already been positioned as "interactive" spectator of the augmented reality at the Square Louise Michel (viewing Amélie through the telescope) by the time he interacts with her through the transparent screen at the café. In chapter 4, I interpreted the scene as Jeunet's digital response to *It Happened One Night*, but postponed elaborating on a telling difference between the scenes. We should now be in a better position to grasp that difference.

The relevant question regarding Amélie's game (as in *It Happened*) is not who will break the rules of the game (as Deleuze asked of Renoir's film) but who will break through the screen, so to speak, or emerge from behind it (by "blowing a trumpet")—an event that nothing in the physical world (of the films) seems to prevent from happening. Yet in *It Happened*, it actually happened: Ellie simply drew the blanket to the side to appear to Peter. Capra then switched around the use of ordinary and special (soft) focus to express Peter's inability to accept the reality of his fantasy. It is only after Peter's refusal of Ellie's revelation of herself (the declaration of her love) that she leaves the hotel room in disappointment.

Since *It Happened* as a whole primarily aligns with Peter in terms of focalization, the appropriate equivalent of the scene in *Amélie* would actually not be for Amélie herself, but for Nino to expose himself. And while he knocks on the glass partition, we are left to ponder why he simply walks out of the café right when, as Amélie's mind tells us, he "has understood." Here I offer various possible interpretations for consideration.

According to the first, Nino's anticlimactic departure simply expresses (enacts, obeys) Amélie's wish. This would be on par with her mind now being in control of his actions ("He's going to dip his finger in the sugar") and would also explain her precautious action to ensure Nino will find out about the next move in her game. That, in turn, would further explain her tactics in playing the game: unwilling to draw the skeptical conclusion (letting him go altogether, rendering her own isolation complete), she establishes this new connection to the world without having to emerge from behind herself (by accepting the reality of her fantasy). D. N. Rodowick's observation about the impact of digital screens may be at stake here, albeit in reverse: the price of our belief in our ability to control other minds, he argued, is that minds have become "information." I already quoted him as saying that, in seeking "new ways of acknowledging other minds," we no longer know whether there are "other selves behind them." In Amélie, however, it is the heroine behind the screen who desires to control Nino's mind rather than the other way around. It then remains an open question as to whether Nino leaves because Amélie forces him to or whether Nino's self is taking its leave as Amélie is trying to manage his "information" (herself failing to emerge from behind her mind).

Another explanation would *not* be that Nino leaves simply because *he* (rather than she) wishes to do so. His action would still be involuntary, though not now because Amélie (or her voice-over) controls his willpower. The suggestion, rather, is to take the lack of motivation for his departure literally: Nino appears to break with the chain of causal action, and yet that break of causation is, as it were, itself but a mechanical consequence. In other words, we could read his departure allegorically as the consequence of digital capture, as the break of automatic analogical causation. At the very moment Amélie's "disembodied" voice-over gains the power to manipulate the world before projecting it, our "sense of reality" "simply" leaves—in this scene by quite literally walking out the door. Amélie's subsequent sigh (and her meltdown into a formless stream of information) then sounds like Laura Mulvey's sigh of relief (which I evoked in the first chapter) at the "abstract information system" for "*finally* sweeping away the relation with reality."

Taken together, these two readings combine the reinforcing implications of digital recording and screening, as D. N. Rodowick does in taking his guess at the riddle of the changing ontological, epistemological, and ethical implications at the digital turn.

These implications are already at stake before Nino takes off, when, still interacting with the screen, he insists on "it" being "you," pointing at the photograph and looking straight through the writing on the screen at Amélie. This, we could argue, plays out the ontological uncertainty Cavell attributed to the analog photograph (as discussed in chapter 1). To be sure, Nino's initial need for confirmation stems primarily from Amélie's disguise *in the photograph*. Yet this obvious difficulty in recognizing the face behind the mask itself obscures the equally obvious, but more profoundly enigmatic, fact that a photograph of Amélie is not Amélie in the flesh. For Amélie to affirm *"that is me"* would sound paradoxical, as it implies an ontological identity between image and model. But then her initial denial of Nino's question would be no less paradoxical, Cavell would say, if she merely means that the picture he is holding up is not a human creature. We could then read Amélie's shrug of the shoulders in response to Nino's insistence ("Yes it's you!") in Cavellian terms as suggesting that "such problems in notating such an obvious fact" bring to light that "we do not know what a photograph is" (Cavell 1979, 18).

But Jeunet gives this uncertainty another twist by placing Amélie "in the flesh" behind a digital screen, disguised as the waitress she nevertheless "really" is (within the diegetic world).[12] Taking her doubly disguised and digitized appearance into consideration, we might read Amélie's shrug of the shoulders differently: as indifference or some generic "who knows"—thus expressing what Elsaesser calls the general acceptance of skepticism in the digital age. I already countered his conception of "ontology mark two," according to which "trust has to be a function of skepticism," by objecting that trust (faith, belief) had already been such a function before the digital and global turns—and it *still* is, only not now because of some generic denial or indifference towards the question of reality. Nino's departure, in that light, would be a response to Amélie's initial denial of and subsequent indifference towards his satisfaction of her reality: facing a farce of skepticism, he takes his leave to look for a more moving image of it.

So Nino leaves the café 1) because, as an object of Amélie's digital fantasy, she makes him leave by wishing it; 2) because in the digital age we are not to know whether there are any selves behind the minds we seek to control; 3) because this previously digitized phantom has now turned into a representative of prefilmic reality, whose material connection to the world on screen has been broken; or 4) because he is facing a fake image of skepticism denying his satisfaction of reality.

That the film allows for these various options makes *Amélie* an exquisite expression of cinematic skepticism on the interface of the analogue and the digital.

5.4. The Cultural Dominance of the Digital, or: Nature's Return

Although the café scene's polyvalence contributes to its value, I do find that the idea of Nino as representative of physical reality, whose causal link to the world on screen is severed (or problematized) by digital capture, particularly powerful in light of the film's denouement. I argued in the previous chapter that the scene forms a turning point for Amélie: just when she gets to control Nino's mind, she all but loses her own. At least she loses control over the narrative (stratagem) she had been developing for Nino. His departure at the café foreshadows his more radical disappearance during their next meeting: when Amélie brings Nino's mystery to a point of resolution, his disappearance shortcuts Amélie's own resolution to reveal herself to him.

But of course, Nino finally does return to her. His appearance at her door is as lacking in motivation as his disappearance through the door at the café had been. And when she still fails to remove the screen between them, he insists on his return, announcing and indeed enacting the return of this return (*"je reviendrai"*). Although it merely displaces rather than explains the mystery of it, Nino's (re-)appearance does seem to be (re-)mediated by Dufayel, the forger-painter on the screen. This, then, is a final ironic twist to Cavell's remarkably apt comment about film: "This is not a return *to* nature but the return *of* it, as of the repressed" (Cavell 1979, 113–14). Nino returns as a representative of nature, which had already been repressed in the analog age, and now doubles down on his return through the interference of this analog-digital composite figure whose own material support is on the verge of collapse due to brittle bone disease.

In this regard, *Amélie* is strikingly similar to its otherwise inverted counterpart. In *Grizzly Man*, Timothy Treadwell appeared to be losing his own mind just when we thought him able to command the minds of the bears (if they can be said to have any). We can witness this, for example when he describes "intruders" to the park, who are seen throwing rocks at a bear in an apparent attempt to ward it off, as a group of "poachers" "stoning" it.[13] Besides his mental state, Treadwell is also losing control over his self-invented Grizzly Man *narrative*, according to which he is out on a mission to protect the bears he in fact endangers, when he slips from one persona into another in the scene meant to wrap up his expedition 2001. Facing this "fear of losing control" (as Jeong and Andrew have it), nature finally returns with such morbid irony that Herzog decides to interfere, first by literally cutting back Treadwell's outraged voice to impose his own, then by listening to the audiotape of Treadwell's fabulous destiny only to push it back into collective repression. That the tape, forged or not, should nevertheless reappear to circulate on the internet befits this series of ironic twists on the analog-digital interface.[14]

This comparative analysis thus challenges the idea that contemporary cinema takes our ability to live in fictional or virtual worlds for granted, claiming instead that the desire to know the world has not lost its provocation and that the question whether the world on screen provides clues does not necessarily bypass questions about its implications regarding reality. At the same time, I find what D. N. Rodowick calls the "will to control information" to pervade postphotographic film exceeding the relation between viewer and screen. Questions of manipulation and control not only concern the image; they are also played out in the narrative *and concern* the narrative, whose protagonists are being "played with"—as are the viewers.

In the final chapter, I provide a comparative analysis of two films, both from 2008, that give their own spin on this new tendency in cinematic skepticism to control information, to play with or manipulate minds, to unground ocular verification only to foreground the need to recover from a break with the world. Lucrecia Martel's *The Headless Woman* (*La mujer sin cabeza*) and Nuri Bilge Ceylan's *Three Monkeys* (*Uç Maymun*) stage this recovery in a way I find paradigmatic, by playing out an ambiguity or tension I am tracing throughout this book, one that finds us oscillating between discovering new connections and covering up the crisis altogether, between openings and closures. Unlike *Amélie* and *Grizzly Man*, neither film is particularly significant as a digital production—Martel shot *The Headless Woman* on analog, whereas Ceylan limits the powers of postproduction in *Three Monkeys* mostly to color manipulation, rendering the sickly narrative in appropriate hues. Yet I will argue that they nevertheless affirm the "cultural dominance of the digital" (D. N. Rodowick) by leading an assault on our ability to believe in *this* world.

Chapter 6

Reveiling the Gap in
The Headless Woman and *Three Monkeys*

An accident breaks a link to the world, opens up a gap, putting *the powers of the false* to work. Thus forced into thinking and on the brink of making fiction, the protagonists of *The Headless Woman* and *Three Monkeys* nevertheless choose to avoid both knowledge and fabulation. Rather than discover or reveal new ways of connecting to the world, they cover up their traces and reveil the groundlessness under their feet as they *reterritorialize* in a numbed and burned everyday.

6.1. Hit and Run: Plot Analogies

The Headless Woman (*La mujer sin cabeza*, 2008), the third and final instantiation of Lucrecia Martel's Salta trilogy,[1] centers on a middle-aged, upper middle-class dentist named Vero (María Onetto), short for Verónica and coincidentally meaning *true* in Italian.[2] After a seemingly minor hit-and-run accident shown in the film's prologue and a subsequent visit to the hospital, where only minor injuries need attention, Vero goes to a nearby hotel where, perchance, she runs into her cousin Juan Manuel, whom she seduces that night. Rather than the tightening of a web around a criminal protagonist digging a grave to hide a body, the main chunk of the film is left to report Vero's daily activities in the wake of this turbulent day.[3] Vero is initially withdrawn, absent minded, and irresponsive to external stimuli. Rendered in a Deleuzian vocabulary, we could say that while her body is intact, her sensory-motor link has been broken. Yet she gradually recovers from this condition: despite a disturbing self-accusation on Vero's part—halfway through the film, she suddenly claims that she may have killed someone on the road—everything seems to have returned to "normal" conditions when a party is held in her honor at the film's closing. The suspicion lingers that the men around Vero have taken care of any possible evidence that might incriminate her in a road kill, yet Vero seems to resign herself to that situation.

This plot description will prove remarkably similar to that of its companion in this comparative study: Nuri Bilge Ceylan's *Three Monkeys* (*Uç Maymun*, 2008). Like Martel's, Ceylan's prologue features a hit-and-run accident; in this case, it involves a middle-aged, upper middle-class politician named Servet (Ercan Kesal), coincidentally meaning "riches" or "fortune." Since he is running for president as leader of a (fictional) political party, he fears that official charges against him will offer his political rivals the opportunity to unleash a disastrous publicity campaign. He therefore bribes his long-time chauffeur Eyüp (played by famous folk singer Yavuz Bingöl) to take the rap and spend his time in jail in exchange for a continued payroll to support Eyüp's wife and son and a lump sum of money upon his release. All the same, Servet's fictional party suffers a crushing defeat at the elections against Erdogan's not-so-fictional APK party—historical footage of celebrating APK supporters is shown on diegetic TV screens.

With Eyüp jailed, his wife, Hacer (Hatice Aslan), seeks to keep their troubled son, Ismail, who just failed his university entrance exam, away from bad friends. In order to get him the car he needs for a temporary job as a daycare driver, she ends up giving in to Ismail's request to ask Eyüp's boss Servet for an advance payment of the promised lump sum. A sexual encounter between Hacer and Servet is part of the exchange, however, and is witnessed by a now even more troubled Ismail. Upon Eyüp's release from prison, Servet finds himself in trouble as Hacer, unwilling to end their affair, is stalking him, while Eyüp finds himself in trouble to avoid his knowledge of this affair, even as he is supposedly looking for the smoking gun that would confirm his wife's infidelity.

Instead of finding that evidence, Eyüp finds himself confronted, towards the end of the film, with his son claiming to have killed Servet. To prevent Ismail from going to jail for this murder, Eyüp first denies to the police that he knows about his wife's infidelity and then reverts to Servet's bribing strategy by asking a local tea house servant, Bayram, to plead guilty in exchange for a lump sum of money upon his release. Eyüp's decision to pass on the money he was offered by Servet to pass off the responsibility on his son's part thus makes the film as a whole come full circle.

Despite obvious differences between *The Headless Woman* and *Three Monkeys*—one, most notably, centers on the perpetrator of the accident, while the other shifts focus to the chauffeur's family to whom responsibility is passed off—the similarities between the films are all but uncanny, especially considering that both entered into the same Palme d'Or competition at the Cannes Film Festival of 2008.[4] Important representatives of the New Argentine Cinema and the New Turkish Cinema, respectively, both films open with a prologue featuring equally enigmatic hit-and-run car accidents—each of which I shall discuss in detail—with slowly unfolding aftermaths forming the main body of the films. Both films also involve adultery and (omitted from the descriptions above, but to be discussed further on) the dis/appearance of a mysterious(ly) drowned boy. Both of these events add to the complexity of the webs of half lies, blind eyes, and blunt denials entangling their protagonists. The main characters have trouble relating to the world, but their attempts to restore their sensory-motor links culminate in the end with a strong sense of closure, in terms of a narrative coming full circle and of protagonists closing their ranks.[5]

Formally, the films share an investment in episodic scenes, false continuities, oblique contexts, and irrational cuts. Martel and Ceylan are equally skilled, in other words, in their use of what Deleuze called the "powers of the false," as I will elaborate in the course of this chapter. To add to the odds, both films feature a technique I will introduce as the *virtual point of view*, which has important implications for cinematic skepticism. I will analyze how some of these formal techniques open up an Outside that contradicts or counterbalances the strong sense of narrative closure. As I discuss the respective films, it should also become clear, however, that they employ opposite narrative strategies, which goes to show that each has its own specific way of giving cinematic expression to the problem of skepticism. In other words, the films provide their own audiovisual and narrative clues that suggest ways of connecting to a world from which its protagonists feel severed and that strikes them as unjust, groundless, frozen, dead. I will start this comparison with a discussion of the accident and the virtual point of view (POV) in *The Headless Woman*.

6.2. The Accident and the Virtual POV in *The Headless Woman*

The scene of the accident opens with Vero driving in broad daylight on a deserted rural road alongside an empty drain. After a short, near-subjective through-a-windshield shot that reveals nothing but an empty road, the camera, ostensibly placed on the passenger seat, laterally frames Vero for the entire duration of the scene (which is well over three minutes long), with the exception of a brief but remarkable interruption which I shall discuss momentarily. While the cheerful tune "Soley Soley" sounds through the car's speakers (performed by the appropriately named band Middle of the Road), we hear Vero's cell phone ring. She takes her eyes off the road to search for the phone in her purse—ours are still fixed on her—when the car hits something. Though the sudden impact seems violent and shocking, the consequences initially appear manageable—for Vero at least. She merely loses her sunglasses and bangs her head slightly against the steering wheel. She stops the car and catches her breath; "Soley Soley" continues to play as though nothing has happened.

Vero reaches for the door handle to get out, but then she hesitates and changes her mind. After a brief pause, she slowly drives away from the scene only to stop again around the next bend in the road. There she does get out, unlike the camera, which slightly (therefore perhaps all the more awkwardly) tilts but remains inside the car. Vero paces up and down, literally headless from the spectator's point of view as her body is truncated by the edges of the car's windshield—an example of Martel's extensive use of what Pascal Bonitzer called "deframing" (*décadrage*) (fig. 6.1).[6] Rain—that allegorical eraser—starts falling in thick drops on the diegetic screen of sorts until the title frame cuts the scene.

Figure 6.1. A literally headless woman.

Reveiling the Gap in *The Headless Woman* and *Three Monkeys* / 131

I have omitted three significant details in this description—details that might easily escape one's attention upon first viewing. I will discuss two of these later on; they concern the nature of the collision itself and a guess at Vero's motivation to drive away from (rather than to investigate) the site of the accident. For now, I will insist on the importance of the third detail, which involves the short interruption of the long take mentioned above. This interruption concerns a brief rear-window shot onto the scene of the accident and occurs when Vero drives away from it. It is so brief indeed that we are probably unable to discriminate what it shows. At best, we may be able to see that *something* is lying in "the middle of the road." With pause buttons and other digital tools at our disposal, however, we can readily determine this to be a dog (fig. 6.2 and inset).

James Quandt makes an interesting point when he writes in his review of *The Headless Woman* that this particular shot "has been described as subjective, as being from Vero's point of view, but probably isn't" (Quandt 2009, 95). And indeed, we do not see the frame of the rearview mirror itself within the frame of the shot, as is customary in such cases—think of Marion anxiously spotting the police car behind her in *Psycho*, or *Taxi Driver*'s amazing final shot. Vero neither glances in the direction of the mirror when we cut back to her—the scene does not follow the editing conventions for an eyeline match—nor does she show any signs of having observed anything significant in the mirror (a sign of relief, say, for having hit a dog rather than a human being). I would doubt, then, what Amy Taubin asserts in her review of *The Headless Woman*: "In the rearview mirror we see, as she [Vero] also

Figure 6.2 + inset. The rear-window shot showing a dog "in the middle of the road."

must, her victim lying in the road but whether it is a dog or a child or both is unclear" (Taubin 2009, 23). Given our pause button, it is clear enough what Taubin doubts: that we see a dog and not a child. What we ought to doubt is what Taubin states with confidence: that we are looking through a mirror and that Vero is (or must be) doing the same. Given that Vero did not get out of the car, thus avoiding the knowledge of what she had hit, it would make sense for her to want to avoid this indirect confrontation as well.

I would rather side with Quandt, then, when he doubts the subjective nature of the rear-window shot, however hesitantly ("it probably isn't"). Yet he too seems to miss an important point when he parenthetically adds: "The film's central mystery rests on the ontological status of that one image" (Quandt 2009, 95). Although Quandt does not elaborate on this suggestive comment, I would argue that the ontological status of this image is an interesting one indeed, even if the film's mystery in no way depends on it—a crucial point that requires elaboration.

By doubting that the rear-window shot offers a subjective perspective, we need not assert that it provides an objective one instead: the point of view is too specifically restricted to a particular place for that, and what it shows from this position is too suspiciously unclear. That is, the point of view is *localized but not materialized* within the diegetic world. Ostensibly, someone must have turned around to see this, yet no one was actually there to make this turn: we lack an actual character to assign this view to. I would therefore suggest calling this point of view a virtual one. The virtuality of the point of view does not necessarily undermine the *reality* of the shot—we need not doubt that there was something (a dog) on the road—but by lacking a clear relation to a stable center of perception, the shot renders its *actuality* inoperable or impracticable.[7]

This virtual ontological status of the point of view is in fact already apparent in the long take interrupted by this rear-window shot. In it, the immobile camera persists in a profile view of Vero sitting behind the steering wheel. As such, this is a conventional camera position for scenes shot inside a car. But if it is awkward already to maintain this lateral framing for so long (especially because nothing very specific is happening or to be seen for the most part), it becomes all the more suspicious at the moment of the collision, as it prevents us from seeing what is happening in front of the car. The position of the camera now strikes not only as one that does not show anything specific, but as specifically *not* showing something, thus restricting *our* knowledge of the nature of the accident. As with the inserted shot, this is neither an objective point of view—the cinematic equivalent of an omniscient narrator, which would have shown us what had happened from the best possible position—nor a subjective one as we have no reason to assume that somebody is actually occupying the passenger's seat. With this uncomfortably insistent yet dispassionate recording of the entire scene, Martel puts a cinematic convention to use by turning it into a very deliberate localization: the point of view is conspicuously situated within the car, but as with the inserted shot of the dog, it lacks the materialization that would justify such a position.

Martel's own descriptions of her camera as "a character with whom I identify very closely" and as "someone who belongs to the world of the narrated" can seem misleading.[8] Such specifications do not accurately describe the instances of the virtual point of view under consideration. Had the camera been a character indeed, it could have picked up Vero's phone and prevented the accident to begin with. The sheer fact that it cannot do this *despite* being located in the car, or more generally the fact that Vero and the camera do not interact with and cannot acknowledge one another, underscores Cavell's insistence that the camera exists on a different plane as the protagonist and is thus marked by a fundamental outsideness. This, we saw, marks one pole of cinematic skepticism, the pole of the skeptical conclusion that renders our distance to the world absolute (which the camera does automatically).

On the other hand, the camera also alludes to the opposite pole of cinematic skepticism—the pole of wanting to defeat the skeptic by overcoming this distance to the world and render our presence and knowledge of it absolute (beyond doubt), even if this requires the overcoming of our human limitations. For despite its lack of interaction, the camera does ostensibly insist on some localized presence within the diegetic world. The specification of this presence as a virtual one, I want to argue, is pertinent not only in the strictly Deleuzian sense of something real but not actual, it also invokes the more loosely defined contemporary application of a "virtual reality," broadly understood as a simulated (actual but ultimately not real) physical presence.[9]

Martel offers what I consider a much better characterization of her camera (than it being a character) when she conceives of herself as "playing doctor" by using the technical aspects of cinema as though they were "medical instruments." The camera, she mentioned in an interview, "is like a microscope. Behind it, I feel as though I am examining my characters—though I [also] have a very strong feeling that the closer I get, the less I know" (Matheou 2010, 30). In another conversation, she puts it as follows:

> There's a medical aspect in my filmmaking in that I try to get as close as possible to my subject in an almost microscopic way and from that draw more general reflections. The set of a film can be similar to an office where X-rays or CAT scans are made of the body. All these technical aspects allow us to come closer and closer to discovering and putting out into the world the mystery that is by nature secret and mysterious [*sic*], and that's the mind itself. (Oumano 2011, 177)[10]

This citation suggests that the central mystery of the film does not primarily concern the question whether Vero hit a dog or actually killed a person on the road, but whether we can gather what goes on in her mind. All we have at our disposal to read Vero's mind is her body, and one of the central mysteries for Martel concerns the gap existing between them ("the closer I get, the less I know"). By situating her camera between subjective and objective positions, Martel seems intent to "record" this gap between body and soul, between mind and world, urging us, in the words I quoted from Elsaesser in the previous chapter, to "read signs for minds."

We can elaborate on this significance of the virtual point of view by understanding it as a particular instantiation or variation of what Deleuze dubbed "free indirect vision," which in turn is a specific rendering of Pier Paolo Pasolini's appropriation of *free indirect discourse* for the cinema. Here, however, we should be careful not to take the term too narrowly, as Matt Losada does in his reading of *The Headless Woman*: if free indirect discourse were limited to a camera assuming a subjective presence *by simulating or mimicking a character's way of seeing* even when objective points of view are used (that is, ultimately, even when the protagonist him- or herself is in view), we run the risk of missing the point entirely.[11] Martel's camera, despite its insistent fixation on Vero, is anything but immersive or mimetic. Likewise, we would miss another, if related, point of Martel's film were we to assume that the "information provided to the viewer is restricted to that known to the protagonist" (Losada 2010, 308). It is true that, by withholding our view onto the road, Martel seems to reduce our knowledge of the accident to Vero's. Yet I will argue in the next section that *The Headless Woman* is precisely premised on a discrepancy between two bodies of knowledge, both restricted but unequally so: the protagonist's and viewers'—Vero's and ours. To grasp this, and to more fully appreciate the relevance of a Deleuzian understanding of free indirect vision, we need to include the preceding two scenes of the film's prologue in our analysis and examine the remaining details from the scene of the accident, as promised.

6.3. Martel's *Changüí*

The film opens with a scene of indigenous teenagers playing along the road where Vero's accident is about to take place. We see a (truncated image of a) running boy and a dog, with off-screen children calling him by his name ("Aldo") and his nickname ("harelip"). This shot combines the virtual point of view (with the camera moving at a different pace and altitude as its subjects) and the technique of deframing (cutting the boy from the waist down) in order to establish a premonition of things to come: we recognize a dog first, and an unidentified boy later (fig. 6.3).

As dog and boy are about to exit the frame on the right, the traveling camera speeds up to reframe them, and when the boy jumps down a slope, his face and the camera quickly match. A pause button would do to verify the obvious reason for his nickname.

The scene cuts to reveal the chasers: three indigenous teenagers jump down a slope onto a road, where the accident is about to happen. Seemingly out of nowhere, Aldo suddenly somersaults across the road, past the boys, into the empty storm drain alongside it. One of the other boys, named Changuila, jumps after him, but unlike Aldo, he finds himself unable to find his way back out of the drain before the image cuts away.

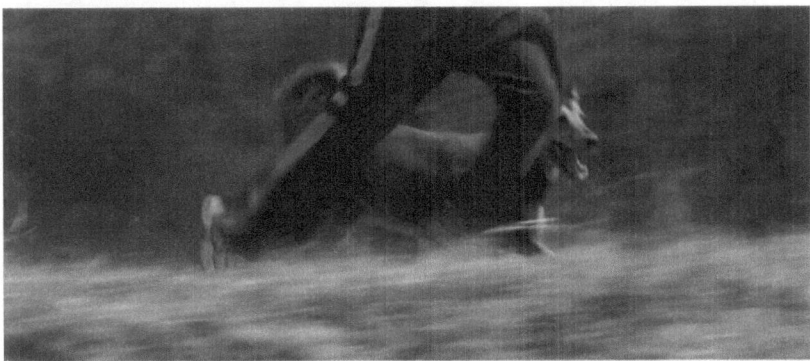

Figure 6.3. Aldo ("Harelip") and his dog.

That cut introduces the first of the film's numerous false sound bridges. While the next scene starts with an image of two middle-aged women reflected in a car window, we hear the voices of off-screen children in the background. Although this acousmatic sound (to use Michel Chion's term for diegetic sound without visible source or cause) is seemingly continuous with that of the previous scene, it turns out that these are not the voices of the children we had seen and heard playing alongside the road (and who had been introduced acousmatically as well, yelling as they were from off-screen spaces).[12] Instead of the indigenous teenagers, we now cut to Caucasian children playing in and around parked cars. This act of pinning sounds onto the "wrong" bodies and its subsequent adjustment thus involves the viewer in drawing racial and class divisions within Argentine society. To underscore the prank Martel is playing on us, one of the women seen in the window repeatedly instructs the other, who is putting on false eyelashes, to close her eyes ("Close, close").[13]

This is when Vero first enters the scene, approaching from a blurry background: with her red sweater and bleached hair, she clearly stands out in the crowd, no matter how shallow the focus. From the scraps of background conversation, we figure that the women are wrapping up a picnic at a swimming pool (pools, bathrooms, and sinks being the tropes that connect all three of Martel's Salta films). We further learn that a new pool, having been built behind a veterinarian hospital, is threatened with contamination by this "disgusting turtle thing." One of the women expresses the hope that the turtles will die of chlorine. Probably oblivious of this comment, Vero inadvertently associates herself with this contaminating threat by responding to the women who congratulate her on her new, blonde look: "Unfortunately, it fades with chlorine." When Vero gets into her car to drive off, the film cuts to the scene of the accident, of which I promised to discuss two details.

The first concerns the literal impact of the collision itself. It appears that the car does not hit something once, but twice. Or rather, it seems to hit two different things, as the violent points of contact, although similar in terms of their impact and quick in succession, are still too far apart in time to suggest that the front and back wheels run over the same obstacle. The second detail concerns a probable cause for Vero to change her mind when she wants to leave the car immediately after the collision: as she turns sideways to look for the door handle, she notices small handprints on the side window (fig. 6.4).

Both details may suggest that Vero did not merely, or did not only, hit a dog. Hence, they are two more reasons for my insistence, earlier on,

Figure 6.4. Indexical signs on the side window.

that the ontological status of the rear-window image of the dog does not bear all the weight of the film's mystery: even if Vero had seen the dog, it would not have been sufficient (to her) to prove what had happened. At the same time, taking into account the information provided by the introductory scenes and the observed details does not necessarily resolve the questionable nature of the event either. The handprints (prototypical indexical signs) are indeed indicative of a causal relationship between child and car, but the particular placement of the impression—flat on the side window/screen—is too awkward to suggest the violent, quick impact a collision would have had. Moreover, we have a much better suggestion available to explain their presence: one of the children playing inside the car in the previous scene had planted his or her hands on the windows while the women were talking about the contamination of the pool (one mother comments off-screen: "Watch those fingers") (fig. 6.5).

Figure 6.5. "Watch those fingers."

Though we can only guess whether *Vero* witnessed or noticed those fingers at that point in time as well, as viewers we can readily verify that the imprints on the side window were visible to us *before* the impact, when Vero bent over to reach for her purse (fig. 6.6).

While this does not rule out the possibility that Vero hit a child—we heard two impacts after all—the point is rather that the film invites us to probe the mystery of Vero's mind rather than to establish the truth of what happened during the accident. Or better: to watch this film is to establish two reconstructions of the event, one based on what we think has happened, and another one based on what we think *she thinks* has happened.

In that context, it is significant that Vero first tells her family, after the accident, that she had hit a dog on the road. To add to this perverse pulling of the rug from underneath our analysis, halfway through the film, she changes her account of things. Seemingly out of the blue (she stands in line in the supermarket with her husband), she says she thinks she killed someone on the road. Vero does not explain her reasons for this self-accusation, but perhaps Martel provided a clue by suggesting that Vero's awareness of the handprints on the side window made her change her mind about leaving the car to examine the damage. If this is the case, we know that Vero is either wrong about her recently expressed suspicion of human involvement in the accident or that she is right for the wrong reasons. It would seem, at any rate, that irony comes full circle as the index, emblem of truth, serves as a false sign for a woman who, despite being named after the truth, tries hard to avoid its knowledge.

Figure 6.6. Vero reaches for the phone in her purse just before the accident.

The gap between the viewer's knowledge and Vero's widens by taking the double impact into account. As viewers we do know, unlike Vero, that Changuila got trapped in the drain at the spot where the accident took place and that the dog was with him when the film's opening scene broke off. Hypothetically, it should be possible that he managed to get out of the drain the very moment Vero passed by, and was knocked back into it by the impact of her car (therefore remaining invisible in the rear-window shot).

This option, although labored, seems to be corroborated later on in the film. I described above that it started raining by the end of the accident scene. We learn afterwards that this was the onset of a heavy storm that filled up the drain. Soon after Vero starts suspecting that she killed someone, she encounters potential corroboration for this suspicion. This occurs when Vero and her family drive by a clogged sewer in the drain; the firemen at work on the site inform them that they have found the body of "a person or a calf"; the newspapers confirm afterwards (per Vero's account) that a drowned boy had been found.

Narrative logic compels viewers to connect Changuila's entrapment in the drain to the drowned boy as well as to Vero's accident (and its double impact), although the conjunction of these two connections itself makes for a labored, crudely constructed, hypothesis. Martel, however, seems intent to thwart all such logical efforts at reconstructing the event: right at the moment when Vero, visiting a local nursery in the wake of the news of the drowned boy, becomes ill at ease to learn that one of the helpers has gone missing, Changuila blandly appears in front of her (*changüí* is Spanish for "joke" or "trick"). It turns out that not he, but Aldo (who, we discover, is his brother) is the one who has gone missing, and that his family has been looking for him for a week now—while we know through Vero's account of the newspaper that the drowned boy had already been found. To the best of our knowledge, Aldo's body never was.

6.4. Identification of a Headless Woman: Margin and Center

It is possible, to be sure, that Aldo's body *was* found; that the body in the drain was *his* but that the corpse was neither returned to his family nor publicly identified, perhaps because the body may have shown signs of a violent impact and hence have incriminated Vero. But at this point, we have arrived at a level of assumption, speculation, and suggestiveness that has little to do with the interpretation of signs or with narrative logic. Far from approaching a stable position from which to finally nail down the truth of what has happened and assess a totalizing view of the film as a whole, we have rather been subjected to what Deleuze calls the "powers of the false"—the operative powers, that is, of the crystalline regime of the image. In this regime, as opposed to the organic regime (regimes that coincide with Deleuze's broader distinction between the movement- and the time-image),

> narration ceases to be truthful, to claim to be true, and becomes fundamentally falsifying. This is not at all a case of "each has its own truth," a variability of content. It is a power of the false which replaces and supersedes the form of the true, because it poses the simultaneity of incompossible presents, or the coexistence of not-necessarily true pasts. . . . Falsifying narration . . . poses inexplicable differences to the present and alternatives which are undecidable between true and false to the past . . . Contrary to the form of the true which is unifying and tends to the identification of a character . . . the power of the false cannot be separated from an irreducible multiplicity. (Deleuze 1989, 131–33)

The accident not only occasioned the present to break down into the simultaneous questions "What has just happened?" and "What is going to happen?"—as is characteristic of the event—it also produced a series of incompossible presents in its aftermath—that is: a number of situations that are equally possible, but not at the same time. Vero may have fallen sway to a false sign of truth (the handprints on the window), but the viewer of *The Headless Woman* is in no better position of knowing what happened: the clues provided give way to a number of plausible options, none of which is sufficiently supported by evidence: Changuila got drowned, Changuila got killed, Changuila is alive; Aldo got drowned, Aldo got killed, Aldo disappeared. All of these are equally possible, but not simultaneously, as they cancel one another out. Far from an unfolding according to the logic of a unifying present, then, the accident occasions the unfurling of diverging series of incompossibilities that force Vero to think. No longer able to distinguish the real from the imaginary or perception from memory and fantasy, her faculties disintegrate as she oscillates between different possible worlds: there is one in which she is guilty, which pushes her into self-accusations, and another one in which she had only hit a dog and got scared. In the next, she suffers from not knowing whether to acquit herself or not, while she really does not want to know what had happened in yet another world. There is a world in which she denies her guilt despite knowing better and one in which the people around her deny her guilt and cover her trails against her will.

In this context, we can better understand the significance of Martel's use of the virtual point of view as a particular instantiation of free indirect discourse—provided we avoid the narrow understanding of the term discussed above. To Deleuze, the various methods grouped under the rubric of cinematic free indirect discourse, or free indirect vision, ultimately challenge "what the camera sees, what the character sees, the possible antagonism and necessary resolution of the two" (Deleuze 1986, 149). Free indirect discourse no longer suggests that we are dealing with two kinds of images—objective and subjective ones—or even with two bodies of knowledge—one associated with the character and one with the author (or what the author allows the viewer to know). Such antagonisms and displacements lead to a more profound transformation and bring to the cinema what Bakhtin had detected in the novel: namely, "a 'plurilingualism'" as Deleuze writes, "that brings together the author, his characters and the world" only by way of a "broken line, a zig-zag line" (Deleuze 1986, 187).[14] Such a cinematic form of heteroglossia replaces the interior monologue of a character—the interiority of the subject and its identification—in favor of a process of becoming. In Deleuze's words:

> Objective and subjective images lose their distinction, but also their identification, in favor of a new circuit . . . What cinema must grasp is not the identity of a character, whether real *or* fictional, through his objective and subjective aspects. It is the becoming of the real character when he himself starts to 'make fiction' . . . and so contributes to the invention of his people. (Deleuze 1986, 149–50)

For Deleuze, "making fiction"—which he sometimes also dubs as "making up legends" (*légender*) or "fabulation"—is neither an act of making up a story and passing it off for true, nor is its potential to create new worlds specifically marked in opposition to the real. Rather, it consists in endowing the actual world with the powers of immanent transformation and becoming.[15] As a character, Vero herself does not necessarily proceed to tell such fictions—she barely speaks at all in the film. But the powers of

142 / Cinematic Skepticism

the false do lead Vero away from "identification of a character" in favor of a becoming leading toward "an irreducible multiplicity," as is already evident in the first scene following the accident of the film's prologue, which shows Vero's visit to the hospital.

After a series of tableaus connected by way of false sound bridges, which serve to indicate that the powers of the false accumulate and accelerate in quick succession, Vero realizes that she cannot recall her own name when prompted by a nurse—a name that the viewer does not know at this point in the film either.[16] Shocked by this, she flees to the hospital's bathroom. Vero washes her face when a demanding voice-off calls out the name "Elisabeth Andrade." Not knowing whether this is her name or not, Vero confusedly looks over her shoulder to see if someone is addressing her. The scene then cuts to a medium shot to display the complexity of the bathroom space with its several mirrors, doors, and abruptly ending walls. A nurse appears to address Vero and approaches her, but then she continues to call out into an empty space behind Vero (figs. 6.7, 6.8).

Figures 6.7, 6.8. Calling for Elisabeth Andrade.

Subsequently, several women appear from different angles into different planes of this space. Each of the women—be it a nurse, a security guard, a patient—is presented as a potential "Elisabeth Andrade," only to refute this identification, until finally an indigenous woman, whose face we barely get to see, emerges from one of the bathrooms in the right margin of the frame. Further framed by two security guards as well as several mirrors and doorposts, she is immediately escorted away into the depth of field. The whole scene itself is shot through one of the mirrors, while Vero witnesses the event via the mirror next to the one through which the camera records the scene (fig. 6.9).

Thus, the identification of a character (as the form of the true—of "Vero") gives way to a complex multiplicity that unfolds with the shifting signifier Elisabeth Andrade. But that is not all. For this mistaken identification with a visually and literally marginalized woman of color is also the first sign of an ethical reveille on Vero's part. As the sense of her own identity continues to wane, Vero's awareness of shadowy figures surrounding her privileged existence increases proportionally. For example, when Vero goes to a hotel after leaving the hospital and has a meaningless conversation with a hotel manager at the doorstep of her room, she keeps staring at a woman behind him waiting to bring towels to her room. When she gets home, she notices the children of her indigenous housekeepers playing inside her house as if for the first time, realizing that she does not know their names. Initially, these figures

Figure 6.9. Vero witnessing Elisabeth Andrade through the mirror next to "ours."

144 / Cinematic Skepticism

invariably appear out of focus, in the background, and in the margins of the shot (figs. 6.10, 6.11).

Gradually, however, they come to occupy the signifying zone of the image. This first happens when Vero, upset by a boy who loses consciousness on a soccer field (confronting her with the possibility that she may have knocked out a boy herself), runs off to yet another bathroom and allows herself to be consoled by a darker skinned plumber. In want of running water, we hear the workman buy a bottle of water from an off-screen vending machine, which he then pours over Vero's hair and neck while she bends over the sink. In this moment of strange intimacy, Vero's head is deframed while the plumber occupies the signifying zone, thus inverting the predominant compositional structures of the film up to this point (fig. 6.12). Even more telling, perhaps, is the next scene in the film—one in which Vero, waiting in line in the super market, confesses to her stunned husband that she killed someone. Just before this confession, and probably spurring her to it, Vero stares at a young indigenous girl sleeping over the shoulder of an adult standing a couple of spots ahead in line (fig. 6.13).

Figures 6.10, 6.11. Vero turns towards the literally marginalized people in her life.

Reveiling the Gap in *The Headless Woman* and *Three Monkeys* / 145

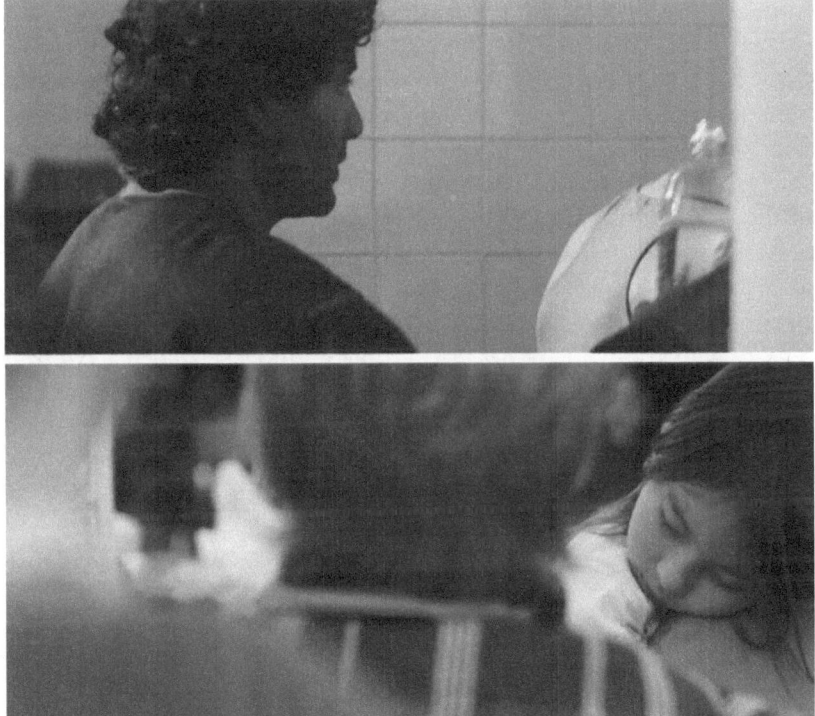

Figures 6.12, 6.13. From the margin to the signifying zone of the image.

The focus on this girl's face and its sharp contrast to the blurry surroundings mark the sharpness of Vero's growing connection to a world that had thus far only existed in the periphery. The initial misidentification with Elisabeth Andrade has thus triggered new affective capacities within Vero, who seems well on her way to fabulate a fiction of the people who have been missing from the signifying zones of her life. This fiction starts with the self-accusation, if not indeed self-sacrifice, of Vero as killer.

Having thus come to occupy the center of the frame halfway through the film, however, the people of color are then gradually pushed back to the margins again, if not out of frame altogether. In this way, Martel provides a cinematographic expression to the gradual recovery of Vero's "true" identity. The change begins to set in when Vero, still wavering between self-guilt and self-acquittal, increasingly feels an indigenous gaze weighing down on her. Instead of turning away from the camera toward these fleeting figures, she now turns away from them (in the case of her gardener for example, cf. fig. 6.14) or pretends ignorance (as when two women discuss the family of the missing boy outside her car (fig. 6.15).

This act of pretending not to see or of willfully looking away culminates in what is arguably the most important and loaded scene of the film: Vero's visit to El Cruce, an "intersection" of slums inhabited by the (metaphorically crucified) indigenous people of Salta. The significance of the scene stands out all the more clearly through its contrast with a previous one. In this earlier scene, Vero revisits the site of the accident at nighttime, along with her husband, Marcos, who is intent to prove to her that she had merely hit a dog; throughout the film, he keeps repeating to the point of *demanding* that nothing happened ("*No pasa nada!*"). Marcos, seated off-screen, drives the car, when Vero (framed in close-up from behind) suddenly bursts out: "Over there! There's something on the roadside. It's right there, Marcos, you've passed it." Meanwhile

Figures 6.14, 6.15. Vero avoiding the indigenous gaze.

the camera remains fixed on the back of Vero's head, which makes it impossible for the viewer to tell whether anything was indeed to be seen, and, if so, what it was. We cannot tell whether Marcos saw more than we did either, though this seems doubtful since he passed "it." All the same, he responds as he turns the car around by saying: "It's a dog," and, "The drain is really full." Passing by the site again, the camera now frames Marcos in close-up from behind, and it stays there while he takes over directing Vero's look: *"There's* the dog!" Vero says, "Don't stop." Marcos replies, "It's a dog. You got scared. It's okay." The camera now cuts to Vero, who insists: "I think I ran over someone." Marcos keeps directing from off-screen space: "You got frightened by the dog. *There*, over there." Vero's head does not move to the roadside, any more than we get to see anything but the back of her immobile head. It would seem, then, that the withheld point of view shot that should have shown the dog expresses Vero's unwillingness to look at it, despite having initially directed attention to it herself—a point underscored when she declines Marcos' suggestion to drive by a third time. Despite persisting in the idea of having killed "someone" rather than (or in addition to) a dog, she equally persists in avoiding the verification of this idea—if the dog would already have proven anything either way.[17]

Now when we compare this scene to the one in which Vero visits El Cruce, we note a subtle but nonetheless significant difference. Vero had been brought to the slum by one of the film's liminal figures, an indigenous girlfriend of Vero's lesbian niece, Candita, who goes by the vulgar name of "Cuquita" (slang for vagina). While Cuquita drops off a gift to and connects with the suffering family, who still does not know Aldo's whereabouts, Vero remains in the car, opening her window only to receive directions for the way out of the slum. Following this, Vero passes by Changuila, who is on his way to get water with a red jerry can (fig. 6.16 on page 148). The moment is brief and barely marked but striking all the same: the camera, positioned on the back seat, pans to connect with the boy, showing him through a window that has an only partially legible word marked on it by a finger (fig. 6.17 and inset on page 148). Changuila, meanwhile, looks through another side window at Vero. We only see the back of her head, but even that indicates that she is oblivious to his presence, pretends she is, or effectively seeks to avoid his look. At any rate, she does not return his look, any more than he acknowledges ours.

Figures 6.16, 6.17, and inset. Indexical, symbolic, illegible: passing by Changuila in El Cruce.

The resonance between the two scenes, then, is evident. In both cases, we have a triangulation of unmatched looks. Yet in the first scene, the virtual point of view is a "classical" case of free indirect vision in the strict sense, as its lack of movement and explicitly restricted view could be said to mimic Vero's state of mind. In the second scene, however, the virtual point of view, and what it allows us to see, explicitly distinguishes itself from Vero's. Moreover, this glimpse of the boy is mediated by a sign that is not only indexical (as were the handprints on the window in the scene of the accident), but symbolic as well. A linguistic, yet illegible sign inserted in a view, not from nowhere, but from no one, suggests a fiction Vero is now hurrying to avoid telling herself.

6.5. Closing Doors, Closing Worlds

At this point in the film, others are taking over Vero's story. It has gradually become evident that the men in her family are invested in getting Vero's life back to normal. Vero discovers, for example, that her brother has removed X-rays from her file in the hospital and that her husband had the dent in the car fixed. The men's involvement in Vero's process of normalization (her *reterritorialization*) is rendered cinematographically when Marcos invites Vero's cousin Juan Manuel over to discuss "a situation." Walking away from Juan Manuel and Vero to turn on the light, Marcos, himself half cut off by the right edge of the frame, reveals the presence of an indigenous housekeeper staring at the adulterous and incestuous cousins. Having been caught as the bearer of the gaze "in center-frame," so to speak, the woman abruptly returns to work, running her errands in the background again with her look turned away from her employers. Sensing that this marginal presence is bothersome still, Marcos, gesturing reassuringly at Juan Manuel, asks the housekeeper to leave the room altogether, and to "close the door, please."

The film's closing scene captures this effective, but for Vero not necessarily comfortable, sense of *reterritorialization*. By this time, Vero has changed the color of her hair. Giving up her blond hair for a much less striking (if still dyed) dark color may well serve as an emblem for the fact that the cover-up is now complete.[18] Paradoxically, Vero's peroxide-blonde hair, for all its unnatural whiteness and contrast, had come to be associated with people of color and the theme of contamination explored throughout the film.[19] The change of dye, then, may well mark Vero's desire to take a distance from that association.

This sense of distance is given further significance by Martel's way of recording the party held in Vero's honor, at which she receives compliments on her new look. The gathering takes place behind glass doors, with the camera remaining outside to follow Vero from a virtual point of view. The glass, appropriately frosted to offer a half transparent, blurry view, may well express Vero's escape from our focus and resonates with the initial view we caught of her. Given the logic of focalization in the film as a whole, it would make sense to claim that the virtual point of view coincides with the gaze that had weighed down on her between these moments, and hence forces the viewer to identify with the indigenous position—a position marked by a denied access to the world of the party in which Vero occupies the center.

But the relation between party and point of view may have other implications, leading to alternative interpretations, as well. After all, Vero may be the center of attention, but she did not organize this party herself. This is significant in the context of the men around her having taken over the telling of her story. Notably, the party takes in the very hotel near the hospital where Vero had spent the night of the accident with her cousin Juan Manuel. Just before joining the festivities, Vero walks up to the front desk and checks to find that no records exist of her stay there. This could mean, of course, that the whole thing never happened. It may also mean that Juan Manuel has "taken care" of this potentially corroborating evidence, not only of their night together, but of the entire day and its events. This, in turn, may mean that he, if not indeed everyone else around her, doubts that Vero had merely hit a dog, despite going out of his way to convince her that she had. As a medical doctor, Juan Manuel had access to all the local officials, whom he contacted to "verify" that nothing had happened during the night of the storm. The missing evidence of her night at the hotel, then, may not so much satisfy Vero's desire of getting her life back to "normal" as it signifies her awareness of the daunting extent to which that life is a bubble—a skeptical conclusion visually rendered by the frosted glass door and her own sense of exclusion from the party/world.

A third interpretation remains open to us, as we—viewers—are not only outsiders looking in through the frosted glass; we are listeners receiving the sound coming out of the room as well. Although subdued, it remains audible enough to understand the more emphatically uttered, though all rather meaningless, phrases of praise. The music playing in the background is rather more telling. From interviews we know that the '70s pop song played at these final moments of the film ("Mamy Blue"), like the one we heard on the radio during the accident ("Soley Soley"), is meant to relate the scene to the time of the military junta.[20] Several commentators have pointed out that the final scene thus invites us to read Aldo's disappearance, and of the lack of responsibility on Vero's part for finding out about him, allegorically as the bourgeois attitude towards the *desaparecidos*. On the other hand, of the various versions and covers of the song, Martel picked Los Pop-Tops English rendering, one that features a front man of color (Trinidadian Phil Trim) in an otherwise white group, rather than, say Julio Iglesias' cover—a choice that would have made more sense if a point about dictatorships had to be made.

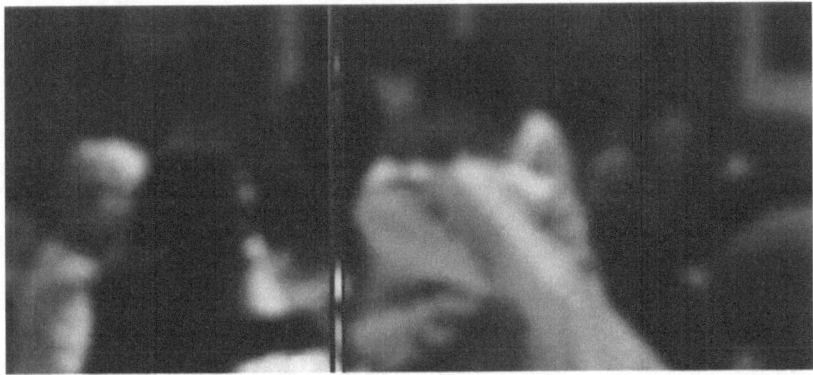

Figure 6.18. Vero at the party behind the slightly ajar door of translucent glass.

There is thus a sense of ambiguity in the final scene that is perhaps best indicated by the fact that the glass doors remain ajar (fig. 6.18). As in the case of *Amélie*'s scene at the café, the polyvalence of *The Headless Woman*'s ending increases its significance in terms of cinematic skepticism, yet here I do have my preferred reading. For the fissure suggests that Vero's isolation may not have been rendered complete, that the metaphysical distance to the world outside the edifice is not an absolute one. Despite the loss of a more radical potential and the recovery of her sensory-motor link, Vero maintains an openness toward the possibility of creating new connections to this world, however limited in scope.[21]

6.6. The Accident and the Virtual POV in *Three Monkeys*

Three Monkeys' assault on any call to believe in this world carries perhaps even more force, but as we shall see, Ceylan's film ends on a similar note as *The Headless Woman*, with a strong sense of closure nevertheless leaving space for an openness to the world, warped as it is through a connection to the Outside. The film also starts on a similar note as Martel's, as the following analysis will show, with a hit-and-run accident withheld from view, offering a virtual point of view instead.

I already mentioned that the prologue shows how Servet gets involved in a collision, even though that accident itself is withheld from view. Apart from an initial objective windshield shot of the tired-looking politician behind the wheel (fig. 6.19), the three-minute prologue is composed of two mirroring scenes, each consisting of a single long take. The first starts when we cut from the windshield shot to a view of the back of a car, which serves as an establishing shot of sorts: we now see that the man is driving at moderate speed on a desolate country road at night, surrounded by trees (fig. 6.20).

Having been trailed by the camera for a while, the car gradually drives away into the distance. To the viewer, the circumference of the car's light beam appears to shrink to a mere dot on a big black screen. Meanwhile, the noise of the car gradually gives way to the ambient sound of the surrounding forest, with its crickets and chirping birds. Break lights provide a last red glow before the car takes a turn and disappears altogether, leaving us literally in the dark about the events

Figures 6.19, 6.20. Servet just before to the accident.

Reveiling the Gap in *The Headless Woman* and *Three Monkeys* / 153

taking place just behind the bend in the road in the distance. Within this total blackness, we can hear a faint noise of screeching tires.

The second half of the prologue reverses the order of things. This time around, the scene starts off with a black screen. The chirping of crickets and birds is all but suppressed by the steady sound of pouring rain. We hear a car approaching before we get to see its headlights occurring from behind a distant bend in the road. The light beam reveals a barely discernable man running from the middle ground of this shot to hide behind a car parked in the foreground; only the roof of this car is visible along the bottom edge of the frame. The approaching car stops when it arrives at an indistinct body lying in the middle of the road, in the middle ground of the shot (fig. 6.21).

We hear car doors opening, but no one gets out. We hear a man asking a woman what she thinks she is doing, to which she replies: "Going to have a look, the guy looks alive." The male voice urges her to stay inside the car: "Don't be ridiculous. We'll call the police." On that note, they drive off. Servet now reappears from behind the car parked in the foreground. He walks around the vehicle, gets in, and wipes the wheel with a tissue. The scene cuts to the title frame as Servet drives off, accompanied by a roaring thunderbolt to punctuate the end of the prologue.

Wanting "to have a look" but not being permitted one: it is as though the man in the car were Ceylan himself, frustrating the viewer no less than the woman next to him. Indeed, the viewing position is so awkwardly restrained that this, more than anything, seems to be the point

Figure 6.21. An indistinct body lying in the middle of the road.

of the entire scene. Since it appears clear enough what has happened (and since Servet, unlike us and unlike Vero in *The Headless Woman*, examined and therefore *knows* what he has hit), we are to figure out why Ceylan robbed us of our view of such an obvious event. What is the function of *this* particular constraint?

The question becomes all the more pressing once we realize that Ceylan, like Martel, puts the *virtual* POV to work. As discussed, the virtual POV can be seen as a particular instantiation, or rather a variation, of free indirect vision. Neither subjective nor objective, it implies a specific viewer positioned within the diegetic world, even while no character can be assumed to incarnate it. Hence, I called this POV *localized but not materialized* in the world shared by the characters. In the scenes I just described, we see this virtual POV at work when the car drives away into the distance, which is not happening because it speeds up, but because the camera slows down and by the same token ceases to offer an objective point of view. Indeed, as the sounds from the forest increase and gradually replace the noise of the car, our sense of physical presence grows accordingly: by all appearances, somebody or something through whose senses we now experience the world not only stopped trailing, but stopped moving altogether. Despite this, no character appears to grant us a subjective vision. The shot shows no signs of a driver or passenger perspective: it is not framed by a dashboard, rearview mirror, or hood, nor do we see headlights shining forth. We are not offered a reverse shot revealing the identity or nature of the perceiver either. As a result, we should not only feel constrained because of our situatedness: we are so ostensibly *here*—left in the dark among the crickets—whereas we really want to be *there*—on the other side of the bend—but *we cannot go there now*.

The effect of this virtual POV is further enhanced in the subsequent scene. Although it consists of a single long take, Ceylan's virtuosity radically destabilizes the POV as he alternates between subjective and objective perspectives.

The initially immobile camera is positioned behind and slightly above Servet's parked car. When the other car enters the scene of the accident, Servet runs to hide behind his vehicle—hence behind the camera. He sides, or coincides, with us as he comes to embody the objective POV, thus turning it into a subjective one (we now see what he sees). This fluctuation between subjective and objective shots is made even more pertinent when Servet's face reappears. Initially he looks off-screen

Reveiling the Gap in *The Headless Woman* and *Three Monkeys* / 155

to the right to watch the couple drive away. To wit: we witness him witnessing the witnesses. Servet then turns his head to look at the body on the road, offering us an over-the-shoulder [OTS] shot—a subjective shot allowing us to look with, or, so to speak, through the character (fig. 6.22). When he turns his head to look off-screen again (fig. 6.23), we no longer look with him (seeing what he sees), but *at* him (seeing him looking at something off-screen): it is as though we are no longer associating with him hiding behind the car, but wish to remain hidden from him, be left unseen by him.

Without moving, then, the viewer has been displaced from a position behind the car to a position behind the screen, which is given further significance when the camera, hitherto immobile, suddenly pans down to allow us to look through the car window—that allegorical screen of sorts—and watch how Servet gets behind the wheel. As if to underscore our invisible presence, the politician anxiously looks around him and

Figures 6.22, 6.23. Oscillating between subjective and objective shots.

Figures 6.24, 6.25. Servet leaving the scene of the accident.

checks his mirrors to make sure he is acting unseen before erasing his fingerprints from the wheel (fig. 6.24). With a final gesture mimicking Servet's earlier turn of the head, the camera pans right to witness Servet driving away (fig. 6.25).

As a whole, the prologue thus comes full circle: from the opening shot, which offered an objective look through the windshield/screen at Servet fighting off sleep behind the wheel, we came to occupy a disembodied position within the diegetic world. After the cut, Servet came to embody our position, until we were finally put back behind the window/screen, only to start the sequence again as we are left behind with the car driving off into the distance. This cyclical loop structure in fact anticipates the structure of the film as a whole.

These fluctuations between objective and subjective positions, and the dynamic between presence and absence, embodiment and disembodiment, insideness and outsideness effectively highlight our sense of distance to the world viewed. In so doing, the prologue points toward *Three Monkeys*' preoccupation with cinematic skepticism. But these "aberrant movements" also point toward another sense of outsideness—to an Outsideness (*le Dehors*) in the Deleuzian sense of the word. Before discussing this, I want to point out a third and final feature of the prologue relevant in this respect, namely, the cut between the two mirroring scenes.

The first scene literally fades to the black of night when the only source of light disappears behind a distant bend, whereas the second scene starts from this same blackness, with a car appearing from behind an equidistant bend. If it were not for these bends to turn in opposite directions, the points of view in both scenes may well have coincided, and we could have been led to believe that there was but a single, continuous (uncut) scene. As is, we should rather infer that we are dealing with two different scenes, the second of which is shot from the opposite side of the same bend, with the camera positioned at a similar distance from it.

These two scenes are indeed separated by a cut that remains invisible: we can only hear the shift between them. As mentioned, a faint sound of screeching tires, all but overwhelmed by the surround sound of chirping nightlife, could be heard when the screen went black: the audible index, we are likely to infer, of the accident that injured or killed the body we see in the next scene. It takes careful listening to detect the even less distinct sound of a dog at that very moment as well. Then, after three quick, barely audible barks, Ceylan literally turns off the microphone altogether.

When he turns it back on, the screen is still black, but the sound of crickets returns, this time all but suppressed by the monotonous clatter of pouring of rain. The silence between the scenes lasts but a second, yet it creates an enigmatic depth. It opens up an invisible crevice, indicating that a cut or black screen has been inserted within the blackness of night. At the point where Ceylan so crudely withholds the scene of the accident from us, he more subtly reveals the sheer nothingness inserted between the moments immediately preceding and succeeding the moment of collision.

6.7. Ceylan's Procedure of Conjecture

The invisible yet enigmatic cut in the prologue does not so much connect as separate the prologue's mirror images. In Deleuzian terms, it is not a simple *interval* that crosses the void, relating one image to the next so as to form chains of logical and chronological sequencing; it is rather an *interstice* disconnecting the before and after. The interstice, in Deleuze's own words, is a "spacing which means that each image is plucked from the void and falls back into it" (Deleuze 1989, 179), and as such it marks an operation of differentiation. In this operation, the so-called irrational cut becomes significant in and of itself: in Ceylan's prologue, the dog flees (or disappears) into it.

We can readily see that the irrational cut and the fluctuation of POVs not only work to reinforce one another; they also collaborate to create *Three Monkeys*' enigmatic, elliptical narrative form. The film proceeds by way of episodic development; it forms sequences of semi-autonomous, differentially related vignettes (spatiotemporal blocks). In fact, each of these vignettes itself already contains *false continuities*. That is, they possess a certain degree of consistency, form seemingly continuous or coherent blocks of optical sound situations, but nonetheless contain incommensurable audiovisual elements, creating "aberrant movements" as a result.[22] Sounds and images are connected by way of irrational or, better yet, a-rational relations: they do not form completely random piles, but they produce assemblages based on very precise mismatches. In Ceylan's work, these often include false sound bridges (a favorite device, as we have seen, of Martel as well).

Consider, for example, the vignette that occurs briefly after the title frame, in which we find a fully dressed Eyüp sitting on his bed at dusk, car key in hand—presumably to indicate that he accepted Servet's ordeal to take the rap—while his wife, Hacer, seems sound asleep behind him. When the sound of a train occurs in the background, Eyüp looks up and over his shoulder (figs. 6.26, 6.27).

A magnificent vista of cargo boats on the Marmara Sea, seen through the living room window, is offered as a POV shot (the one Eyüp turned to see; fig. 6.28). With the sound of the invisible train continuing, Hacer, now fully dressed, walks into this shot to water the plants in the windowsill (fig. 6.29).

The train is still passing when we see her wake up their son, Ismail (Ahmet Rıfat Şungar), in the room next door, telling him he is about to miss his train. A quick series of shots show Ismail eating his breakfast in the living room, walking out of the house, crossing the railroad separating the house from the sea, and sticking his head out of a running train, until we finally cut to a meeting with his father in jail. In short, while these few shots certainly appear in chronological order, they introduce very

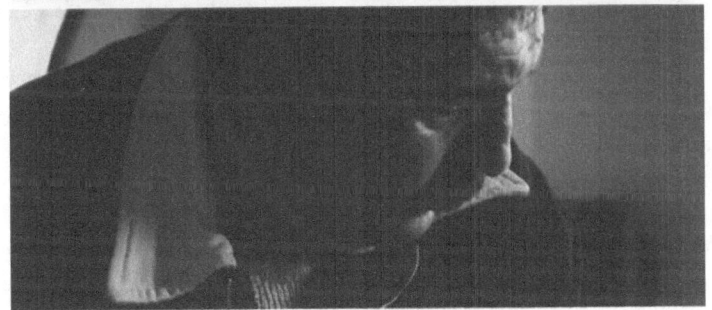

Figures 6.26, 6.27. Eyüp hears a train pass by.

Figures 6.28, 6.29. False reverse shot.

precise mismatches to suggest that things are not connected as smoothly as they appear: the sound bridge of the train suggests a continuity in real time, as does the eyeline match of the first cut. Yet Hacer undermines this suggestion of continuity by walking into Eyüp's view while she was supposedly sleeping behind him. The suggestion that the brief shots form a sequence of events taking place during one and the same morning is further contradicted by the fact of Eyüp's imprisonment at the end of the sequence. This temporal mismatch is underlined by other little slippages, such as the one that makes us pin the sound of the invisibly passing train first onto a ship seen out of the window and then connects with Hacer's warning to her son not to miss a train yet to come.[23]

Such slippages are not simple "goofs"—unintentional continuity errors reminding us that the film is an elaborate production rather than a snapshot taken of reality itself. Nobody, as Cavell reminds us, needs reminding that a film is (only) a film. Rather, Ceylan's aberrations engage and indeed implicate the viewer in the construction of his narrative. Just as we figured that an accident must have taken place between the two scenes of the prologue, we retrospectively adjust our impression of the unfolding of a single morning in this scene—the one that starts and ends with Eyüp—by inserting an entire trial in the interstice. And this is, in fact, the blueprint for the entire movie, which develops according to a *procedure of conjecture*, as a synopsis of the film, like the one I offered at the beginning of this chapter, will readily point out.

I think there is little room for doubt that the events I summed up there—from Hacer's request for money from Servet to Ismael's confession of having killed him—are indeed the most significant actions making up the story. Yet this lack of room for doubt is precisely what is at stake in the film, considering that none of the (diegetic) facts I mentioned in my synopsis actually *describes* actions or events depicted in the film. This is not because the descriptions are inaccurate, but because the actions or events are not depicted at all. This indeed conditions Three Monkeys' conjectural procedure: it does not *show any* of its nuclei; it *implies* them. Anything that would normally perform a cardinal function in a narrative and thus allow the viewer to reconstruct the logical and chronological order of events into a "story" is in fact withheld from view in the film.[24] For the most part, all we get are the moments before and/or after, never the actual events themselves. From these situations, as well as from the characters' reactions and responses, we can gather, infer, guess, or assume what must have happened. This was already the case with Servet's accident in the prologue and with Eyüp's trial right after; it is no different with the sexual encounter between Hacer and Servet or with Servet's murder. In the former case, Ismail, having returned home unexpectedly, peeps through the bedroom's keyhole. Instead of providing us with an eyeline shot matching what he sees, however, Ceylan inserts a reverse shot showing a close-up of Ismail's eye framed by the keyhole. It is from his response and his subsequent actions that we can figure what we would probably expect but were not allowed to see for ourselves.[25] In a similarly indirect way, we learn of Servet's murder when Eyüp, having been led through a series of false continuity shots into a police station, is asked during an interrogation whether he, as Servet's long-time driver, has any idea who might have killed him. Fait accompli, apparently. It is as though the film proceeds by way of a-rational cuts and yet does not allow for room to doubt the rational (logical and chronological) sequence of events.

6.8. Letting Ambiguity Linger

During Eyüp's interrogation process, the officers showcase another strategy abounding in the film: the high degree of ambiguity in the use of their language. In technical terms, the officers, as all characters in the film, employ signs in so-called oblique or opaque contexts.[26] Thus, when they tell Eyüp that the last text message on Servet's phone came from his wife and ask him, "Didn't you know?" the question is so ambiguously formulated that we have no precise idea just what Eyüp denies when he nods his head and clicks his tongue (or what he, properly speaking, affirms when he denies a negatively formulated question). Is he merely (affirming or) denying that he knew about his wife's text message or that it was the last one Servet received? Does Eyüp affirm/deny that he knew his boss and wife were on "texting" terms with one another, perhaps even that they had arranged to meet one another, or had been meeting all along, or that they had an affair? "Didn't you know?" By lacking a stable referent, the question grows in all directions over the film as a whole. What, indeed, didn't Eyüp know that we do, or vice versa?

This idea of oblique linguistic contexts is further developed through the ringtone on Hacer's phone: Yıldız Tilbe's arabesque song "Emi." The song's text, including its title, puts a curse on the addressee, but the implied addressee varies throughout the movie. The phone rings frequently without Hacer being able to find it or pick it up, forcing others, along with Hacer herself, to endure lines like "I hope you love and are not loved back," or "I hope despair is always at your door."

That the addressee is indeed depending on context becomes particularly striking when the song is used as a false sound bridge. In one scene, we watch Servet and his wife leave their house. Suddenly, the ring tone starts, and we see Servet searching in the direction of the camera for its source. A sudden reverse shot reveals that we had been looking on through Hacer's eyes, whom we now see gazing at the couple, with the song putting a curse on their love ("I hope despair is always at your door"). The song continues uninterruptedly when the scene cuts to Hacer's purse hanging outside a running shower. Eyüp peers into the bag, initially leaving the phone untouched. But when the song starts over again ("I hope you suffer from love"), he picks up to hear a male voice fulminating: "What do you think you were doing outside our house!" Eyüp underscores that the question of the addressee is at stake by asking to whom the speaker had expected to talk—upon which the line gets disconnected.

This use of oblique contexts is once again put to work when Ismail confesses that he killed Servet. He does not, properly speaking, confess anything in particular when he says to Hacer, out of the blue, that he "did it." Nothing in particular indicates that "it" should refer to Servet's murder, and Hacer initially reacts confusedly, indicating that she is not sure what he is talking about. Yet even when it does start to dawn that he must be confessing to a murder, we should still be suspicious of his claim. Caution is called for, not because his claim does not really make sense, but because it is at least as plausible as Eyüp causing a hit-and-run accident with Servet's car—something Eyüp must have confessed under oath.

This is how Ceylan's conjectural procedure implicates the viewer. While the film deliberately leaves significant gaps on the level of its discourse, we make up for this "direct experience" and "actual knowledge" of "actual events" taking place on the level of the story though our knowledge of genres (*Three Monkeys* follows the blueprint of a conventional crime story), of narrative clichés, and through our ability to read film as a system of signs. Hence, we no longer need to see the crucial events themselves to connect the dots; a web of slight, casual, indirect, and insinuating signs will do to confirm or seal our conjectures. Indeed, were we to deny our knowledge of what is going on, we would find ourselves in the same awkwardly naive position as Eyüp assumes.

Ceylan nevertheless calls for caution, or evokes some critical distance against our credulity, when commenting on the scene of Servet's final appearance—a scene that precedes Eyüp's interrogation at the police station. This scene starts with the camera following Hacer to an open field along the Bosphorus. Surrounded by the ruined Byzantine city walls and overcast by heavy clouds, the field has every appearance of a theatrical setting. It is introduced to us as a reverse shot of Hacer's gaze. But then Ceylan has her enter *her own* visual field as she walks up to Servet, who is waiting for her in the distance (figs. 6.30–6.32). A fight ensues between the two, with Servet offensively trying to rid himself of

Figures 6.30–6.32. Hacer entering her own POV.

164 / Cinematic Skepticism

a smitten Hacer. The ruder he reacts, the more she clings to him, until she literally falls onto her knees to embrace his kicking legs.

The entire scene is shot in a single long take (almost three minutes in duration) with an immobile camera keeping its subject (the couple) at a distance. There are no close-ups to reveal the wrath and despair on their faces, no fast-paced editing to match the fiery exchange. As viewers, we are put back in the position Ceylan had assigned for us in the prologue: we are being kept at a distance just when we wanted to "have a look." But here Ceylan offers another turn of the screw: not only does he refuse to cut to a close-up, but he cuts to a shot taken from the same angle at even greater distance, with the striking difference that the vista is now framed by foliage (figs. 6.33, 6.34).

Ceylan does not offer a reverse shot to reveal the identity of the person hiding away in the bushes. Commenting on this decision, Ceylan said that he "wanted to let some ambiguity linger. [Hacer and Servet] could also be observed by the father."[27] By using such phrases as "*some*

Figures 6.33, 6.34. The cut to the framed view.

ambiguity" and "could *also*," the director, even while offering an alternative reading of the plot, indirectly acknowledges that we are more likely to interpret the final shot as seen through the eyes of Ismail hiding away in the bushes, waiting to launch his assault.

In my reading, however, the significance of the scene does not depend on the ambiguous identity of Servet's supposed killer—that is, in knowing whether it was the father or the son (or who knows) who "did it." What matters still more than a declaration of an unknown murderer's actual presence through a subjective POV is the virtual presence implied by the preceding viewpoint. The long take of Hacer and Servet's fight involves the most enigmatic virtual POV yet, not least because it initially appears as a subjective shot (of Hacer) and is supplanted by a shot that *again* strikes us as a subjective one.

The transitions here are significant in and of themselves. The first is an unmarked transition: there is no cut (or reframing, or any other technical trick) inserted between what appears as Hacer's POV and the view in which she appears. This resonates with a previously discussed scene in which Hacer magically walked into Eyüp's view while she was supposedly asleep behind him: both cases are marked by an incommensurability between perceiver and perceived, whereby the actuality of one eclipses that of the other. It is what Deleuze (after Leibniz) calls a case of incompossibility: both shots are perfectly normal and certainly possible, but not at the same time—a trademark, as mentioned in discussing *The Headless Woman*—of the powers of the false.[28]

The second transition, the one from the virtual POV to the final subjective shot, is perhaps even more significant. We could describe it from a technological perspective as a variation of the jump cut. In the strict sense, a jump cut occurs when two successive shots of the same subject matter are taken from an ever so slightly different angle. Such a violation of the thirty-degree rule of continuity editing, part of Godard's claim to fame, tends to make its subject seem to jump in time; it is (to put it in contemporary terms) as though our online video or media player momentarily froze and now picks up a continuous scene a few seconds later. In the case under consideration, however, the effect is quite different. Since the subjects of our view—Hacer and Servet—are filmed from a significant distance, and since it is not primarily the angle but the distance to them that slightly varies, the result is that the viewpoint jumps more than they do. This jump, moreover, is not a temporal as much as a spatial form of displacement. Given that the displaced viewpoint is attributed to an unknown viewer who is hiding away from Servet and Hacer, the preceding and much longer shot now stands out for being taken from a position that should be in plain view in a double sense: being caught between the fighting couple and the person in the bushes, it ought to be visible to both, whereas it in fact appears visible to neither.

As in the prologue, Ceylan thus combines fluctuations between points of view and a-rational cuts to create a virtual presence within the diegetic (if stagelike) world. And just as the invisible (if audible) cut in the prologue revealed an enigmatic crevice, a sheer nothingness inserted in lieu of the accident, the cut to the subjective shot in this scene, far from revealing the identity of the killer, reveals that nothing is actually present to stand in the way between killer and victim, subject and object. In so doing, the scene opens onto a *virtual* presence, of something that is yet to come. "Nothing," in other words, should not be understood as an absence or a negativity—it is not anything lacking. We should rather take it in the positive sense of a void or a point of connection with the Outside. By locating the virtual position *within* the diegetic world—that is, by relating images to "a point of outside beyond the outside world"—Ceylan effectively brings about what Deleuze had called a "suspension of the world," a power the film-philosopher attributes to modern film (or the time-image) generally (Deleuze 1989, 181).[29]

Drawing here on Blanchot's notion of *le Dehors* (Blanchot also speaks of it as *le Neutre*—the Neutral), this point of outside is not, for Deleuze, a point of transcendence: it is not as though modern film projects a beyond in any religious sense, or even only a better, more perfect world than the one we inhabit.[30] Nor does the suspension of the world amount to a phenomenological reduction—a way of bracketing the world as we "naturally" experience it for the sake of examining consciousness (or its cinematic equivalent, the "apparatus"). Rather: as a space without a place, it is a disjoining force residing outside of Being, image, and language, opposing gravitating forces of a center of origin, of harmony and of unity. Already in *Difference and Repetition*, Deleuze had argued that thought is marked by its relation to the outside; thinking, as I discussed previously, is not a form of contemplation, but it happens to us in an encounter. We are only forced to think when some x (something eluding identification, recognition and judgment) imposes itself on us and disintegrates the faculties, putting *them* into a state of exteriority. That thought comes to us from the Outside, then, is clearly not to say that it pre-exists in some way (in a world of ideas, say). On the contrary: if thought is opposed to judgment, identification, and recognition, it is because the latter depend on past conditioning and the harmonious co-functioning of faculties, whereas thought occurs as an openness toward the future. Deleuze thus appropriates the notion of the Outside for his philosophy of immanence: thought is forced onto us by the powers of qualitative change and of self-differentiation by the forces that keep pushing into an unknown, as yet unthinkable future whose possibilities may not yet be contained within the actual conditions of the given.

Modern cinema, as we have seen, has its own relationship to thought. Rather than creating concepts, as philosophy does, it produces audiovisual assemblages of a specific kind. Whereas classical cinema may have produced images of thought that correspond to notions of knowledge, truth and interiority in so many variations of the Cartesian cogito, modern cinema, according to Deleuze,

> develops new relations with thought from three points of view: the obliteration of a whole or of a totalization of images, in favor of an outside which is inserted between them; the erasure of internal monologue in favor of a free indirect discourse and vision; the erasure of the unity of man and world, in favor of a break which now leaves us with only belief in this world. (Deleuze 1986, 187–88)

I have discussed the tools Ceylan employs to create *Three Monkeys* as an instantiation of modern cinema: incompossible viewing situations, false continuities, virtual and fluctuating points of view, oblique linguistic contexts, differentially related vignettes, and a conjectural narrative procedure all work to develop the new relations between cinema and thought from outside. Still, it may seem a far cry to argue that *Three Monkeys* should be capable of evoking belief in this world.

6.9. *Three Monkeys* and the Suspension of the Ethical

Indeed, the tone of the film, rendered in sickly, drained colors (postproduced pale greens, yellows, and orange-red hues prevail),[31] along with its isolated characters, claustrophobic spaces, and its strong sense of closure, rather seems to point at the sheer lack of belief in this world. One could easily argue that Eyüp's unholy bribe at the end of the film goes to show that the political defeat and even the murder of Servet—the contractor-cum-politician whose name translates as "riches" or "fortune" and who stands for mutual implications of the new money of global capitalism, fraud politics, and clientelism—will not stop his mentality from trickling down, preventing ordinary people from living a morally acceptable life. In his review of *Three Monkeys*, film critic Vecdi Sayar sums it up:

> How related are the stormy lives of small people, who are indifferent when AKP's election victory is announced in the televisions, who watch Yeşilçam movies in admiration, whose telephones ring with tunes of arabesque songs, to what is really happening in the society? Is it possible to live in this society without being a prostitute? Who is, which classes are, responsible for the fact that people take refuge in mosques? (Sayar 2008, trans. Basak Yuce)

While Servet did not ultimately manage to buy himself the presidency, he did manage to affect "small people" like Hacer, who did not find it possible to offer a worthy life to her son without prostituting herself, as well as Eyüp, who took refuge in a mosque on his way to Bayram, not to pray so much as to reinforce himself while appropriating Servet's contractor mindset. Significantly, Sayar formulates his rhetorical question in terms of ordinary people's relation to the world: what *Three Monkeys* displays, in a reading I share with him, is a sense of indifference, of resignation and withdrawal. Sayar is undoubtedly right to suggest that the film points an accusative finger at Servet (or his "classes"), though I would not think of him as the *cause* of *this* particular malady. Even if Servet is morally corrupt and exploitative, he can only get things his way as long as "small people" like Eyüp and Hacer, who are indeed small enough to be economically dependent on the likes of Servet but not so small as to lack any resources to pursue what is right, find themselves turning their backs on one another under the pretense of covering those backs. The world of *Three Monkeys* is a world of moral stagnation and impasse, which is marked by the paradox that established values are held up by, and inspire, immoral actions.

All of this is to say that, in *Three Monkeys*, the link between humans and the world has been broken. This world is not peopled by morally upright characters ready for purposeful action, but by human beings who no longer know what to do without reverting to the hypocrisy represented by the three monkeys of the film's title. In fact, this title accurately captures the paradoxical sense of moral stagnation. For in the Japanese pictorial maxim, which itself adapts Confucius' description of morally upright behavior in the Code of Conduct, the three monkeys embody the proverbial dictum "see no evil, hear no evil, speak no evil." In the West, however—as in the film's title—the proverb rather signifies the hypocritical turning of a blind eye (along with deaf ear and mute mouth). "In the film," Ceylan sums up in an interview, "the son pretends that he hasn't seen his mother commit adultery, the father pretends he hasn't heard his boss's voice on the phone, and the mother lies to the other two: her husband and the child. In our day, then, the metaphor of the three monkeys is used in a negative way, to denounce the hypocrisy of appearances" (Cardullo 2015, 106).

Yet in the midst of this "hypocrisy of appearances," another appearance is made to announce an altogether different dimension of the story. When Ismail drives Eyüp home upon his release from prison (with the car financed through Servet's money), they stop, per the father's request, at the grave of Ismail's (unnamed) brother. Later in the film, the dead boy makes two ghostly appearances: in the first, Ismail reaches out longingly when he sees the boy, drenched in water and seemingly violated, coming towards him in a hallucinatory vision (fig. 6.35).

The boy later silently embraces Eyüp, who is lying in bed in a defeated mood. In both cases, the respective men had just pretended not

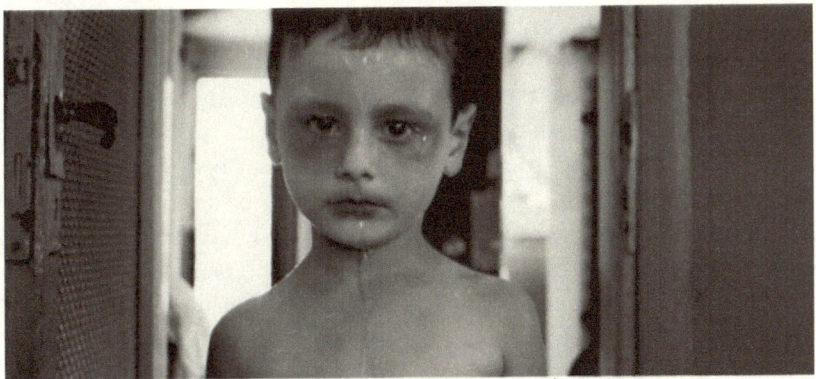

Figure 6.35. The drowned boy: Ishmael's brother.

to know what they must have found hard to deny. Ismail denied to his father, then still in jail, that Hacer was unfaithful, while Eyüp himself denied whatever the police officer expected him to know about his wife and his boss. In that sense, the boy may well represent a confession of sorts, if not for sacrificing truth, then for the need of consolation. More pertinently: if Ismail, son of Hacer, suddenly has a brother—another one of his father's sons—we are surely invited to read *Three Monkeys* allegorically against the background of the story of Abraham.

In the Hebrew Bible and the Quran alike, an aged but still childless Sarah (Sara) convinces her Egyptian handmaiden Hagar (Hajar, Hacer) to bear her husband Abraham (Ibrahim) a child so as to live up to the covenant with God that Abraham be progenitor of nations.[32] Thus, Hagar gives birth to Ishmael (Ismail). Fourteen years later, Sarah, despite having long passed the childbearing age, still has a prophesized child with Abraham herself—Isaac (Isḥāq). Per Sarah's request, and reinforced by God, Abraham then sends Hagar and Ishmael away. When the two endure hardship and are about to die of thirst, God creates a well right under their feet, at the point where today's Zamzam provides holy water to the hajji in Mecca. But this is also the point at which consensus between the Judeo-Christian and the Islamic versions of the story ends, and indeed where their paths as world religions decisively diverge. *Three Monkeys* places itself at this religious, historical, and cultural junction.

In the Judeo-Christian version of Abraham's story, Isaac becomes the more important of his children, as he was the one whom his father would have sacrificed to God were it not for the latter's divine intervention on Mount Moriah. By contrast, most Muslims believe that Abraham was to sacrifice Ishmael to God: since the Scriptures state that Abraham was asked to offer "his only son," the sacrifice is assumed to have taken place before Isaac was even born. The significance of this controversy can readily be seen from the fact that Jesus descends from Isaac's lineage, whereas Mohammad belongs to Ismail's offspring.[33]

Read against this background of the biblical and Quranic narratives, the dead boy in *Three Monkeys* may well be taken to represent the premature death of the Christian lineage. We could further speculate that something must have prevented a divine intervention, as a result of which Isaac was "sacrificed" "by accident" (as though, to wit, he were a poacher of sorts). This throws an unexpected light on Eyüp's final decision to "sacrifice" Bayram, the orphaned teahouse servant, rather than yet another son.

This allegorical reading puts *Three Monkeys* in stark contrast with Kierkegaard's interpretation of (the Judeo-Christian rendering of) Abraham's sacrifice. In *Fear and Trembling*, Kierkegaard offers four different retellings of this story. These are meant to unravel a paradox not unlike the one we encountered in *Three Monkeys*, namely, that the killing of Isaac is ethically wrong but religiously right. Kierkegaard ultimately pleas for a theological suspension of the ethical based on the difference between faith and resignation. Abraham, Kierkegaard argues, could not have acted on account of the latter: he did not simply submit to the will of God because God had told him to sacrifice his only son, and he *knew* God is always right. Instead, he *believed* that God would never do (command) something unethical, yet he was still prepared to go ahead with the ordeal if demanded. Kierkegaard further specifies that Abraham did not believe he was to be redeemed in the next life for obeying God's will in this one. Rather, Kierkegaard writes,

> Abraham believed and believed for this life. To be sure, had his faith only been for a future life, he could indeed more easily have cast everything away in order to hurry out of the world to which he did not belong. But Abraham's faith was not like that, if there be such a faith, for that is not really faith but only the remotest possibility of faith, which faintly spies its object at the edge of the horizon yet is separated from it by a yawning abyss within which despair plays its tricks. But Abraham believed precisely for this life, that he would grow old in the land, honored by the people, blessed by posterity, forever remembered in Isaac, his dearest one in life. (Kierkegaard 2006, 17)

In this reading, then, Abraham did not turn his back on the world in order to go through with God's command. That is, he did not manage to cope with the prospect of sacrificing what was dearest to him in life by turning his faith into the world of the afterlife. He kept his faith in God's intervention even when it seemed no longer possible: his belief was for *this* life and for *this* world to which he *did* belong.

Kierkegaard's rendering of Abraham's belief is the kind Deleuze has in mind when he programmatically claims, as aforementioned, that "cinema must film, not the world, but belief in this world" (Deleuze 1989, 272). In order to restore our broken link to the world and to be able to reconnect to what we hear and see, we need to believe in *this* world *as in the impossible*, Deleuze writes, claiming that modern cinema in particular possesses to power to provide us with the reasons to believe in it—reasons we are in want of, he adds, "whether we are Christians or atheists" (ibid.).

With Ceylan we could perhaps include Muslims in the equation. With *Three Monkeys* he not only comments, as has been pointed out, on the allegorical significance of the way Turkish society approaches "the Kurdish issue or the Armenian issue" (Magden, quoted in Suner 2011), meaning the loops the country goes through in order not to acknowledge atrocities committed against minorities living along and across its eastern borders (including the 1915 genocide); he also points to Turkey's precarious location, historically and geographically, as the threshold between the Muslim and Judeo-Christian worlds, and indeed between Europe and Asia, as the shift of meaning of the film's title in the East and the West signifies.[34]

Kierkegaard all but names skepticism when he speaks, in the quotation above, of "only the remotest possibility of faith" which "spies its object at the edge of the horizon yet is separated from it by a yawning abyss within which despair plays its tricks." Since we could also apply the description almost *verbatim* to the unknown murderer in *Three Monkeys* spying on Hacer and Servet, perhaps even the dead boy's consolation no longer suffices to provide reasons to believe in this world. Eyüp's family's suspension of the ethical is neither justified on theological grounds, nor does it foster his belief in *this* world. On the contrary: it tilts over the other side of Kierkegaard's crucial distinction between faith and resignation. But while Eyüp and his family are thus drawing the skeptical conclusion, Ceylan makes sure to insert the virtual point of view so as to offer an opening to an Outside of their morally stagnant world.

6.10. Avoiding Knowledge, Unmaking Fiction

In this comparative analysis, I first argued how Vero, named after the truth but seeking hard to avoid knowledge of it, fails to pick up an opportunity at making fiction after a car crash breaks her sensory-motor link—a failure Lucrecia Martel renders allegorically and cinematographically by filming through an illegible, broken-off word written with a finger on the dirty side window of Vero's car, not far from where a child's handprints had been visible at the time of her accident. The handprints, I had already argued, function as false indexical signs of truth, and as such it gives way to a whole series of mismatches, false continuities, and similar powers of the false, all pushing Vero beyond self-identification, forcing her to think, to start fabulating, and to discover new connections with the world and the marginalized people around her. For a while, her world trembles and shakes with potential significance—perhaps a sign of guilt, perhaps a sign of promise—when people of color gradually come to occupy Vero's mind as well as (what Bonitzer calls) the signifying zone of the image. But by the time she passes Changuila at El Cruce, she cannot bear to look at him, unlike the virtual point of view Martel offers from the seat behind her. Hurrying out of the slum, Vero allegorically sacrifices "El Cruce" and turns her back, in Treadwellian fashion, to the social world outside of her threatened "sanctuary."

I discussed how the idea that Martel's virtual point of view in fact differs from Vero's own generated two bodies of knowledge—the viewer's and her own. And while attempts at measuring the distance between them may be part of the game Martel plays with the viewer, it turns out that neither body of knowledge proves to be of decisive importance. We may not know exactly what Vero knows, or whether what she claims to know has any ground in (diegetic) reality, but we do know that she, despite a sense of guilt and her half-hearted desire to know what had happened, ultimately gives way to the avoidance of knowledge—which itself marks a moral attitude. Thus, giving way, Vero also gives in. The men around her take her self-accusative narrative out of her hands by taking care of potentially incriminating evidence; Vero, albeit reluctantly, appears to resign to that situation.

Not only is Vero subject to manipulation; the viewer's mind is also played with. Even if we assume that ocular verification settles the ontological status of a given image (of the handprints on the side window or of a dog seen through the rear window), the evidence remains insufficient to explain away the event. Each time we seem to have gathered the information necessary to gain further insight into the nature of the accident, Martel pulls another *changüí* on us, leading us to postulate increasingly labored hypotheses that are never confirmed, leaving ample room for doubt about what happened. The question we are left with is whether grasping the exact nature of the accident would make a difference to Vero's ability of making fiction out of it.

With *Three Monkeys*, Nuri Bilge Ceylan takes this strategy in the opposite direction. Ceylan plays with the viewer through what I have called his procedure of conjecture: he withholds all crucial events from view, yet he leaves virtually no room for doubt about the nature of events: if *The Headless Woman* hardly ever confirms our stipulations, *Three Monkeys*, by contrast, barely puts anything (or anyone) in the way to challenge or contradict our conjectures. As in *The Headless Woman*, then, the question of knowledge is still at the forefront, since Eyüp, like Vero, gladly avoids corroborating unverified and unwelcome "facts." When Eyüp dodges the policemen's question about the text message, he may not exactly be lying, yet he is certainly not making fiction either. It may well be the case, in other words, that there was *something* he did not know with certainty, in the strict sense of the word, but beyond this epistemological nonclaim, his denial has a more substantial ethical bearing. Far from cracking the crystal of the "old morality" by way of fabulation, Eyüp rather aims to seal it up again in an attempt to protect his "only son."

Despite their inverted narrative strategies—one force-feeding its plotline, which it withholds from view, whereas the other invites myopic scrutiny only to pull the rug from under our feet—*Three Monkeys* and *The Headless Woman* paint equally gloomy pictures of protagonists drawing the skeptical conclusion. Far from trying to recover from their fall into skepticism by discovering new ways of relating to the world (through acts of making fiction), they rather foreclose or forego such opportunities, resorting or giving in to webs of half lies and "alternative facts" that cover the gaps the respective accidents had opened up. This is underscored by the strong sense of closure in both films, as narratives come full circle. Despite this sense of being caught up in closed circuits, cracks occur that allow for glimpses of an Outside, as my discussions of the virtual point of view and the fissure in the frosted glass door point out, even if these do not actually lead their protagonists out of their crystals.

Conclusion

The Digital Will or a New Romanticism?

Ever since the global recognition for her role as *Amélie*, actress Audrey Tautou has developed a life as a photographer alongside her performing career. In July 2017, she literally exposed what *The New York Times* called the "very private" and "unseen side of her identity" at the most public event in the world of still photography, the renowned *Rencontres d'Arles* photography festival.

As Tautou changes her position in relation to the camera (no longer acting in front of it, but controlling it from behind), she assures us that she refrains from digital processing: "Once I take the photos, I don't retouch and I don't change the framing at all. I don't cheat on anything" (Judah 2017.) At the same time, she *does* mimic the gesture of the heroine she played in the film by finally revealing her unseen identity at the festival after fifteen years of practicing photography privately. Says Tautou: "I've been keeping it to myself for so much time, even those around me don't know this work" (ibid.). Commenting on this exhibition, the *New York Times* critic Hettie Judah wrote: "Counterbalancing her pictures of the journalists responsible for creating her public image are small, spontaneous snapshots Tautou takes of her own reflection." Like Amélie, then, Tautou reverts to *pétisme* in an attempt to counter the global scale of things, taking control over her imago only to find herself on the verge of isolation. As was the case for the waitress from Montmartre, Tautou now says: "For me it was a necessity to deliver myself from this work" (ibid.).

Just weeks before the exposition, on June 19, 2017, Werner Herzog addressed an audience at the Walker Art Museum in Minneapolis, the venue where he had delivered his Minnesota Declaration in 1999. He was asked whether he would "reconsider" that earlier Declaration in light of the Trump Era. "With the arrival of the new term 'alternative facts' in the political arena," Herzog now claims in his first of six statements, "the question of facts and the question of truth have acquired an unexpected urgency" (Herzog 2017). Further positing that "facts cannot be underestimated as they have normative power," Herzog nevertheless returns to his initial position of preferring a poetic truth over a factual one: facts, he explains, may well lay claim to truth, they do not provide insight in it. By way of support, he "quotes" André Gide (alongside Shakespeare and Michelangelo) as saying: "I modify facts in such a way that they resemble truth more than reality" (ibid).

Cavell found a similar idea of modified facts resembling truth more than reality in the marquis from *Rules of the Game*: when the latter excused his gamekeeper for a "deplorable accident," Cavell accused him of (or credited him with) telling poetic truths, or what Cavell himself rather called telling a *fiction*, that is, either way, telling the truth by lying. Deleuze on his part warned that *making fiction* (he also called it *fabulation*) is neither an act of making up a story and passing it off for true nor a potential for creating new worlds, if these are specifically marked in opposition to the real. Rather, as I discussed in the context of *The Headless Woman*, making fiction is an effort to endow the actual world with the powers of immanent becoming. In *This New Yet Unapproachable America* Cavell called such a continuous process of transformation a *reformation* if it leads away from an "anonymous, burned everyday" to an *eventual* everyday (Cavell 1989, 64).

With recent global and political developments, questions of manipulation, control, "cheating," and "alternative facts" have gained urgency indeed. So much so that Herzog accepts a call to defend his notion of poetic truth—a call that apparently did not occur to anyone when he delivered his Minnesota Declaration at the turn of the millennium (when the digital turn, with its "open-access" rhetoric and potential for piracy, was perhaps more widely seen as furthering democratic and liberal, if not anticapitalistic, agendas).[1] When Herzog now says that "facts cannot be underestimated as they have normative power"—a statement brought in against the idea of "alternative facts"—we may assume that it was for this reason they had been treated with suspicion in the not too distant past. Facts, Herzog stated in the earlier Declaration, are so many "truths of accountants," and what they account for is the *actual* state of affairs (if not a world *past*), whereas the ideas of poetic truths or making fiction are creative, concerned as they are with the *eventual*. And if the eventual concerns a constant state of becoming, hence the emergence of the new, it falls outside the model of knowledge and the scope of facts—an important reason for Cavell and Deleuze to call for a model of belief instead. What we needed first and foremost were *reasons* to believe in this world, *supporting* faith in the eventual as being less numbing or burning than the actual. Deleuze called upon cinema to do so, to help us recover from our fall into skepticism, even if it could not be expected to overcome skepticism once and for all. It would have to go beyond the "fact-image," since for Deleuze, I explained, a "fact," reduces the sensible to an established recognition, whereas film as the "art of the encounter" names that kind of sense-experience that jams our sensory-motor system and prevents our cognitive faculties from corroborating in an effort of recognition, thereby ultimately forcing us to think.

With Cavell, we may well say that our modern fate (or modern "fact") thus alludes to *a new romanticism*. The *old* wish of romanticism, he explained in The World Viewed, sought *redemption* in the possibility of some intimate way of knowing nature, of possessing knowledge of its conditions—its power of destruction and of healing—in thought. The new romantic, on the other hand, no longer demands nature's presence to us, nor our knowledge of it, least of all when understood in terms of a *possession in thought*. Rather, its conditions "present themselves as nature's autonomy, self-sufficiency, laws unto themselves" (ibid.).

This is what Cavell meant when he said: "This is not a return *to* nature but the return *of* it, as of the repressed." In the context of old and new romanticism, the return of nature marks the world's independence from us. In other words, it stands for the limitations of subjectivity and of its ability to grasp nature in thought. "It is the release of nature from our private holds" and "draws my limits," Cavell writes (Cavell 1979, 114). The return of nature thus marks what he elsewhere, in an essay on Emerson, called the world's "standoffishness," in relation to which the idea of "thinking as clutching" (as Emerson calls the attempt to grasp the world in thought) now appears as "the most unhandsome part of our condition" (Cavell 1989, 86).

This is Cavell's interpretation of what he considers the key passage from Emerson's essay "Experience": "I take this evanescence and lubricity of all objects, which lets them slip through our fingers when we clutch hardest, to be the most unhandsome part of our condition."

"Look first," Cavell comments, "at the connection between the hand in unhandsome and the impotently clutching fingers." He then suggests opposing the concept of thinking as clutching with another Emersonian term, *attraction*, or *attractiveness* ("the most handsome part of our condition"), which names "the rightful call we have upon one another, and that I and the world make upon one another . . . Heidegger's term for the opposite of grasping the world is that of being *drawn* to things" (Cavell 1989, 86–87).

In his recent book, *Philosophy and the Patience of Film in Cavell and Nancy* (2016), Daniele Rugo extends the relation Cavell finds between Emerson and Heidegger to Jean-Luc Nancy's writing on the cinema. With Cavell and Nancy, Rugo argues, we can see how film releases us of our will to mastery by provoking the power of passiveness (or power of patience as Rugo prefers to call it), by "grant[ing] us entrance into the calm of things, before or beyond human purpose" (Rugo 2016a, 124). Especially those filmmakers who insist on the camera's outsideness (Rugo himself made a case in point for Asghar Farhadi) keep the world at arms' length, at a distance that should not now despair us (see Rugo 2016a, 146–46, and Rugo 2016b).

Nancy further foregrounds thinking's attachment to the unthought and discusses how the films of Abbas Kiarostami and Claire Denis open to "the outside that opens right in the middle of the world" (Rugo 2016a, 100). I have shown the significance of such openings in the films of Ceylan and Martel as well and connected the ability to release nature from our "private holds" while maintaining the capacity of being drawn to what Deleuze called the "impower" of thought. Yet Deleuze goes beyond a call upon cinema to grant entrance into the "calm of things" by calling for the creation of new relations and for providing reasons to believe in the world. By opening on to an Outside, Deleuze would argue, cinema provokes the force of thought rather than a calm of things, although this is far from a call for a stronger clutching hand. We are only forced to think, but in so doing, thought is forced to think the "dispossession of itself *and of the world*," as Deleuze had it (Deleuze 1989, 169). There is, then, an inherent struggle with skepticism, requiring force as much as faith in a daily balancing act on a rope that refuses to lead across the abyss.

In line with this, I quoted Cavell as saying: "The faith of this [new] romanticism, *overcoming* the old, is that we can still be moved to move . . . that nature's absence . . . is only the history of our turnings from it" (Cavell 1979, 114, emphasis added). This new faith is thus a matter of overcoming indeed—but *not* now *of skepticism*. On the contrary, what the new romanticism seeks to overcome is the *old* romantic wish of overcoming skepticism—say its demand for *redemption*. It is along these same lines that I interpreted Deleuze's call for belief as one that urges us to foster new connections despite our aversions to do so.

I insisted on the idea that neither Cavell nor Deleuze aims at an overcoming of skepticism. Deleuze especially has been interpreted as calling upon the cinema to defeat the skeptic. I took my time to counter arguments along these lines by Malcolm Turvey (who claimed that Deleuze renewed the revelationist tradition by taking the cinema to overcome the limitations of human forms of perception) and Philipp Schmerheim (who found him to promise *salvation*). Whereas my disagreements with Turvey and Schmerheim were based on a different understanding of Deleuze, I did find D. N. Rodowick's reading to be on par with mine, yet he too took Deleuze's insistence on choosing to believe in this world (with its immanent forces of becoming and self-differentiation) to amount to an overcoming of skepticism. At the same time, D. N. Rodowick acknowledged that such a choice would need to be sustained by a daily practice, which in my view amounts to a recognition of the standing threat of skepticism. I therefore used the Cavellian division of three skeptical positions (its impetus, conclusion and defeat) to suggest that Deleuze's demand or wish for belief amounts to an acknowledgment of the skeptical impetus (a broken link between man and world), while avoiding the skeptical conclusion (which would render our isolation complete), without, however, countering this conclusion by defeating it (which would require an overcoming of the limitations of the human).

This balancing act between the radical skeptical positions basically defined my take on cinematic skepticism. I reserved this term for films in which this continuous negotiation is played out on the level of the film's narrative (with protagonists struggling to recover from a perceived break with the world) and by giving it specific audiovisual significance through the creative use of cinematic techniques.

My insistence on a Cavello-Deleuzian embrace of the skeptical impetus, or on their refusal to refute it, crucially informs my take on the digital turn in cinema. For D. N. Rodowick and Thomas Elsaesser have both argued that a shift has taken place since the 1990s under the pressure of this turn—and, for Elsaesser, at least, of the global turn as well. Both agree that, as viewers in front of their digital screens become more likely to accept the creation of other, virtual worlds, the question of our (cinematically mediated) relation to *this* world appears to have lost urgency. Contemporary films would therefore steer away from the idea that evidence should be based on ocular proof. Along with the digital and global turns, then, Elsaesser and D. N. Rodowick both detect an ontological turn in cinema, which moves away from an overcoming or "liberation" (Elsaesser) of skepticism to an acceptance of it. But such an ontological turn only makes sense if we accept that the now old ontology of film indeed did (attempt to) liberate us, for example through the "presence of the contingently real through photographic indexicality," as Elsaesser took Cavell to suggest. My basic claim in this book is that the ontological turn and the digital turn did not coincide: the skeptical threat had already been accepted in the Cavello-Deleuzian paradigm, which "ontology mark 2" seeks to replace. Indeed, the very idea of truth grounded in ocular proof implies a model of thought and a concept of subjectivity against which I brought in a Cavello-Deleuzian model of thought's *impower*, of *releasing* nature from our private holds. Call it a new romanticism.

That, however, was only part of the argument. For while I made a point of saying that cinematic skepticism was neither finally accepted nor finally rejected by the digital-global turn, I did pick up on Elsaesser and Rodowick's suggestion that the turn pressed a "digital will" onto contemporary culture at large, and film culture in particular, a will, that is, to control and manipulate information, images, narratives and minds—to which I added its flipside, the fear of losing control over any and all of the above, including the mind we like to think is our own. Either way, such contemporary concerns are at odds with anything the Cavello-Deleuzian paradigm called thinking (dispossession, stand-offishness, impower, attraction, being drawn). If we further take the recent political developments into account, we may well wonder whether "facts" are still modified to "resemble truth more than reality," as Herzog did, or whether fiction is still made with the aim of endowing the actual world of the powers of immanent becoming, or for the sake of preventing it from happening. In short, haven't the powers of the false ironically been turned against themselves? If these questions sound rhetorical in the political realm of our day, I hope they sound differently when posed in the context of the (docu)fictions on our screens.

Should we ask whether the digital will to control is just like any other will to control, the oldest will in the world? I argued in the introduction that cinematic skepticism is not just like any other skepticism, nor is it as old as philosophy itself. Film knows what is known in philosophy as skepticism, but it responds to it in a cinematic way, which is to say, automatically. When cinematic skepticism takes the digital will to control to heart, it does so in contrast with an analog will that *cannot* control the world it records—call it the impower of automatism. The analog will leaves the viewer powerless as a result, for being kept outside of its world. The digital will, by contrast, wants to control by gaining access, by getting inside, by not merely pointing but actually touching: it wants to poke the bear's nose with its finger (*Grizzly Man*), dip it into the sugar (*Amélie*), use it to write on a dirty car window (*The Headless Woman*). It wants to access the diegetic world, even if only in dematerialized form: it wants a virtual point of view (*The Headless Woman*, *Three Monkeys*). It wants a view of its own and to enter right into its own view, becoming the object of its own gaze (*Three Monkeys*); it wants to absorb its subject, wants its subject to become its gaze (*Three Monkeys*). It wants to change someone else's stories, take over someone else's voice, take control over the narrative itself (all four films). It wants to access other minds ("Now he has understood"), command it ("go back and play"). It wants to play with the mind of the viewer.

In a word, if the cinema used to stand for our distance to the world—for our standing at a distance from it—and indeed aimed to carry out a suspension of the world, the new cinemas emerging since the 1990s do appear to challenge this idea of film. As the will gains access, comes closer, crosses lines, we may well feel compelled to draw new ones, as Herzog did with Treadwell. "The closer I get, the less I know," said Martel. And just when Amélie got to dictate Nino's actions from behind the digital screen, he bluntly walked out the door. Even (or especially) Ceylan, who controls narrative information so tightly he does not need to show any of its cardinal points, feels compelled to "let some ambiguity linger" when there really seems no room for doubt.

Notes

Introduction

1. For the reference to grand theory, see Bordwell and Carroll 1996.

2. See Mullarkey 2009; Mulhall 2008; Sinnerbrink 2011 and 2016; Rodowick 2007 and 2015.

3. For Cavell on literary skepticism, see, among others, Fischer 1989, Rudrum 2013.

4. On this point of cinema speaking to us, see, for example, Sandra Laugier's "L'ordinaire du cinéma": "[T]he interest of a film does not lie in what a brilliant mind may have to say or invent about it . . . but in what it explicitly has to tell and show to us" (Laugier and Cerisuelo 2001, 267; my translation). I have rather qualified the "explicitness" of its address.

5. Several articles published in Dennison and Lim's 2006 anthology *Remapping World Cinema: Identity, Culture and Politics in Film* highlight the decreasing significance of the distinction between Hollywood and world cinemas. See, in particular, the editors' introduction and Lúcia Nagib's contribution, "Towards a Positive Definition of World Cinema." For Cavell's doubt about the usefulness of distinctions between classical and modern film (film as the last traditional and as modernist forms of art, as he calls it), see Cavell 1979, 219.

6. Like the subgenre of the home-invasion film, which Thomas Elsaesser discusses in the context of the "mind-game film" (Elsaesser 2009, cf. ch. 5 below), what I propose to call the "collision film" started occurring regularly in the 1990s, with Kieślowski's *Three Colors: Blue* (Poland / France, 1993) Cronenberg's *Crash* (Canada / UK, 1996), Egoyan's *The Sweet Hereafter* (Canada, 1997) and Alejandro Amenábar's *Open your Eyes* (Spain / France / Italy, 1997), and its Hollywood remake, *Vanilla Sky* (2001) as most notable examples. The subgenre has expanded exponentially since the turn of the century with films such as the following (listed in alphabetic order): *A Separation* (dir. Asghar Farhadi, Iran, 2011); *Adaptation* (dir. Spike Jonze, USA, 2002); *Amores Perros* (dir. Alejandro

González Iñárritu, Mexico, 2000); *Child's Pose* (dir. Calin Peter Netzer, Romania, 2013); *Louder than Bombs* (dir. Joachim Trier, Norway / France / Denmark, 2015); *Mulholland Drive* (dir. David Lynch, France / USA, 2001); *Premonition* (dir. Norio Tsuruta, Japan, 2004); *Reservation Road* (dir. Terry George, USA / Germany 2007); *The Watchtower* (dir. Pelin Esmer, Turkey / France / Germany, 2012); *Whiplash* (dir. Damien Chazelle, USA, 2014). The list is neither meant to be exhaustive, nor is it to deny the existence of collision films prior to the 1990s. Notable precursors range from *Lolita* (Stanley Kubrick, 1962, remade in 1997 by Adrian Lyne) to Peter Weir's Ozploitation film *The Cars That Ate Paris* (Australia, 1974) and from Joseph Losey's *The Accident* (1967) to Kazan's *The Arrangement* (USA 1969).

7. As with any specification of a genre or subgenre, a certain degree of arbitrariness cannot be avoided in determining its scope. It is not impossible to imagine a subgenre that includes other sudden events with high impact, such as airplane crashes or gun violence. Yet whereas the airplane crash indeed features frequently enough since the success of Marshall's 1993 film *Alive*, to say nothing of its hype in post 9/11 cinema, I would set it apart from the collision film as it does not meet the crucial criterion of a momentary loss of control and the subsequent question of responsibility. It would rather belong to the category of disaster movies. Gun violence, on the other hand, seems overdetermined in this respect: even when stray bullets or shooting accidents are considered, the sense of responsibility is assumed rather than put under pressure and for that reason lacks allegorical significance. Other films consider questions of moral responsibility and push protagonists to reconsider their relation to the world, while they do not strictly involve cars. Hirukazo Koreeda's *Maborosi* (1995) is an excellent example of this.

Chapter 1

1. See, for example, Gerrits 2012 and 2014a.
2. In the growing French scholarship on Cavell, Élise Domenach likewise foregrounds the relation between epistemological skepticism and moral perfectionism. See Domenach 2011.
3. For my analysis of this book in light of her seminal essay "Visual Pleasure and Narrative Cinema" as well as the challenges it faces in the context of new media, see Gerrits 2007.
4. Doane attributes the lamenting attitude to Paul Willemen and Dai Vaughan. For their respective views, see Willemen's "Reflections on Digital Imagery" (in *New Screen Media: Cinema/Art/Narrative*, ed. Martin Rieser, Andrea Zapp, London: BFI Pub., 2002), and Dai Vaughan's "From Today, Cinema Is Dead" in his book *For Documentary: Twelve Essays* (Berkeley: University of

California Press, 1999). Both Mulvey and Doane elaborate on these reactions by means of Roland Barthes's analysis of the powers of the analog photograph in *Camera Lucida* (Barthes 1982).

5. Barthes used the term "punctum," which he defined in distinction from the "stadium" (as the intended photographic meaning) to name the prick, wound, sting, speck, cut, little hole caused by a singularly interesting aspect or detail of a photograph that does not have a place within its functional aspect or logical design and is thus indicative of "a pressure of the unspeakable that wants to be spoken" (Barthes 1981, 19).

6. This is what Barthes called the paradoxical point of the punctum: it depends on the individual viewer to stand out, and yet it does not signify this subjective response. In his chapter on Barthes in *Why Photography Matters as Art as Never Before*, Michael Fried argues that the punctum manages to punctuate the crust of our visual literacy by making us see something without it having being shown; the picture thus presents the past beyond our own doing. So it is not so much the subjective response itself that matters as the fact that this response is needed to draw attention to the viewer's existential relationship to a photograph (Fried 2008).

7. Cavell's engagement with Austin and Wittgenstein was first outlined in a book of essays published between the Harvard seminar and *The World Viewed*'s publication, entitled *Must We Mean What We Say*.

8. A misreading of this kind can be found, for example, in Rosalind Krauss's review of *The World Viewed* published in ArtForum, may 1974, entitled "Dark Glasses and Bifocals: A Book Review." Although an elaboration of the topic lies outside the scope of this chapter, it is worth noting that the relation between the medium and individual films is crucially a dynamic one for Cavell.

9. As is common practice, I will use section numbers rather than page numbers for references to the first part of the *Investigations*.

10. For Bazin's phrase (quoted by Cavell), see Bazin 2004, 110.

11. In *Theorizing the Moving Image*, Noel Carroll (who had already discussed the matter in *Philosophical Problems of Classical Film Theory*) attributes the following line of reasoning to Cavell: "[I]f it is not the 'sight' or the 'appearance' of the object that a photographic image re-presents, then it must be the object itself that is re-presented" (44). Carroll here assumes that Cavell arrives at a conclusion rather than at a paradoxical, if not aporetic, situation. To Carroll, Cavell's "premise that photographic images either re-present objects themselves or sights of objects . . . begs the question about the nature of cinematic representation by assuming that the photographic image must re-present something from the past." To my mind, however, it is Carroll's own suggested solution that begs the questions: "[W]e may say that what photography does is to produce a recognizable proxy for its model" (ibid). Whatever the nature of the proxy, it either obscures or renames the problem, but it does not solve it.

The same can be said of Cavell's own attempt, in "What Photography Calls Thinking," to replace the term "representation," with that of "visual transcription" so as to register the fact that the object plays a causal role in the taking of the photograph and is not made "in the likeness" of it. Cavell writes that "a representation emphasizes the identity of its subject, hence it may be called a likeness; a photograph emphasizes the existence of its subject, recording it; hence it is that it may be called a transcription" (Cavell and Rothman 2005, 118, emphasis added). However, to Cavell, the paradoxical or aporetic situation forms the starting point of philosophy, whereas Carroll suggests that it marks a dead end: "Patently," Carroll writes, "a shot of Denzel Washington is not the same thing as the man himself. So in what sense *is* the image its model? Unless a reasonable answer can be supplied to this question, photographic realism seems dead in the water" (Carroll 56).

12. The notion of philosophical intuition is about as old as Western philosophy itself, but the notion has changed dramatically over the course of its history. Yet it was Kant who radically changed its application from ideas to percepts—from a direct grasp of Platonic forms unmediated by perception to a perceptual experience of this world unmediated by forms of thought—only, again, to deny its very possibility.

13. What Bazin called the "myth of total cinema" in his essay of the same name—the idea of the world re-created in its own image; the exhibition of the world in itself—Cavell calls "the promise of candor" (1979, 111, 119), the candid being that which occurs independently of me (or any audience), thus also that which displays my powerlessness over the world. While Cavell admits that this idea of overcoming subjectivity had always been one of the myths of art in general, cinema satisfies it in a new way: *automatically*, or, what comes to the same thing, *magically*, which either way is to say that the camera reveals the world without *my* having to do anything for it (without me being able to do anything about it). Thus, the term "automatism" also serves to differentiate photographic media from painting (which do not render the world we live in at all but consist of a world of its own) and especially theater.

14. Cavell understands the idea of modern film in terms of the modernist endeavor generally, explained by Michael Fried (Fried 1998) as addressing a felt loss of conviction in the conventional ways of proceeding: no longer able to take the tradition for granted, the artist, instead of continuing to produce within the medium's conditions and conventions, feels called upon to acknowledge these aspects of his or her art by explicating them in works of art that can stand the comparison to the those of other modernist artists as well as those whose value in the tradition seem incontestable. For film to be part of an investigation of modernism, it ought to be able to investigate what has always been taken for granted about it—it has to *declare* its necessary conditions and material basis—; it ought to be able "to run up," as Cavell writes, "against a problem

quite unforeseen in what we had experienced in film's possibilities" (1979, 70). Cavell goes on to say that a film as a modernist work will give significance to these unforeseen possibilities by leading them to their limits, declaring itself in so doing not as another instance of its art but "a new medium within it" (103).

15. The relativity of the distinction is a subject of intense debate in both Cavellian and Deleuzian scholarship. Cavell, addressing criticism from unnamed sources (but likely including Rosalind Krauss' review of *The World Viewed* in the Artforum issue of May 1974, in which she rhetorically wondered whether "one can construct an 'ontology of film' in which its conditions and limits are set out without knowing about (or 'acknowledging') the serious engagements with those conditions and those limits . . ."), writes in "More of the World Viewed" that he is prepared to modify his previous claims on the modernist break in cinema by saying "either that movies from their beginning have existed in a state of modernism . . . ; or else that movies from their beginning have existed in two states, one modern, one traditional . . . ; or else that the concept of modernism has no clear application to the art of film" (MWV 219). Noting that not having a clear application is still a way of having one, I should add that Cavell insists on his feeling that none of his adjustments undermines his earlier conviction that film was the "last traditional art."

Within Deleuzian scholarship, David Martin-Jones distinguishes two "schools of thought" based on the respective conception of the relationship between the two cinema books. The first, to which D. N. Rodowick and Patricia Pisters belong, claims that *The Movement-Image* and *The Time-Image* depict different ways of thinking, the difference between them thus marking an epistemic shift. The second, attributed by Martin-Jones mostly to András Bálint Kovács, though we could add Jacques Rancière as well (see esp. the latter's "From One Image to Another? Deleuze and the Ages of Cinema" in *Film Fables*), maintains against Deleuze's own claims to the contrary that the cinema books posit a linear history of cinema organized around a historical break.

Far from aiming at resolving these issues at this occasion, I rather wish to mark the controversy in light of my larger claim that, while cinematic skepticism as I conceive it is prevalent throughout film history and does not start after the Second World War, both Deleuze and Cavell do find an intensified need, expressed in cinema, to re-establish a broken link to the world; a need which is then also expressed differently and involves a modernist investigation into the medium's necessary conditions and material basis.

16. On his "fact-image," see Bazin 2004, vol. 2, p. 37, and Deleuze 1989, 1.

17. Among the many works that do in fact provide such an analysis, the most influential ones on my thinking have been Paola Marrati 2008 and D. N. Rodowick 1997. Both Rodowick and Marrati have also been important interlocutors in helping me think through the relation between Cavell and Deleuze. For their respective views on this relation, see Marrati's essay "A Lost Everyday:

Deleuze and Cavell on Hollywood," appendix to the English translation of the abovementioned book, and Rodowick's *Philosophy's Artful Conversation.*

18. This crucial distinction is exemplary of Bergson's methodology, which Deleuze adopted as well: while things are always mixed in practice, we nevertheless need to distinguish between them in principle so as to avoid mistaking a difference in kind for a difference in degree. To see a mere difference in degree between perception and memory, for example (taking a recollection to be of the same nature but in weakened form as the perception it had been) would undermine the very possibility of a philosophical intuition and lead, in Bergson's view, to numerous false philosophical problems. On Bergson's methodology and its impact on Deleuze, see the "Intuition as Method" chapter in Deleuze 1988.

19. Apart from the metaphor, though, the relation to Plato does not stretch very far. On the contrary, when criticizing Kant, Bergson accuses him precisely on grounds of his Platonism: "the whole *Critique of Pure Reason* rests . . . upon the postulate that our thought is incapable of anything but Platonizing, that is, of pouring the whole of possible experience into pre-existing molds" (1990, 197).

20. In *Creative Evolution*, Bergson goes a long way explaining the function of the intellect from an evolutionary perspective, for example by arguing that the concept of homogeneous space must be seen as an aid in the decomposition of matter for the want of tools (man's "artificial organs"). Bergson's primary target in Kant concerns the latter's conception of time in terms of space, that is, as a homogeneous and discontinuous quantitative notion, rather than as qualitatively differential heterogeneous yet continuous blocks of duration.

21. See, for example, Deleuze 1988, 85, and Deleuze 1986, 17.

22. "Empiricism," Deleuze writes, "truly becomes transcendental . . . only when we apprehend directly in the sensible that which can only be sensed, the very being *of* the sensible" (Deleuze 2004, 56–57).

23. See Bergson 1974, especially pp. 161–62.

24. There are good reasons for wanting to distinguish the films from the 1950s and onwards from neorealism in the strict sense, as, for example, Bondanella has argued (see Bondanella 2009, esp. ch. 8 ff). Here, however, I follow Deleuze in finding continuities between them.

Chapter 2

1. Among the many book-length studies of Renoir's work that foreground the role of theater in the film, André Bazin's *Jean Renoir* (1971; English trans. 1973) is explicitly referenced by Deleuze; it is a likely source for Cavell as well, as is Alexander Sesonske's (at the time of Cavell's writing, forthcoming book) *Jean Renoir: The French Films* (Sesonske 1980). Deleuze's interpretation of the film is further inspired by an unreferenced text by Jean-Pierre Bamberger as

well as texts by François Truffaut (the introduction to Bazin's book) and Eric Rohmer's *Le goût de la beauté* (trans. *The Taste for Beauty*, 1989).

2. Here, I am following the tendency in Anglophone writing to spell Jurieux's name with an *x* at the end, as opposed the French convention of spelling his name without it. (On this difference, see Goldhammer 1992.) For reasons of consistency, I adjusted the French spelling in this quotation from Cavell.

3. In a now famous footnote to "A Plea for Excuses" (the 1956 presidential address for the Meeting of the Aristotelian Society published in his *Philosophical Papers*), J. L. Austin provides the "story" of shooting a donkey, which makes evident that doing so "by mistake" or by "by accident"—apparently interchangeable expressions—signifies entirely different actions or different assessments/descriptions of them. To Cavell, who discusses Austin's example in "Austin at Criticism" (Cavell 1969, 105 ff), the philosophical significance of such dis/agreements in language is of major importance.

4. When the marquis blesses Jurieux's plan to leave with Christine, he says he is only troubled by one thing: the risk that Christine might be left behind alone seems significant; given her new lover's profession, young age, and fame, chances are that he may get involved in an "accident." How or whether this worry—not to say wish or prophesy—complicates Cavell's reading will have to be considered at another occasion.

5. I imagine one could object that films remain open to revision after they have had their first screening, as was the case with *Rules of the Game*. Expressing his curiosity over the fact that Bazin only wrote a brief introductory note to what was clearly his favorite Renoir film, François Truffaut speculated that, by the time of his death almost twenty years after the initial release of *Rules of the Game*, Bazin was still "waiting to see the definitive version of the film, which Jean Gaborit and Jacques Maréchal had started to put together" (and which would be released a year later, when it was presented at the Venice Film Festival) (Bazin 1973, 70 note). I do take it that the "putting together" of the final cut, even if approved by the director, cannot be said to be the work of the director (as Truffaut's mentioning of Gaborit and Maréchal underscores). Nevertheless, this aspect of Cavell's position on film may be in need of revision in the context of digital postproduction.

6. Based on statements like this one, Bazin would fit squarely into the tradition that Malcolm Turvey calls "revelationism." I will argue against Turvey's attempt at extending this tradition to include Cavell and Deleuze as well in the next chapter.

7. The circuit refers specifically to one of Bergson's graphic representations in *Matter and Memory*, which served to explain the relation between perception and memory in "ever deeper strata of reality" (Bergson 1988, 105). Deleuze himself added another graphic to Bergson's to elaborate a fundamental operation of time: the splitting of the present into two dissymmetrical jets, one

making the present pass into the past as such and another pressing into the future. I will discuss some of the implications of the crystal as time image in the next chapter.

8. Per Deleuze's account, Bergson equates the pure past with Being, whereas the present must be understood in terms of becoming. "We have great difficulties in understanding a survival of the past in itself" Deleuze explains, because we believe the past is no longer, that is has ceased to be. We have thus confused Being with being-present. Nevertheless, the present *is not*; rather, it is pure becoming, always outside itself. It *is* not, but it acts . . . The past, on the other hand has ceased to act or to be useful. But it has not ceased to be. Useless and inactive, impassive, it IS, in the full sense of the word: it is identical with being in itself" (Deleuze 1991, 55).

Chapter 3

1. The apparent reference here is to Noel Carroll's *Philosophical Problems of Classical Film Theory*. Turvey's line of reasoning is indeed akin to Carroll's, sharing in particular the latter's impatience with aporetic and paradoxical situations, which are readily dismissed as "the sort of logical or empirical errors" Turvey speaks of here. On Carroll's dismissal of Cavell's alternative mode of thinking, see ch. 1, note 11, p. 185.

2. See Ryle 1949. For Turvey's take on Ryle, see the introduction to Turvey 2008, esp. pp. 14ff.

3. See Deleuze 1991 for his account of Hume's dictum.

4. See Chatman 1978. This distinction between story and discourse time should not be conflated with the one between "film time" and "cinema time," terms used to distinguish the time of recording (also called the "time of the index") and the time of projection. On this latter distinction, see for example Mulvey 2006, 30, 173.

5. In *Gilles Deleuze's Time-Machine*, which precedes *Philosophy's Artful Conversation* by almost two decades, D. N. Rodowick had already developed an argument along these lines. See especially chapter 5: "Critique, or Truth in Crisis."

6. Vertov, like Epstein, ranks among Turvey's four revelationist theorists, and Turvey indeed finds further support for his dismissal of Deleuze in the latter's enthusiasm for Vertov's concept of the kino-eye. Turvey argues that Vertov's visual skepticism, unlike Epstein's (which was grounded in Bergsonian "Romanticism"), finds its source in the "cult of the machine" (Turvey 2008, 34; he takes the term from Stites 1989). Vertov, per Turvey's account, finds human vision to "suffer" from two fundamental limitations. First, it is chaotic and scattered and hence needs an editing table to be organized into an "effective whole." Second,

it is spatiotemporally immobile (or slow, confined), whereas cinema—he quotes Vertov—can "put together any given points in the universe, no matter where [it has] recorded them" (Turvey 2008, 32–33; quote Vertov 1984, 18). Turvey brings Deleuze to bear on this second point, quoting him as saying about Vertov's kino-eye: "This is not a human eye—even an improved one. For although the human eye can surmount some of its limitations with help of contraptions and instruments, there is one which it cannot surmount, since it is its own condition of possibility" (Turvey 2008, 37; quote Deleuze 1986, 81).

To engage with this part of Turvey's argument requires expositions of the Bergsonian status of the image (as something that can be without being perceived) and Deleuze's concept of the plane of immanence. A counterargument would also need to explain that the "perception of an atom" is neither yet another self-contradictory nonsense claim Turvey takes it to be, nor does it capture reality any better than human perception (cf., Turvey 2008, 95, and Deleuze 1986, 58).

7. Translation modified. The reference here is to Schefer's recently translated *The Ordinary Man of Cinema* (2016)

8. Marrati and Rodowick each provide their own frames of reference for the new sense of subjectivity Deleuze develops in relation to time, though both relate them to this splitting of time. D. N. Rodowick focuses on Deleuze's challenge to the unified interiority of the Cartesian ego through Kant. The impersonal form of time itself, which, as discussed above, consists of the splitting of the present in dissymmetrical jets, enacts a division of the subject as well. In Deleuze's reading of Kant, the subject splits into a passive ego (Moi) existing in time, which constantly undergoes and witnesses change, and an I (Je) that, through an active synthesis of time, understands that what does not change is change (that is, time) itself. Hence Deleuze's assertion that "I am separated from myself by the form of time" (Deleuze 1984, ix, quoted in Rodowick 1997, 129). While Descartes' notion of the ego is presumably present to itself (I = I), Kant's thinking I is by default divided from what it predicates. And just as the I does not coincide with itself, time cannot be known in itself, nor can we witness time's passing and forking in itself: "once intuited, it divides, branches, and slips away" (Rodowick 1997, 129).

Marrati likewise grounds a new sense of subjectivity in the splitting of time, though her analysis runs primarily through Bergson's conception of the present. Bergson goes beyond Husserl and subsequent phenomenologists by holding that the present not only has qualitative extension (and is therefore not reducible to a quantitative point on a line); it also doubles. In order to account for the continuous passing of the present into the past, Bergson holds the present perception simultaneously turns into a recollection: the actual image perceived in the present coexists with the virtual image of itself as past. One of these "makes all the present pass on, while the other preserves all the past. Time consists of this split, and it is this, it is time, that we see in the crystal" (Deleuze 1989, 81, quoted in Marrati 2008, 74). If this indeed amounts to a reversal of the concept of the subject, it is because subjectivity understood through this split is no longer an interiority, just as time is not an a priori form of perception inside a transcendental subject (as Kant would claim). Instead, as Deleuze writes, "Subjectivity is never ours, it is in time, that is, the soul, the spirit, the virtual" (Deleuze 1989 83, quoted in Marrati 2008, 76).

9. The concept if *impouvoir*, sometimes also translated as *unpower*, is important in the context of contemporary French thought generally. In an interview with Jean-Luc Marion (published under the title "Unpower" in De Vries and Schott 2015), Hugues Choplin offers the hypothesis that "contemporary French philosophy is defined by its inventiveness when it comes to power [*pouvoir*], more precisely, to *authority* and *force* [*puissance*]" (De Vries and Schott 2015, 36). Deleuze takes the concept of *impouvoir* from Artaud, though it is mediated by Blanchot's reading of Artaud in the eponymous entry in *The Book to Come*, from which this citation is also taken (Blanchot 2003, 36).

10. Schmerheim does not clearly situate himself in relation to Früchtl's arguments, so unless he explicitly distances himself from the latter's assertions, I take him to be in agreement with them.

11. Deleuze's comments about thought versus dream here must in part be read against the background of Artaud's ambiguous relation to the surrealist movement and more his dispute with Germaine Dulac on *The Seashell and the Clergyman* (1928). See, for example, Flitterman-Lewis 1996).

12. Beyond D. N. Rodowick's argument, which I will discuss, see also Marrati 2008, 115, and Sinnerbrink 2015.

13. Schmerheim also reconnects Deleuze to Cavell here, finding resonance with the latter's take on fantasy as indistinguishable from reality (which I shall explore in chapter 3). See Schmerheim 2016: 6.7 (pp. 161–63).

14. On different grounds, D. N. Rodowick finds that *The Matrix*, despite its innovative, postphotographic manipulation of space, does not mark a new genre or type of film either. With its stereotypical plot structure, strong sense of closure, and transparent ideological message, *The Matrix* is rather a "cliché" classical film (Rodowick 2007, 182). This disappointment is related to D. N. Rodowick's "deeper point" that a digital perceptual realism (which aims for optimal photographic credibility) "wrongly [assumes] that the primary powers of photography are spatial semblance" (Rodowick 2007, 103). These powers, in his view, must rather be found in the analogue's ability to transcribe duration. A digitally composed world, by contrast, does not *transcribe* but *synthesize* time, which is to say that "time itself is transformed as a purely quantitative function defined by calculation." As a result, the digital moving image is confined to a "continuous present" (Rodowick 2007, 118, 171).

Chapter 4

1. Docufiction films are usually differentiated from the more familiar docudramas, which are fictional reenactments of true events, as well as from the less common mockumentaries, in which obviously fictional events are reported in documentary style. On this differentiation and for a highly informative collection of texts on docufiction, see the 2005 anthology *Docufictions*, edited by Gary Don Rhodes and John Parris Springer.

2. Interview with Norman Hill (Exploring with Werner) on the DVD of *The Wild Blue Yonder* (2005), quoted in Prager 2007, 8.

3. With yet another twist, Herzog's features often spill over into making-of documentaries (Les Blank's 1982 *Burden of Dreams* in the case of *Fitzcarraldo*) and are surrounded by production stories that appear stranger than fiction. Such stories then give rise to (and become the subject of) new documentaries, as in the case of another Les Blank film, his 1980 *Werner Herzog Eats His Shoe*, or in Herzog's own account of his complex relation with Klaus Kinski (his lead actor in both Aguirre and Fitzcarraldo, among others) in his 1999 film *My Best Fiend*. If the title of that last film readily captures Herzog's taste for paradox, the title of Weisenborn and Keusch's 1978 documentary portrait of Herzog—*I Am My Films*—bluntly states the ambition of intertwining maker and film, life and work.

4. Eric Ames provided another twist to docufictions by discussing a scene from *Encounters at the End of the World* (2007) in his recent book on Herzog's documentaries. He points out that in one of Herzog's interviews with a diver-scientist on Antarctica, they rehearse almost verbatim the last point of the Minnesota Declaration: "Life in the oceans must be sheer hell. A vast, merciless hell of permanent and immediate danger. So much of a hell that during evolution some species—including man—crawled, fled onto some small continents of solid land, where the Lessons of Darkness continue" (Herzog 1999).

5. In *Camera Lucida*, Barthes used the phrase in relation to Alexander Gardner's 1865 portrait of Lewis Payne, a man awaiting his execution who will be dead by the time the viewer gets to see this portrait. Barthes reserved the term "punctum," which he distinguished from the "studium," for a detail that stands out to a viewer of a photo because it was not an intentional feat on part of the photographer. The possibility of its existence is therefore conditioned by the camera's automatism, bypassing the artist's subjectivity. In *Grizzly Man*, Herzog likewise notes that part of the beauty he found in Treadwell's footage occurs at moments that appear to elude Treadwell's intention.

6. On Herzog's relation to Caspar David Friedrich and the German Romantic tradition of painting that takes landscapes to represent inner states of mind, see, among others, Prager 2009 and Gandy 2012.

7. Alexander Sesonske presented on the potential challenge of cartoons to Cavell's idea of film as a moving image of skepticism at the American Society

of Aesthetics symposium "The World Viewed," held in Sarasoto, FL, 1971. The presentation is published, along with "More on The World Viewed," in *The Georgia Review* (See Sesonske 1974).

8. Amélie has just returned to Paris by train from a visit to her lethargic and withdrawn father, carrying her father's garden gnome along with her. The gnome—that fantasmatic creature turned commodity—is the only object in the world Amélie's father still appears to have some feelings for; it is a displaced figure metonymically related to his late wife (who had gifted it to him). Amélie is about to turn the gnome into a protagonist of a game parallel to the one she is to set up for Nino: she has asked a stewardess friend to take it along with her on a work tour around the globe and to send snapshots of the statuette posing in front of the great monuments of the world to its rightful owner—Amélie's father. That Amélie's aim of awakening her father's desire to travel the globe himself turns out to be successful by the end of the film should not prevent us from seeing that the images of a fake travel narrative would themselves be fairly easy to fake, even without digital intervention (with a simple backdrop, say). But apparently, and significantly, Amélie prefers to offer real world projections of a fake travel narrative.

9. In the film, the booth itself is called a "photomaton," as are related machines used for mechanical reproduction (such as the photocopier). This was indeed the original name coined by the inventor of the photo booth, Anatol Josepho, but that historical fact is barely as relevant as the more poetic force emanating from the name, with its amalgam of conceptually related phenomena associated in the film with Nino himself as well as with the man he is pursuing, namely, photo, automaton, and phantom.

10. Andrew 2004, 43–45. Nino's female colleague at the sex shop suggests an additional allegorical significance when she calls the fun fair attraction the Genius of the Carpathians, a name referring to one of Ceaușescu's self-imposed titles, though in common parlance rather connoting him as master inventor of complicated schemes.

11. This point of discrete images, autonomy, and control is underscored in the subsequent scene, in which the four identical pictures of a set of passport photos come to life, waking up Nino to talk about Amélie. Describing Amélie, who is yet unknown to Nino, the reproduced talking heads initially act in sync, but soon start moving independently of one another and eventually quarrel among themselves as they disagree about Amélie's qualities and intentions.

12. On the connection between contingency and necessity in the analogue, see Doane 2007.

13. Cf. Ezra 305. Ezra elaborates on the allegorical significance of Dufayel (and his interactions with Lucien, whom Dufayel calls "le roi des magiciens"—viz. Méliès) in the context of the cinema and the concept of indexicality, though

she does not appear to see any significance in the rather obvious fact of him being a painter—and a forging one at that.

14. The TV set was set up, we should note, by Lucien (who has a key to deliver groceries) at Dufayel's suggestion. This underscores the reversal of authorship, as Lucien thus counters Amélie's own invasion of Collignon's home to punish him for bullying Lucien.

Chapter 5

1. On this division, see Schmerheim 2016, chapter 7: "Varieties of Skepticism Films."

2. For an alternative reading of the significance of this power within a feminist context, see Laura Mulvey's *Death 24X a Second* (Mulvey 2006). In "The Remote Control as Political Weapon" (Gerrits 2007), I relate the ability to control the "relentless forward drive of cinema" to Mulvey's groundbreaking essay "Visual Pleasure and Narrative Cinema" (1975, reprinted in Mulvey 2009).

3. Buckland 2009 and 2014; Cameron 2008; Daly 2010; Manovich 2001; Mittell 2006; Panek 2006; Pisters 2012; Simons 2007; Staiger 2006.

4. In the 2018 follow-up essay, Elsaesser complicates this initial postulation by discussing cases of commercially successful films that, while themselves based on video-game logic, failed to generate aesthetically or commercially interesting spin-offs (TV-series, computer games).

5. Elsaesser, to be sure, actually does reference Deleuze's "Postscript on the Societies of Control" (see chapter 5 note 11), but this rather points away from his cinema books.

6. Elsaesser thus falls in line with other theorists of world cinema, claiming that it is not a mere conglomeration of national cinemas but one held together by aesthetic and theoretical concerns. See Denison and Lim 2006, Nagib and Perriam 2012.

7. In an earlier paper, entitled "Truth or Dare: Reality Checks on Indexicality, or the Future of Illusionism" (1998), Elsaesser had already exempted Deleuze from this "horror of proximity," speculating that this is may be an important reason for Deleuze's congeniality to theorists of new media.

8. For Baudry's point about the cinematic viewer as transcendental subject, see his essay "Ideological Effects of the Basic Cinematographic Apparatus" (Baudry 2009).

9. Seung-hoon Jeong's reconceptualization of indexicality is part of a larger project that aims to rethink the relation between image and subject through the concept of "interfaciality"—a term he "creatively appropriate[s]" from new media discourses to "retrofit it through film theory" (Jeong 2013, 3). Although

his way of relating Freud to Bergson and especially Lacan to Deleuze appears at times problematic, Jeong's discussion of "the intradiegetic outside" (Žižek) in relation to Deleuze's cinematic rendering of the plane of immanence seems particularly fruitful to me (Jeong 2013, 51).

10. In the 2018 essay on the mind-game film, Elsaesser adds "a more philosophically inflected and conceptually interconnected account" to the earlier sociological and economic perspective on subject. In so doing, he doubles down on his claim that contemporary cinema responds to a generalized skeptical condition. He asks: "How can cinema—or in my case, a meta-cinema like the mind-game film—be an answer to the modern wounds of radical scepticism or philosophical nihilism? How can it restore our trust in the world, when it is all make-believe, and dangerous or beautiful illusion?" (Elsaesser 2018, 16) Elsaesser's immediate response—which is not his whole response, but all I will discuss here—is as surprising as it is troublesome. "First, because its automatism acknowledges this rift between a world utterly indifferent to humans and the fact that these humans are nonetheless utterly responsible for this world, as Stanley Cavell has so cogently argued in *The World Viewed*" (ibid.). The response is surprising because of its departure from his previous interpretation of contemporary film as having moved away from the ontological and epistemological concerns that had occupied Cavell, towards a position I am taking. Yet it is also troublesome, for it is hard to see how Cavellian *automatism* can offer a response to "restore our trust in the world" or how the "nonetheless" should be accounted for under such conditions, even when bracketing the complication Elsaesser is most interested in ("when it is all make-believe.")

11. Deleuze developed the idea of Societies of Control in response to what he saw as a break away from the disciplinary societies of industrial modernity, which Foucault analyzed so well. These developments are neither for the better nor for the worse, but they do significantly change the way we relate to the world and to others. We no longer grow up by moving from one disciplinary cast or mold to another in gradual succession (the family, the school, the barracks, the factory), but live in various "modulations" simultaneously. No longer kept "in chains" in enclosed spaces, we are kept in debt while we are distributed and tracked in open spaces. See Deleuze 1992; for Elsaesser's reference, see Elsaesser 2009a, 31.

12. Nino expects her to arrive as a client, as is evident from the fact that he seats himself facing the entrance door. Just before the scene described, he lights up when a pretty young woman enters, heading toward him. He is visibly disappointed when she turns to kiss another young man sitting in the next booth over. Witnessing the scene, Amélie in turn appears to be disappointed at Nino's expectations, fearing at the same time his disappointment in her appearance. That the two women do not resemble one another in the least underscores Nino's obvious difficulty in identifying the woman in the picture.

13. Herzog furthers the sense of growing paranoia on Treadwell's part in a subsequent scene, in which Treadwell finds a neatly piled stack of boulders near his camp. Treadwell comments: "Now we're not gonna call this the building of the pyramids, but we *are* saying there's a bit of trouble." He points his camera at a happy face "indelibly painted into the rock, like it's looking at me" and shares his interpretation with his implied viewer: "Very very freakin' frightening, huh? It's a warning. It's better than a 'you're dead' type of thing; it's Freddy Kruger creepy, baby."

14. See for example, the reddit blog and lost media archive's wiki at https://www.reddit.com/r/UnresolvedMysteries/comments/5lresx/audio_recording_of_the_death_of_timothy_treadwell/. http://lostmediaarchive.wikia.com/wiki/Timothy_Treadwell_%22Grizzly_Man%22_Death_Audio_(Recorded_in_2003).

Chapter 6

1. Beyond *The Headless Woman*, the Salta trilogy, named after the Argentine region in which the films were set and shot, further includes Martel's directorial debut, *The Swamp* (*La Ciénaga*, 2001), and its successor, *The Holy Girl* (*La niña santa*, 2004).

2. While the film is in Spanish, the Italian reference is unlikely to get lost on Argentine viewers. Not only is the Spanish *verdad/veras/verosimilitud* closely enough related to the Italian to gauge the significance of the protagonist's name; we should also note the fact, highly relevant in the context of this film, that Italian immigration forms one of the largest and central ethnic origins of modern Argentinians, with 62.5 percent of the total population having some degree of Italian descent.

3. See Matheou 2010 for this self-declared characterization of the film on Martel's part.

4. Neither ended up winning the Palm, which went to Laurent Cantet's *The Class* (*Entre les murs*), though Ceylan was awarded the prize for best director.

5. Beyond its similarities to Martel's film, which I take to be entirely coincidental, Ceylan's film takes its blueprint from Güney's *The Father* (*Baba*, 1971), which Ceylan himself acknowledged as the "point of origin" for *Three Monkeys* (Cardullo 109). Güney's film, in fact, revolves around a conflict of *two* fathers. The first, played by Güney himself, is a man struck by poverty desperate to support his family. Just when he resolves to leave his country and try his luck as a migrant worker in Western Europe, the son of his rich landlord/employer commits a murder in an act of drunken stupor. The second, rich father now asks the poor one to take the responsibility for the crime, promising to support his wife and children financially during his imprisonment and a lump sum of money upon his release. The poor father's decision to accept the offer suggests

that time in jail under such conditions is preferable to being a migrant worker abroad, which in turn had already ruled out the option of staying at home under the current circumstances.

6. See Bonitzer 1985. For an English introduction to the concept of deframing, see Aumont's entry "The Apparatus" in *Postwar Cinema and Modernity: A Film Reader*. Deframing reverses of the common tendency to put the most meaningful objects or people in the foreground, center, and focal point of the frame.

7. The term "virtual point of view" borrows from Deleuze's interpretation of the Bergsonian concept of the virtual. For Bergson's take on the "virtual image" as differentiated from both objective and subjective images, see Bergson 1988, 130–31. On Deleuze's interpretation, see especially Deleuze 1988, 40–43, and note 12.

8. Oubiña, quoted in Page 2013, 79.

9. In this sense, Martel's film makes for an interesting comparison with Kim Ki-Duk's *3 Iron* (a.k.a. *Bin Jip*, 2004), a film that Thomas Elseasser interpreted in terms of the virtual and hence with the "new ontology characterized by 'ubiquity' . . . (and its corollary, invisible presence . . .)" (Elsaesser 2013, 12, 14).

10. This citation explains the significance of the X-ray office, visited by Vero during her brief hospitalization after the accident in a scene marked by a disturbing false sound bridge.

11. Losada uses this narrow definition in his reading of *The Headless Woman* to suggest that Martel's stylistic decisions are based on her "immersion in the mind of a character" (Losada 2010, 308). He does not, to be sure, specifically have the scene of the accident in mind when discussing the concept. Indeed, he claims that the film's opening is to be excluded from his analysis, claiming that in the "opening eight minutes or so the narration is fairly objective and omniscient . . . but then comes the trauma" (310). I am arguing rather that these minutes are not objective and omniscient, any more than they are indicative of free indirect discourse in this narrow sense.

12. Several commentators have discussed the significance of sound in Martel's films, including Losada (who also includes Michon's terminology in his analysis) and Quandt (who briefly discusses the false sound bridge). For Michon's use of the term "acoustmatic" (which he borrows in turn from his forebear Pierre Schaeffer), see especially his recently translated *Sound: An Acoulogical Treatise*.

13. This anticipates a scene later on in the film, in which Vero's aunt Lala complains about the presence of ghosts in the house and urges Vero: "Don't look at them"—an utterance that coincides with Vero looking at the shadowy figures of indigenous children in the background.

14. Bakhtin developed his notions of plurilingualism and heteroglossia in "Discourse in the Novel," published in Bakhtin 1981.

15. For a more detailed discussion on Deleuze's concept of fabulation in relation to *The Headless Woman*, see Page 2013.

16. In a regular sound bridge, the sound continues from one shot into the next, thus establishing a spatiotemporal continuity between the two. False sound bridges, however, connect discontinuous images, establishing more poetic resonances and discordances between them. In *The Headless Woman*, a whole series of false sound bridges accumulates in the scenes following the title frame. For example, while the sound of rain falling onto the car carries over this title frame into the next scene, we do not cut back to where we left off, with Vero walking "headlessly" in front of her car; instead, we find Vero staring out of the side window as she is being driven to the hospital. At this point, we hear a female voice stating that "this water is going to be good for your hair" (as opposed, we may note, to the water from the pool)—a statement we can only attribute to the young woman driving this car (probably Candita), despite the fact that her mouth is not moving. However, the same voice continues to speak in the following shot ("Good thing someone brought you"), which shows Vero standing in a doorpost with a piece of adhesive tape on her temple. We still seem to lack a body to attribute the voice to, until a hand reaches to touch Vero's hair. Only then do we realize that a woman is standing right next to her. Barely visible behind a rain-covered glass panel and tightly framed between doorpost and film frame stands the woman who does the speaking—it turns out to be a nurse, a woman of color, in the following shots. Martel thus combines the false sound bridge with a visual technique she will explore further in the course of the film: the literal marginalization of staff, workers, and helpers, especially when people of color are concerned.

17. The scene is interesting too because it initiates a complex dynamic going on between Vero and Marcos. While he infantilizes her with his hushing comments ("*no pasa nada*"), it is not Marcos but Vero who actively avoids the knowledge of what happened. At the same time, Marcos never asks Vero why she thinks she killed someone, being all too ready to accept the dead dog as the cause of her scare. He effectively uses Vero's refusal to go examine the site more closely against her in their subsequent discussion with Juan Manuel. When Marcos tells the latter that Vero got a scare from having killed a dog, and she interrupts him saying she thinks she killed a person instead, he effectively shuts her up: "No." And, turning to Juan Manuel as if she weren't there: "Vero had quite a scare. She ran over a dog." Vero, for her part, does not continue to explain her suspicion, insisting instead on the lack of accuracy of lesser important details in her husband's story ("it didn't rain yet"). Throughout the remainder of the film, Vero maintains this attitude of venting her general skepticism through cynical and sarcastic comments about seemingly minor details. Thus, when she hears towards the end of the film that her daughter and husband bought an outdoor heater as a wedding gift, she cynically asks: "For Tucumán?" (Salta's

neighboring province with barely two cold weeks a year), though she did not make any suggestions when asked what to get as a gift herself.

18. Several commentators connected this makeover to Hitchcock's guilty women, most notably Kim Novak in *Vertigo*. The analogy with Monica Vitti's blonde and disheveled coiffure in Antonioni's films has also been pointed. See, for example, Taubin 2009, Martin 2013, and White 2015.

19. Beyond already mentioned occasions—the intimacy with the plumber and the association with contamination at the pool in the film's prologue—there are several other occasions on which Martel explicitly links the tropes. For example, when Vero arrives at the hospital, one of the nurses, a woman of color, runs her hand through Vero's disheveled coiffure, commenting that "this water is going to be good for your hair." This contrast with a scene in which Josefina (the woman with the false eyelashes) rants about her daughter Candita for hanging out with indigenous "ladies." While we see Candita and her girlfriend Cuquita through the open door in the background, a "headless" Josefina (decapitated by the frame) gives Vero a Chinese hair wash, saying: "I don't know where she finds these people, all day on their bikes, like guys. Some days I can't stand them." In the same breath, she shifts registers and addresses Vero: "Your hair is disgusting." For an excellent elaboration on the theme of contamination and on Candita's liminal role in the film, see Martin 2013.

20. On these and other references to the junta period, see, among others, Sosa 2009 and Matheou 2010.

21. This is evident also from the fact that, instead of retreating behind the doors of her private clinic, Vero embarks on a public-school dentistry program ("la semena de la sunrisa"). While Deborah Martin maintains that these "redemptive possibilities," however important, mark but a "*limited* coming to consciousness" on Vero's part (Martin 2013, 146, emphasis added), Joanna Page shifts the emphasis we she notes: "Although Vero eventually colludes with the conspiracy of silence, we are left with a sense . . . of the radical potential of the accident to crack open a fissure in the edifice" (Page 2013, 83).

22. Aberrant movements, then, are not movements of a character, but of the movement-image. The term "aberration" is frequently employed in French poststructuralism and deconstruction. In De Man's work, for example, ideological aberrations result from the attempt to conceptualize reference as a perfect merging of language and being, or linguistic and natural reality (De Man 1997).

23. This complex temporal layering gets another turn of the screw since Ismail, who does seem to catch his train this time around, will indeed miss his train later on in the film and so discovers Servet's visit to Hacer's bedroom.

24. Nucleï or cardinal functions are narratological pivot points that decisively push the action in one direction or another. See Barthes's "Structural Analysis of Narratives" (in Barthes 1977).

25. At this moment, a man can be heard coughing in Hacer's room, and after we see Servet leave the building via subjective shots of Ismail spying on

him, Hacer seems to be giving herself away. Mistakenly assuming she has a moment unwatched by her son, she straightens out a wrinkle in the blankets of her (otherwise impeccably well-made) bed. She then seems to lie by telling Ismail that the cigarettes in the ashtray are from a female friend paying an unannounced visit. While the actual audio-visual signs—the man coughing, the impeccable bed—do not in fact corroborate the idea of a sexual encounter, our potential doubt about it seems powerless compared to Ismail's reaction and Hacer's subsequent infatuation with Servet.

26. On oblique contexts in linguistics, see Ducrot and Todorov 1979.

27. Levy 2015, 107.

28. On Deleuze's concept of incompossibility, see Deleuze 1996, 130–31, as well as chapter 5 in Deleuze 1993.

29. Although he takes it in a very different direction, my interpretation is here indebted to Suner's, who relates Ceylan's narrative strategy to the concept of the void as well, as I discuss in the conclusion to this book (see Suner 2011). Peter J. Schwartz explored the notion of the void at the center in relation to Haneke's films (see Grundmann 2010).

30. For Deleuze's take on Blanchot, see esp. Deleuze 1986, pp 167–68. For Blanchot's concept and his indebtedness to Artaud, see especially the entry of the latter in Blanchot 2003.

31. Cf. Andrew 2009, Suner 2011.

32. Of course, Eyüp is not named after the biblical patriarch. Eyüp is the Turkish name for Job, who is known in the Islamic tradition as a prophet characterized by his patience and endurance in the face of adversity. Yet Ceylan weaves these characters together into a biblical mesh-up. The accounts of Hagar/Hacer and Eyüp/Job share the fact that God caused a cool spring of water to emerge from the earth right under their feet, which may well account for the boy appearing (to Ismail) as having suffered a violent death by water. But the more pertinent analogy between the biblical narratives of Job and Abraham consists in God's intervention to release the respective men of a burden they were ordained to carry out. Job was released from his oath to beat his wife with a hundred strokes when God told him to hit her softly with a bundle of soft grass instead. Ceylan adapted this into a powerful scene in which Hacer, in seductive night gear, receives Eyüp upon his return from jail. While Eyüp, whose lust mixes with anger and disgust, pushes his wife about the details of the financial transaction between her and Servet, she switches between states of laughing and crying. Their dynamic, dense, mostly wordless interaction breaks off before either a sexual climax or a violent explosion is reached. In other words: while the biblical figure is released from the burden of having to torture his wife without having to break his word, in Ceylan's hands, Eyüp becomes the emblem of an emasculated patriarch.

33. There are, in addition, two differences between the biblical and Quranic accounts of Abraham's sacrifice that are relevant for our reading of *Three*

Monkeys. First, in the Quran, as opposed to the Old Testament, Abraham's dream of having to sacrifice his son is not confirmed to be a divine command. Although in most mainstream translations of the relevant verse we can still *assume* this to be the case, other, nonmainstream translations explicitly deny the dream the status of a command from God. See, for example, Ghulam Ahmad Parwez' nonmainstream translation: "We immediately removed this thought from Abraham's mind and called out to him, O Abraham. You considered your dream as Allah's command and laid your son for the purpose of slaughtering him! This was not Our command, but merely a dream of yours. Therefore We have saved you and your son from this. We have done so because We keep those who lead their lives according to Divine guidance safe from such mishaps." (37 As Saaffaat 2017, 104–5). Second, whereas the biblical account has Isaac kept in the dark about his father's plan to sacrifice him even as they climbed Mount Moriah together, the Quranic version relates that Abraham openly spoke about his plan with Ishmael, who thus knew of his fate and loyally encouraged his own sacrifice.

34. Although Asuman Suner ultimately argues regarding *Three Monkeys* that the film "does not refer to a particular historical event . . . Rather, the film as a whole turns into an *actual* thought process through which the state of oblivion in Turkey . . . gets refracted" (Suner 2011, 23, emphasis added), thus shifting focus from past to present, his allegorical reading still looks at the state *in* Turkey, whereas mine shifts focus to the state *of* Turkey within a global setting—a shift I find significant in light of the transition from national Turkish cinema (Yeçilçam) to a transnational (post-Yeçilçam) New Turkish Cinema.

Conclusion

1. See, for example, the work of such different writers as Manuel Castells, Gary Hall, or Mark Poster, as well and a variety of new media theorists who embraced Deleuzian concepts of the rhizome, the virtual, and assemblage theory to make a case for the Internet as a nomadic playground.

References

Ahmad, Aijaz. 1987. "Jameson's Rhetoric of Otherness and the 'National Allegory.'" *Social Text* 17: 3.
Amenábar, Alejandro. 1997. *Open Your Eyes*. Santa Monica, CA: Artisan Home Entertainment.
———. 2002. *The Others*. Burbank, CA: Dimension Home Video.
Ames, Eric. 2012. *Ferocious Reality: Documentary according to Werner Herzog*. Minneapolis: University of Minnesota Press.
Andermann, Jens. 2012. *New Argentine Cinema*. Tauris World Cinema Series. London; New York: I. B. Tauris.
Andrew, Dudley. 2004. "Amélie, Or Le Fabuleux Destin Du Cinéma Français." *Film Quarterly* 57 (3): 34.
Andrew, Geoff. 2004. "Beyond the Clouds: An Interview with Nuri Bilge Ceylan." *Senses of Cinema*: 32.
Annaud. Jean-Jacques. 1997. *Seven Years in Tibet*. Mandalay Entertainment.
Antonioni, Michelangelo. "L'avventura: Cannes Statement." *Criterion*. Accessed 07/28/ 2017. https://www.criterion.com/current/posts/100-l-avventura-cannes-statement.
———. 1960. *L'Avventura*. Irvington, NY: Criterion Collection.
———. 1964. *Red Desert*. United States: Criterion Collection.
Antonioni, Michelangelo, and Pierre Leprohon. 1963. *Michelangelo Antonioni: An Introduction*. New York: Simon and Schuster.
"Argentina's Flourishing Film Industry." *WIPO Magazine*. Accessed 07/28/, 2017. http://www.wipo.int/wipo_magazine/en/2005/03/article_0011.html.
Arslan, Savas. 2011. *Cinema in Turkey: A New Critical History*. New York: Oxford University Press.
Audiard. Jacques. 2015. *Dheepan*. Paris: Why Not Productions.
Aumont, Jacques. 2001. "The Apparatus." In *Postwar Cinema and Modernity: A Film Reader*, edited by John Orr and Olga Taxidou. New York: NYU Press.
Austin, J. L. (1979). Philosophical Papers. 3rd ed. / Edited by J. O. Urmson and G. J. Warnock. Oxford: Oxford University Press.

Bakhtin, M. M. (Mikhail Mikhaĭlovich), and Holquist, Michael. 1981. *The Dialogic Imagination: Four Essays*. Austin: University of Texas Press.
Barthes, Roland. 1981. *Camera Lucida: Reflections on Photography* [Chambre claire. English]. New York: Hill and Wang.
Barthes, Roland, and Stephen Heath. 1977. *Image, Music, Text*. Fontana Communications Series. London: Fotana.
Baudry, Jean-Louis. 1975. "Ideological Effects of the Basic Cinematographic Apparatus." *Film Quarterly* 28 (2): 39.
Bazin, André. *Jean Renoir*. 1973. Trans. W. W. Halsey II and William H. Simon. New York: Simon & Schuster.
Bazin, André, and Hugh Gray. 1971. *What Is Cinema? Volumes I and II*. Berkeley: University of California Press.
Bergson, Henri. 1974. *The Creative Mind: An Introduction to Metaphysics* [Pensée et le mouvant. English]. Carol Publishing Group ed. New York: Carol.
———. 1988. *Matter and Memory* [Matière et mémoire. English]. New York: Zone Books.
———. 2007. *Creative Evolution*. Henri Bergson Centennial Series. [Evolution créatrice. English]. Basingstoke England; New York: Palgrave Macmillan.
Blair, David. "Waxweb." Accessed 07/28/2017. http://www.waxweb.org.
Blanchot, Maurice. 2003. *The Book to Come*. Stanford, CA: Stanford University Press.
Blank, Les. 2005. *Burden of Dreams*. Special ed. S.l: Criterion Collection.
———. 2015. *Werner Herzog Eats His Shoe*. San Francisco, CA: Kanopy Streaming.
Bondanella, Peter E. 2009. *A History of Italian Cinema*. New York: Continuum.
Bonitzer, Pascal. 1995. *Peinture Et Cinéma*. Paris: Ed. de l'Etoile.
Bordwell, David and Noël Carroll. 1996. *Post-Theory: Reconstructing Film Studies*. Madison, WI: University of Wisconsin Press.
Braudy, Leo. 1971. "Rev. of the World Viewed, by Stanley Cavell." *Film Quarterly*: 28–29.
Braudy, Leo, and Marshall Cohen. 2009. *Film Theory and Criticism: Introductory Readings*. 7th ed. New York: Oxford University Press.
Brunette, Peter. 2009. "The Headless Woman." *Film Journal International* 112 (9): 43.
Buckland, Warren. 2009. *Puzzle Films: Complex Storytelling in Contemporary Cinema*. Chichester, West Sussex, U.K.: Wiley-Blackwell.
Cameron, Allan. 2008. *Modular Narratives in Contemporary Cinema*. New York: Palgrave Macmillan.
Cantet, Laurent. 2009. *Entre Les Murs: The Class*. Paris: Haut et Court.
Capra, Frank. 2008 (1934). *It Happened One Night*. Culver City, CA: Columbia Pictures, and Sony Pictures Home Entertainment. DVD.
Cardullo, Bert. 2015. *Nuri Bilge Ceylan*. Berlin: Logos Verlag.
Carroll, Noël. 1988. *Philosophical Problems of Classical Film Theory*. Princeton, N.J: Princeton University Press.

———. 1996. *Theorizing the Moving Image*. Cambridge Studies in Film. Cambridge UK; New York: Cambridge University Press.

Cavell, Stanley. 1976. *Must We Mean What We Say: A Book of Essays*. Cambridge UK; New York: Cambridge University Press.

———. 1979. *The World Viewed: Reflections on the Ontology of Film*. Enl ed. Cambridge: Harvard University Press.

———. 1981a. *Pursuits of Happiness: The Hollywood Comedy of Remarriage*. Harvard Film Studies. Cambridge, MA: Harvard University Press.

———. 1989. *This New Yet Unapproachable America: Lectures after Emerson after Wittgenstein*. Albuquerque, NM: Living Batch.

———. 1982. *The Claim of Reason: Wittgenstein, Skepticism, Morality, and Tragedy*. Oxford Paperbacks. Oxford; New York: Oxford University Press.

———. 1985. "What Photography Calls Thinking." *Raritan* 4 (4): 1.

———. 1988. *In Quest of the Ordinary: Lines of Skepticism and Romanticism*. Chicago: University of Chicago Press.

———. 1996. *Contesting Tears: The Hollywood Melodrama of the Unknown Woman*. Chicago: University of Chicago Press.

———. 2005. "What Becomes of Thinking on Film: Stanley Cavell in Conversation with Andrew Klevan." In *Film as Philosophy: Essays in Cinema after Wittgenstein and Cavell*, edited by Rupert Read and Jerry Goodenough, 167–209. Houndsmill: Palgrave Macmillan.

Cavell, Stanley, and William Rothman. 2005. *Cavell on Film*. SUNY Series, Horizons of Cinema. Albany: State University of New York Press.

Ceylan, Nuri Bilge. 2002. *Distant*. Istanbul, New York: NBC Ajans.

———. 2007. *Climates*. New York: Zeitgeist Films.

———. 2008. *Three Monkeys*. New York: Zeitgeist Films.

———. 2011. *Once upon a Time in Amatolia*. New York: Cinema Guild.

Chatman, Seymour Benjamin. 1978. *Story and Discourse: Narrative Structure in Fiction and Film*. Ithaca, N.Y: Cornell University Press.

———. 1985. *Antonioni, Or, the Surface of the World*. Berkeley: University of California Press.

Chaudhuri, Shohini, and Howard Finn. 2003. "The Open Image: Poetic Realism and the New Iranian Cinema." *Screen* 44 (1): 38.

Chazelle, Damien. 2014. *Whiplash*. Culver City, CA: Sony Pictures Home Entertainment.

Chion, Michel, and James A. Steintrager. 2015. *Sound: An Acoulogical Treatise*. Durham: Duke University Press.

Corrigan, Timothy. 2013. *The Films of Werner Herzog: Between Mirage and History*. Routledge Library Editions: Cinema. Florence: Routledge.

Cronenberg, David. 2014. *Crash*. Burbank, CA: Warner Home Video.

Cronin, Paul, and Werner Herzog. 2014. *Werner Herzog: A Guide for the Perplexed*. Rev and updated. London: Faber & Faber.

Crowe, Cameron. 2002. *Vanilla Sky*. Hollywood, CA: Paramount.

Cuarón, Alfonso. 2001. *Y tu mamá también*. Santa Monica, CA: Metro Goldwyn Mayer Home Entertainment.

Daly, Kristen. 2010. "Cinema 3.0: The Interactive-image. (Essay)." *Cinema Journal* 50, no. 1 (September 22, 2010): 81–98.

Deleuze, Gilles. 1986. *The Movement-Image*. Cinema Vol. 1 [Image-movement. English]. Minneapolis: University of Minnesota Press.

———. 1988. *Bergsonism* [Bergsonisme. English]. New York: Zone Books.

———. 1989. *The Time-Image*. Cinema. [Image-temps. English]. Vol. 2. London: Athlone Press.

———. 1991. *Empiricism and Subjectivity: an Essay on Hume's Theory of Human Nature*. New York: Columbia University Press.

———. 1992. "Postscript on the Societies of Control." *October* 59: 7.

———. 1993. *The Fold: Leibniz and the Baroque* [Pli. English]. Minneapolis: University of Minnesota Press.

———. 2004. *Difference and Repetition* [Différence et répétition. English]. New ed. London: Continuum.

Deleuze, Gilles, and Claire Parnet. 2007. *Dialogues II*. European Perspectives. [Dialogues. English]. Rev ed. New York: Columbia University Press.

Delgado, Maria M. 2013. "La Mujer Sin Cabeza/the Headless Woman (Lucrecia Martel, 2008): Silence, Historical Memory and Metaphor." In *Spanish Cinema 1973–2010: Auteurism, Politics, Landscape and Memory*. Manchester: Manchester University Press.

De Man, Paul, and Andrzej Warminski. 1997. *Aesthetic Ideology*. Theory and History of Literature. Vol. 88. Minneapolis: University of Minnesota Press.

Dennison, Stephanie, and Song Hwee Lim. 2006. *Remapping World Cinema: Identity, Culture and Politics in Film*. London; New York: Wallflower.

Doane, Mary Ann. 2007. "The Indexical and the Concept of Medium Specificity." *Differences: A Journal of Feminist Cultural Studies* 18 (1): 128.

Domenach, Élise. 2011. *Stanley Cavell, le cinéma et le scepticisme*. Paris Presses universitaires de France.

Ducrot, Oswald, and Tzvetan Todorov. 1979. *Encyclopedic Dictionary of the Sciences of Language* [Dictionnaire encyclopdique des sciences du langage. English]. Baltimore: Johns Hopkins University Press.

Egoyan, Atom. 1997. *The Sweet Hereafter*. United States: New Line Home Video.

Elizabezquez, K. 2015. "La potica del enrarecimiento en La mujer sin cabeza (2008), de Lucrecia Martel." *Hispanic Research Journal* 16 (1): 31.

Elsaesser, Thomas. 1989. *New German Cinema: A History*. New Brunswick, NJ: Rutgers University Press.

———. 1998. "Truth or Dare: Reality Checks on Indexicality, Or the Future of Illusionism." In *Cinema Studies into Visual Theory?* edited by Anu Koivunnen and Astrid Soderbergh Widding, 31–50. Turku: D-Vision.

———. 2009a. "The Mind-Game Film." In *Realism and the Audiovisual Media*, edited by Lúcia Nagib and Ceĭlia Mello, 3–19. New York: Palgrave Macmillan.

———. 2009b. "World Cinema: Realism, Evidence, Presence." In *Realism and the Audiovisual Media*, 3–19. New York: Palgrave Macmillan.

———. 2018. "Contingency, Causality, Complexity: Distributed Agency in the Mind-Game Film." *New Review of Film and Television Studies* 16:1.

Elsaesser, Thomas, and Hagener, Malte. 2010. *Film Theory: An Introduction through the Senses*. New York: Routledge.

Esmer, Pelin. 2018. *The Watchtower*. UK: Network.

Ezra, Elizabeth. 2004. "The Death of an Icon: Le Fabuleux Destin D'Amlie Poulain." *French Cultural Studies* 15 (3): 301.

Falicov, Tamara Leah. 2007. *The Cinematic Tango: Contemporary Argentine Film*. London: Wallflower.

Farhadi, Asghar. *A Separation*. Culver City, CA: Sony Pictures Home 3 Entertainment, 2011.

Fischer, Michael. 1989. *Stanley Cavell and Literary Skepticism*. Chicago: University of Chicago Press.

Flaxman, Gregory. 2000. *The Brain Is the Screen: Deleuze and the Philosophy of Cinema*. Minneapolis: University of Minnesota Press.

Flitterman-Lewis, Sandy. 1996. "The Image and the Spark: Dulac and Artaud Reviewed." In *Dada and Surrealist Film*, edited by Rudolf E. Kuenzli, 110–27. Cambridge, MA: MIT Press.

Foucault, Michel, and Maurice Blanchot. 1987. *Foucault / Blanchot: Maurice Blanchot: The Thought from Outside and Michel Foucault as I Imagine Him*. New York: Zone Books.

Fried, Michael. 1998. *Art and Objecthood: Essays and Reviews*. Chicago: University of Chicago Press.

———. 2008. *Why Photography Matters as Art as Never Before*. New Haven: Yale University Press.

Früchtl, Josef. 2013. *Vertrauen in Die Welt*. München: Fink.

Fukunaga, Cary Joji. 2009. *Sin Nombre*. CA: Focus Features.

Gale, Bob. 1995. *Mr. Payback*. Interfilm Technologies.

Gandy, Matthew. 2012. "The Melancholy Observer: Landscape, Neo-Romanticism, and the Politics of Documentary Filmmaking." In *A Companion to Werner Herzog*, 528. Chichester, West Sussex; Malden, MA Wiley-Blackwell.

Garrone, Matteo. 2008. *Gomorrah*. United States: E1 Entertainment.

George, Terry. 2007. *Reservation Road*. New York: Focus Features LLC.

Gerrits, Jeroen. 2007. "The Remote Control as Political Weapon: Death 24x a Second: Stillness and the Moving Image by Laura Mulvey." *Senses of Cinema* 44.

———. 2010. "Disagreement as Duty: On the Importance of the Self and Friendship in Cavell's Morals Philosophy." *European Journal of Pragmatism and American Philosophy* 2 (1): 65.

———. 2012. "When Horror Becomes Human: Living Conditions in Buffy the Vampire Slayer." *Mln* 127 (5): 1059.

Goldhammer, Arthur. "On *The Rules of the Game.*" *French Politics and Society* 10, no. 2 (1992): 66.
"Grizzly People." Accessed 07/28/, 2017. http://www.grizzlypeople.com.
Grundmann, Roy. 2010. *A Companion to Michael Haneke*. Wiley-Blackwell Companions to Film Directors. Chichester, West Sussex; Malden, MA: Wiley-Blackwell.
Güney, Yılmaz. 1996. *Baba: The Father*. United States: Hollywood's Attic.
Hagin, Boaz. 2011. *Just Images: Ethics and the Cinematic*. Newcastle upon Tyne: Cambridge Scholars.
Haneke, Michael. 1997. *Funny Games*. Vienna: Filmfonds Wien.
———. 2000. *Caché*. Paris: Les Films du Losange; Culver City, CA.
———. 2007. *Funny Games*. Burbank, CA: Warner Home Video.
Harper, Graeme, and Jonathan Rayner. 2010. *Cinema and Landscape*. Bristol, UK: Intellect.
Herzog, Werner. 1972. *Aguirre, the Wrath of God*. Shout Factory; San Francisco, CA: Kanopy Streaming, 2017
———. 1999. Fitzcarraldo. Troy, MI: Anchor Bay Entertainment.
———. 1999. "Werner Herzog Reads His Minnesota Declaration: Truth and Fact in Documentary Cinema." *Walker Art Magazine*. Accessed 07/28/, 2017. https://walkerart.org/magazine/minnesota-declaration-truth-documentary-cinema.
———. 2000. *My Best Fiend: Klaus Kinski*. Troy, MI: Anchor Bay Entertainment.
———. 2005. *Grizzly Man*. Widescreen. Santa Monica, CA: Lions Gate Home Entertainment.
———. 2006. *The Wild Blue Yonder*. Seattle, WA: Subversive Cinema.
———. 2008. *Encounters at the End of the World*. Widescreen. Silver Spring, MD: Discovery Communications.
———. 2011. *Cave of Forgotten Dreams*. Widescreen version. Los Angeles, CA: Creative Differences Productions, Inc..
———. 2017. "Werner Herzog Makes Trump-Era Addition to His Minnesota Declaration." *Walker Art Magazine*. Accessed 07/28/2017. https://walkerart.org/magazine/werner-herzog-minnesota-declaration-2017-addendum.
Hitchcock, Alfred. 1958. *Vertigo*. Universal City, CA: Universal Home Video.
Holfelder, Moritz. 2012. *Werner Herzog: Die Biografie*. München: Langen Müller.
Horak, Jan-Christopher. 1986. "W.H. or the Mysteries of Walking on Ice." In *The Films of Werner Herzog: Between Mirage and History*, edited by Timothy Corrigan, 23–44. New York: Methuen.
Iñárritu, Alejandro Gonzalez. 2000. *Amores Perros*. Marina Del Rey, CA: Lion's Gate Home Entertainment.
James, Nick. 2009. "The Devil within Us." *Sight & Sound* 19 (3): 12.
Jeong, Seung-hoon. 2013. *Cinematic Interfaces: Film Theory after New Media*. NY: Routledge.

Jeong, Seung-hoon, and Dudley Andrew. 2008. "Grizzly Ghost: Herzog, Bazin and the Cinematic Animal." *Screen* 49 (1): 1.
Jeunet, Jean-Pierre. 2013 (2001). *Amélie*. Burbank, CA.: Miramax films, Lionsgate. DVD.
———. 2014 (1997). *Alien Resurrection*. Beverly Hills, CA: Twentieth Century Fox Home Entertainment.
Jeunet, Jean-Pierre, and Mark Caro. 2016 (1995). *The City of Lost Children*. Culver City, CA: Sony Pictures Home Entertainment. Blu-Ray.
Johnson, Christopher. 2014. "Science in Three Dimensions: Werner Herzog's 'Cave of Forgotten Dreams.'" *The Modern Language Review* 109 (4): 915–30.
Jonze, Spike. 2002. *Adaptation*. Culver City, CA: Columbia TriStar.
Judah, Hettie. 2017. "Audrey Tautou's Very Private Self-Portraiture." *The New York Times*, June 20, 2017. https://www.nytimes.com/2017/06/20/t-magazine/entertainment/audrey-tautou-photographs-self-portraits-superfacial.html.
Kaes, Anton. 2011. "Requiem for a Lost Planet: Notes on Werner Herzog's *Fata Morgana*." In *Just Images: Ethics and the Cinematic*, edited by Boaz Hagin, 94–104.
Kaganski, Serge. 2001. "'Amélie' Pas Jolie." *Libération*, May 31.
Kant, Immanuel, Paul Guyer, and Allen W. Wood. 1998. *Critique of Pure Reason*. The Cambridge Edition of the Works of Immanuel Kant. [Kritik der reinen Vernunft. English]. Cambridge; New York: Cambridge University Press.
Kassovitz, Mathieu. 1995. *La Haine* Irvington, NY: Criterion Collection, 1995.
Kaurismki, Aki. 1989. *Leningrad Cowboys*. New York: Criterion Collection.
Kazan, Elia. 1969. *The Arrangement*. New York: Athena Productions.
Kelsey, Robin Earle, and Blake Stimson. 2008. *The Meaning of Photography*. Clark Studies in the Visual Arts. Williamstown, MA: Sterling and Francine Clark Art Institute, New Haven.
Kim, Ki-duk. 2005. *3-Iron*. Culver City, CA: Sony Pictures Home Entertainment.
Kieslowski, Krzysztof. 1993. *Three Colors: Blue*. Burbank, CA: Miramax Home Entertainment.
Koreeda, Hirokazu. 1995. *Maborosi*. New York: New Yorker Video.
Krauss, Rosalind. 1974. "Dark Glasses and Bifocals: A Book Review." *Artforum* 12 (9): 59.
Kubrick, Stanley. 1961. *Lolita*. Burbank, CA: Warner Home Video.
Kuenzli, Rudolf E. 1996. *Dada and Surrealist Film*. 1st MIT Press ed. Cambridge, MA: MIT Press.
Kurosawa, Akira. 2012. *Rashomon*. Irvington, NY: The Criterion Collection.
Lançon, Philippe. 2017. "Le Frauduleux Destin D'Amélie Poulain." *Libération*, June 1.
Landis, John. 1980. *The Blues Brothers*. Universal Pictures.
———. 1998. *Blues Brothers 2000*. Universal Pictures.

Laugier, Sandra, and Marc Cerisuelo, eds. 2001. *Stanley Cavell: Cinéma et philosophie*. Paris: Presses de la Sorbonne Nouvelle.

Levy, Emmanuel. 2015. "Three Monkeys: An Interview with Turkish Director Nuri Bilge Ceylan." In *Nuri Bilge Ceylan*, edited by Bert Cardullo. Berlin: Logos Verlag.

Losada, Matt. 2010. "Lucrecia Martel's La Mujer Sin Cabeza: Cinematic Free Indirect Discourse, Noise-Scape and the Distraction of the Middle Class." *Romance Notes* 50 (3): 307.

Losey, Joseph. 1967. *Accident*. Royal Avenue Chelsea.

Lynch, David. 1977. *Eraserhead*. Irvington, NY: Absurda; The Criterion Collection.

———. 2008. *Lost Highway*. Universal City, CA: Universal Studios.

———. 2001. *Mulholland Dr.* Universal City, CA: Universal Studios.

Lyne, Adrian. 1998. *Lolita*. United States: Trimark Home Video.

Manovich, Lev. 2001. *The Language of New Media*. Leonardo. Cambridge, MA: MIT Press.

Marion, Jean-Luc and Hugues Choplin. 2015. "Unpower." In *Love and Forgiveness for a More Just World*, edited by Hent De Vries and Nils F. Schott. New York: Columbia University Press.

Marrati, Paola. 2012. *Gilles Deleuze: Cinema and Philosophy*. Baltimore: Johns Hopkins University Press.

Marshall. Frank. 1993. *Alive*. Paramount Pictures, 1993.

Martel, Lucrecia. 2005 (2001) *The Swamp*. Chicago, IL: Home Vision Entertainment. DVD.

———. 2005 (2004). *The Holy Girl*. New York: HBO Video. DVD.

———. 2008. *The Headless Woman*. Culver City, CA: Strand Releasing Home Video. DVD.

Martin, Deborah. 2013. "Childhood, Youth, and the In-between: The Ethics and Aesthetics of Lucrecia Martel's La Mujer Sin Cabeza." *Hispanic Research Journal* 14 (2): 144.

———. 2016. *The Cinema of Lucrecia Martel*. Spanish and Latin American Filmmakers. Manchester, UK: Manchester University Press.

Martin-Jones, David. 2006. *Deleuze, Cinema and National Identity: Narrative Time in National Contexts*. Edinburgh: Edinburgh University Press.

———. 2011. *Deleuze and World Cinemas*. London; New York: Continuum.

Martins, L. 2011. "En contra de contar historias. Cuerpos e imgenes hpticas en el cine Argentino (Lisandro Alonso y Lucrecia Martel)." *Revista de Critica Literaria Latinoamericana* 37 (73), 401.

Matheou, Demetrios. 2010. "Vanishing Point." *Sight & Sound* 20 (3): 28.

McGowan, Todd. 2007a. *The Impossible David Lynch*. Film and Culture. New York: Columbia University Press.

———. 2007b. *The Real Gaze: Film Theory after Lacan*. SUNY Series in Psychoanalysis and Culture. Albany: State University of New York Press.

Mittell, Jason. 2006. "Narrative Complexity in Contemporary American Television." *Velvet Light Trap* 58 (January 1, 2006): 29–40.
Moore, Rick Clifton. 2006. "Ambivalence to Technology in Jeunet's *Le Fabuleux Destin D'Amelie Poulain*." *Bulletin of Science, Technology and Society* 26, no. 1: 9–19.
Morales, Guillem. 2004. *The Uninvited Guest*. Drain + España.
Mulhall, Stephen. 2002. *On Film*. Thinking in Action. London; New York: Routledge.
Mullarkey, John. 2009. *Refractions of Reality*. 1. publ. ed. New York [u.a.]: Palgrave Macmillan.
Mulvey, Laura. 2006. *Death 24x a Second: Stillness and the Moving Image*. London: Reaktion Books.
———. 2009. *Visual and Other Pleasures*. 2nd ed. Houndmills, Basingstoke, Hampshire: Palgrave Macmillan.
Naficy, Hamid. 2001. *An Accented Cinema: Exilic and Diasporic Filmmaking*. Princeton, NJ: Princeton University Press.
Nagib, Lúcia. 2011. *World Cinema and the Ethics of Realism*. New York: Continuum.
Nagib, Lúcia, and Cecília Mello. 2009. *Realism and the Audiovisual Media*. Basingstike, Hampshire; New York: Palgrave Macmillan.
Nagib, Lúcia, Christopher Perriam, and Rajinder Kumar Dudrah. 2011. *Theorizing World Cinema*. Tauris World Cinema Series. London: I. B. Tauris.
Netzer, Calin Peter. 2013. *Child's Pose*. Parada Film.
Nusselder, Andre. 2012. *The Surface Effect*. Hoboken: Taylor and Francis.
Orr, John, and Olga Taxidou. 2007. *Post-War Cinema and Modernity*. Edinburgh: Edinburgh University Press.
Oumano, Elena. 2011. *Cinema Today: A Conversation with Thirty-Nine Filmmakers from around the World*. New Brunswick, NJ: Rutgers University Press.
Page, Joanna. 2009. *Crisis and Capitalism in Contemporary Argentine Cinema*. Durham NC: Duke University Press.
———. 2013. "Folktales and Fabulation in Lucrecia Martel's Films." In *Latin American Popular Culture: Politics, Media, Affect*, 71. Woodbridge, Suffolk; Rochester, NY: Boydell & Brewer.
Panek, Elliot. 2006. "The Poet and the Detective: Defining the Psychological Puzzle Film." *Film Criticism* 31, no. 1/2 (January 1, 2006): 62–88.
Panofsky, Erwin. "Style and Medium in the Moving Pictures." In *Film Theory and Criticism: Introductory Readings*, edited by Leo Braudy and Marshall Cohen, 279–93. 7th ed. New York: Oxford University Press.
Parwez, Ghulam A. "Exposition of the Holy Quran." *Bazme Tolue Islam*. Accessed 07/28/2017. http://tolueislam.org/exposition-of-the-holy-quran-37-as-saaffaat-g-a-parwez/.
Pasolini, Pier Paolo, and Louise K. Barnett. 1988. *Heretical Empiricism* [Empirismo eretico. English]. Bloomington: Indiana University Press.

Pisters, Patricia. 2012. *The Neuro-Image: a Deleuzian Film-Philosophy of Digital Screen Culture*. Stanford, California: Stanford University Press.
Prager, Brad. 2007. *The Cinema of Werner Herzog: Aesthetic Ecstasy and Truth*. Directors' Cuts. London; New York: Wallflower.
———. 2009. "Landscape of the Mind: The Indifferent Earth in Werner Herzog's Films." In *Cinema and Landscape*, edited by Rayner Harper. Chicago: Intellect.
———. 2012. *Companion to Werner Herzog*. Wiley Blackwell Companions to Film Directors. Vol. 18. Somerset: Wiley.
Quandt, James. 2009. "Art of Fugue." *Artforum International* 47 (10): 95.
Rancière, Jacques. 2006. *Film Fables*. Trans. Emiliano Battista. Oxford, UK; New York: Berg.
Read, Rupert J., and Jerry Goodenough. 2005. *Film as Philosophy: Essays in Cinema after Wittgenstein and Cavell*. Houndmills, Basingstoke, Hampshire; New York: Palgrave Macmillan.
Renoir, Jean. 2004 (1939). *The Rules of the Game*. New York: Criterion Collection. Special Edition Double-disc Set.
Rhodes, Gary Don, and John Parris Springer (eds.). 2006. *Docufictions*. Jefferson, NC: McFarland.
Rieser, Martin and Andrea Zapp (eds.) 2002. *New Screen Media: Cinema/Art/Narrative*. London: BFI Pub.
Rodowick, David Norman. 1997. *Gilles Deleuze's Time Machine*. Post-Contemporary Interventions. Durham, NC: Duke University Press.
———. 2007. *The Virtual Life of Film*. Cambridge, MA: Harvard University Press.
———. 2015. *Philosophy's Artful Conversation*. Cambridge, MA: Harvard University Press.
Rohmer, Eric. 1989. *The Taste for Beauty*. Trans. Carol Volk. Cambridge, UK: Cambridge University Press.
Ropars-Wuilleumier, Marie-Claire. 1970. *L' Écran De La Mémoire*. Paris: Éd. du Seuil.
Rothman, William, ed. 2005. *Cavell on Film*. Albany: State University of New York Press.
Rothman, William, and Marian Keane. 2000. *Reading Cavell's* The World Viewed: *A Philosophical Perspective on Film*. Contemporary Film and Television Series. Detroit: Wayne State University Press.
Rudrum, David. 2013. *Stanley Cavell and the Claim of Literature*. Baltimore, MD: Johns Hopkins University Press.
Rugo, Daniele. 2016a. *Philosophy and the Patience of Film in Cavell and Nancy*. London: Palgrave Macmillan.
———. 2016b. "Asghar Farhadi: Acknowledging Hybrid Traditions: Iran, Hollywood and Transnational Cinema." *Third Text* 30 (3–4), 173–87.

Rushton, Richard. 2011. "A Deleuzian Imaginary: The Films of Jean Renoir." *Deleuze Studies* 5 (2): 241–60.
Rusnak, Josef. 1999. *The Thirteenth Floor*. Culvert City, CA: Columbia Pictures.
Ryle, Gilbert. 1949. *The Concept of Mind*. London: Hutchinson's University Library.
Scatton-Tessier, Michelle. 2004. "Le Pétisme: Flirting with the Sordid in Le Fabuleux Destin D'Amlie Poulain." *Studies in French Cinema* 4 (3): 197.
Schefer, Jean Louis. 2016. *The Ordinary Man of Cinema*. Transl. Max Cavitch, Noura Wedell and Paul Grant. South Pasadena, CA: Semiotext(e).
Schmerheim, Philipp. 2016. *Skepticism Films: Knowing and Doubting the World in Contemporary Cinema*. New York: Bloomsbury Academic.
Schrader, Paul. 1972. *Transcendental Style in Film: Ozu, Bresson, Dreyer*. Berkeley: University of California Press.
Schwartz, Peter J. 2010. "The Void at the Center of Things: Figures of Identity in Michael Haneke's Glaciation Trilogy." In *A Companion to Michael Haneke*, 337. Chichester, West Sussex; Malden, MA: Wiley-Blackwell.
Sesonske, Alexander. 1974. Rev. of *The World Viewed*, by Stanley Cavell. *The Georgia Review* 18 (4): 561–70.
———. 1980. *Jean Renoir: The French Films*. Cambridge, MA: Harvard University Press.
———. 2011. "*The Rules of the Game*: Everyone Has Their Reasons." Criterion Collection essay. https://www.criterion.com/current/posts/308-the-rules-of-the-game-everyone-has-their-reasons.
Simons, Jan. 2007. *Playing the Waves: Lars Von Trier's Game Cinema*. Amsterdam: Amsterdam University Press.
Singer, Alan. 1986. "Comprehending Appearances: Werner Herzog's Ironic Sublime." In *The Films of Werner Herzog: Between Mirage & History*, 183. New York: Methuen.
Sinnerbrink, Robert. 2011. *New Philosophies of Film: Thinking Images*. London; New York: Continuum.
———. 2016. *Cinematic Ethics: Exploring Ethical Experience through Film*. Milton Park, Abingdon, Oxon; New York: Routledge.
Sippl, Diane. 2005. "Ceylan and Company." *Cineaction* (67): 44.
Sosa, Cecilia. 2009. "A Counter-Narrative of Argentine Mourning: 'The Headless Woman' (2008), Directed by Lucrecia Martel." *Theory, Culture and Society* 26 (7–8): 250.
Staiger, Janet. 2006. "Complex Narratives, An Introduction." *Film Criticism* 31, no. 1/2 (October 1, 2006): 2–4.
Stites, Richard. 1989. *Revolutionary Dreams: Utopian Vision and Experimental Life in the Russian Revolution*. New York: Oxford University Press.
Suner, Asuman. 2010. *New Turkish Cinema: Belonging, Identity, and Memory*. Tauris World Cinema Series. London; New York: I. B. Tauris.

———. 2011. "A Lonely and Beautiful Country: Reflecting upon the State of Oblivion in Turkey through Nuri Bilge Ceylan's Three Monkeys." *Inter-Asia Cultural Studies* 12 (1): 13.

Tati, Jacques. 2014 (1971). *Trafic*. In *The Complete Jacques Tati: Special Edition Collector's Set*. Criterion Collection. New York: Criterion Collection.

Taubin, Amy. 2009. "Identification of a Woman." *Film Comment* 45 (4): 20.

Trier, Joachim. 2015. *Louder than Bombs*. Culver City, CA: Sony Pictures Home Entertainment.

Tsuruta, Norio. 2004. *Premonition*. Entertainment Farm.

Turvey, Malcolm. 2008. *Doubting Vision: Film and the Revelationist Tradition*. Oxford; New York: Oxford University Press.

Van Warmerdam, Alex. 2014. *Borgman*. Austin, TX: Drafthouse Films.

Vaughan, Dai. 1999. *For Documentary: Twelve Essays*. Berkeley: University of California Press.

Wedel, Michael, and ProQuest. 2011. *Filmgeschichte Als Krisengeschichte: Schnitte Und Spuren Durch Den Deutschen Film*. Film. Bielefeld: Transcript Verlag.

Weir, Peter. 1974. *The Cars that Ate Paris*. Australian Film Development Corporation.

White, Patricia. 2015. *Women's Cinema, World Cinema*. Durham: Duke University Press.

White, Rob. 2011. "Nuri Bilge Ceylan: An Introduction and Interview." *Film Quarterly* 65 (2): 64.

Willemen, Paul. 2002. "Reflections on Digital Imagery: Of Mice and Men." In *New Screen Media: Cinema/Art/Narrative*, 14: British Film Institute.

Wittgenstein, Ludwig, P. M. S. Hacker, and Joachim Schulte. 2009. *Philosophical Investigations*. Chichester: John Wiley & Sons.

Wong, Kar-wai. 1997. *Happy Together* New York: Kino on Video.

Zalewski, Daniel. 2001. "Going Sweet and Sentimental Has Its Rewards." *New York Times*, October 28.

Index

Note: Page numbers in *italics* indicate illustrations.

Abbott, Mathew, 20
Adaptation, 183n6
Alien series, 82, 83
Althusser, Louis, 19
Amélie, *11*, 11–15, 82–107, *90*–*104* passim, 120–124, 175
Amenábar, Alejandro, 183n6
Ames, Eric, 193n4
Amores perros, 183n6
Andrée, Ellen, 104
Andrew, Dudley, 75, 76, 83, 92–93
Antonioni, Michelangelo, 39
Archimedes, 67
Armenians, 172
Artaud, Antonin, 63, 192n9
Aslan, Hatice, 128
Atanarjuat, the Fast Runner, 10, 75
Audiard, Jacques, 9
Austin, J. L., 24, 43, 185n7, 189n3
"automata, spiritual," 61–63
"automatic analogical causation," 8, 21, 95
automatism, 40, 62, 186n13; Cavell on, 22, 30, 95; photographic indexicality and, 75
Avatar, 82

Bakhtin, Mikhail, 141, 198n14

Barthes, Roland, 76, 185nn5–6, 193n5
Baudry, Jean-Louis, 33, 116, 195n8
Bazin, André, 20, 186n13; Bergson and, 47; Cavell and, 22–23; "fact-image" of, 39; on neorealism, 33; on Renoir's *Rules of the Game*, 47, 188n1, 189n5
Beaumarchais, Pierre, 42
Bergson, Henri, 54–55; Bazin and, 47; Deleuze and, 17–18, 33–39, 48, 61, 188n18; Freud and, 196n9; Husserl and, 191n8; Kant and, 188nn19–20
Bicycle Thief, 39
Bingöl, Yavuz, 128
Blair, David, 112
Blair Witch Project, The, 113
Blanchot, Maurice, 63, 166, 192n9
Blank, Les, 193n3
Blues Brothers, The, 13–14
Bob le flambeur, 83
Bondanella, Peter E., 188n24
Bonitzer, Pascal, 130, 173, 198n6
Bordwell, David, 6–7
Braudy, Leo, 19
Buckland, Warren, 112

Cameron, Allan, 112

215

Cameron, James, 82
Capra, Frank, 87–89, 98, 110, 121
Carroll, Noel, 185n11, 190n1
Cavell, Stanley, 7, 85–88, 178–179; Austin and, 189n3; Carroll on, 185n11; on cinematic skepticism, 133; Deleuze and, 2–8, 10–11, 14, 17–18, 32–33, 38–40; Emerson and, 178; film theory and, 18–22; on ontological turn in cinema, 46, 115; on photography, 2–8, 25–26, 30, 123, 185n11; on Renoir's *Rules of the Game*, 41–47, 49–51, 176; Rodowick on, 110–111, 119; Schmerheim and, 109, 110, 192n13; Turvey and, 54, 61; Wittgenstein and, 17, 22–25; on world cinema, 10
Ceylan, Nuri Bilge, 14–15, 125, 128–129, 151–174
Chatman, Seymour, 58
Chauvet cave paintings, 78
Chazelle, Damien, 184n6
Chion, Michel, 136
Choplin, Hugues, 192n9
cinematic skepticism, 1–2, 5, 39–40, 71–72, 133, 179; Renoir and, 41–51
Colbert, Claudette, 87
collision films, 13–14, 56, 183n6; *Headless Woman* and, 131–133, 136–137; post 9/11 cinema and, 184n7; *Three Monkeys* and, 151–152, 157
Confucius, 169
crystal image, 48–51, 56–57, 73, 140, 174, 192n8
Cuarón, Alfonso, 9
Cukor, George, 72

Daly, Kristen, 112
danse macabre, 42–43, 48
De Sica, Vittorio, 39

deframing (*décadrage*), 130, 198n6
Deleuze, Gilles, 178–179; Artaud and, 63; Bergson and, 17–18, 33–39, 48, 61, 188n18, 190n8; Cavell and, 2–8, 10–11, 14, 17–18, 32–33, 38–40; on "clarified reality," 42, 53, 69; on crystal image, 48–50; on empiricism, 188n22; on fabulation, 176; on Kant, 191n8; on ontological turn in cinema, 115; on Outsideness, 157, 166–167; on "powers of the false," 129, 140–142, 165; on Renoir's *Rules of the Game*, 47–51, 188n1; Schmerheim and, 53, 68–71; on simulation, 133; on Societies of Control, 196n11; on time, 60; Turvey on, 56–57, 60, 63; as visual skeptic, 57–60; on world cinema, 10
Denis, Claire, 178
Descartes, René, 3–4, 27, 64, 70, 167, 191n8
Dheepan, 9
digitization techniques, 6–7, 176, 179; as cinema of simulation, 9; indexicality and, 105; Nagib on, 10; Rodowick on, 8, 110–112, 122, 125
Doane, Mary Ann, 21, 22, 95
"docufiction," 73, 193n1
Domenach, Élise, 20, 184n2
Dreyer, Carl Theodor, 72
Dulac, Germaine, 192n11

Egoyan, Atom, 183n6
Elsaesser, Thomas, 6–7, 15; on digital turn in cinema, 112, 119–120, 179–180; on mind-game films, 112–120, 183n6, 196n10; on "new materiality," 117–118; on world cinema, 115
Emerson, Ralph Waldo, 3–4, 28, 177–178

Epstein, Jean, 54–57, 190n6
Erdogan, Recep Tayyip, 128
Escher, M. C., 43–44
Esmer, Pelin, 184n6

Farhadi, Asghar, 178, 183n6
Flaherty, Robert, 73
Fleming, Victor, 72
Frankfurt School, 19
free indirect vision, 141, 148, 154
Freud, Sigmund, 85, 196n9
Fried, Michael, 185n6, 186n14
Friedrich, Caspar David, 193n6
Früchtl, Josef, 64, 68, 192n10
Fukunaga, Cary Jôji, 9
Funny Games, 9

Gable, Clark, 87
Gaborit, Jean, 189n5
Gale, Bob, 112
gangster movies, 9
Garbo, Greta, 25
Gardner, Alexander, 193n5
Garrone, Matteo, 9
Gemorrah, 9
George, Terry, 184n6
Germany Year Zero, 39
Gertrud, 72
Gide, André, 176
Godard, Jean-Luc, 165
González Iñárritu, Alejandro, 184n6
Grizzly Man, 11, 11–15, 28, 74–82, 77, 105–107, 113, 124–125

Haneke, Michael, 9
Happy Together, 9
Headless Woman, The, 14–15, 125, 127–151, 130–151 passim, 172–174
Heidegger, Martin, 3–4, 28, 29, 178
Herzog, Werner, 73–74, 175–177, 193n4; *Aguirre, the Wrath of God*, 74; *The Cave of Forgotten Dreams*, 78; *Fitzcarraldo*, 74, 193n3; *Grizzly Man*, 11, 11–15, 28, 74–82, 77, 105–107, 113, 124–125
Hirukazo Koreeda, 184n7
Hitchcock, Alfred, 131
home-invasion films, 9, 183n6
Hume, David, 3–4, 58
Husserl, Edmund, 191n8
hypermedia interactive films, 112

Iñárritu, Alejandro G., 184n6
indexicality, photographic, 19, 20, 21; automatism and, 75; Elsaesser on, 115, 180, 195n7; Jeong on, 116–117, 195n9
It Happened One Night, 87–89, 88, 110, 121

Jeong, Seung-Hoon, 75, 76, 116–117, 125, 195n9
Jeunet, Jean-Pierre, 11, 11–15, 82–107, 90–104 passim, 120–124, 175
Jonze, Spike, 183n6
Josepho, Anatol, 194n9
Judah, Hettie, 175

Kaganski, Serge, 83
Kaiser, Henry, 76
Kant, Immanuel, 3–4, 12, 26–28, 186n12; Bergson on, 34, 36, 188nn19–20; Deleuze on, 191n8
Kassovitz, Mathieu, 88–102, 90, 95, 97
Kaurismäki, Aki, 9
Kazan, Elia, 184n6
Kelsey, Robin, 20–21
Kiarostami, Abbas, 73, 178
Kierkegaard, Søren, 29, 171
Kim Ki-Duk, 9, 118
Kinski, Klaus, 193n3
Kovács, András Bálint, 187n15
Kracauer, Siegfried, 54

Kraus, Rosalind, 185n8, 187n15
Kubrick, Stanley, 184n6
Kunuk, Zacharias, 10, 75

Lacan, Jacques, 196n9
Lançon, Philippe, 83
Landis, John, 13–14
Last Year at Marienbad, 57–58
Laugier, Sandra, 20, 183n4
Leibniz, Gottfried Wilhelm, 165
Leningrad Cowboys Go America, 9
Losada, Matt, 134, 198n11
Losey, Joseph, 184n6
Lost Highway, 9
Louder than Bombs, 184n6
Lynch, David, 9, 184n6

Maborosi, 184n7
Makavejev, Dusan, 72
Manovich, Lev, 93, 112
Maréchal, Jacques, 189n5
Marion, Jean-Luc, 192n9
Marley, Bob, 100
Marrati, Paola, 61–62, 187n17, 191n8
Martel, Lucrecia: *The Headless Woman*, 14–15, 125, 127–151, *130–151* passim, 172–174; Salta trilogy of, 127, 136, 197n1
Martin-Jones, David, 10, 187n15
Marx, Karl, 42
Matrix, The, 6, 27, 71, 82, 192n14
Méliès, Georges, 194n13
Melville, Jean-Pierre, 83
Mermet, Gérard, 83
mind-game films, 112–120, 183n6, 196n10
Mittell, Jason, 112
Möbius strip, 38
montage, 2, 47, 100, 105, 106
Mujer sin cabeza. See *Headless Woman, The*

Mulhall, Stephen, 7, 20, 84–86
Mulholland Drive, 184n6
Mullarkey, John, 7
Mulvey, Laura, 21–22
Musset, Alfred de, 42
Muybridge, Eadweard, 55
Myrick, Daniel, 113

Nagib, Lúcia, 10, 75, 183n5
Nancy, Jean-Luc, 178
neorealism, 33, 39, 188n24
Netzer, Calin Peter, 184n6
"new materiality," 117–118
"new Real," 42, 53, 69
New Social Cinema, 84
Nietzsche, Friedrich, 3–4
nihilism, 40, 86, 196n10
9/11 films, 184n7
Norio Tsuruta, 184n6
Nozick, Robert, 64

ontological turn in cinema, 8, 12, 22–26, 46, 114–120, 122, 180
Ophüls, Max, 47
Outsideness (*le Dehors*), 157, 166–167
Ozon, François, 84

Panek, Elliot, 112
Panofsky, Erwin, 20, 24
Pascal, Blaise, 68, 115
Passion of Joan of Arc, The, 72
Peirce, Charles Sanders, 94, 95, 96
pétisme, 83–84, 175
photography: Cavell on, 2–8, 25–26, 30, 123, 185n11
"photomaton," 92, 96, 99, 121, 194n9
Pisters, Patricia, 112, 187n15
Plato, 186n12, 188n19
Prager, Brad, 74
Psycho, 131

Putnam, Hilary, 64
"puzzle films," 112, 116

Quandt, James, 131, 132

Rancière, Jacques, 187n15
referentiality, 117
Renoir, Jean, 40–51, 73; Bazin on, 47, 188n1; Cavell on, 41–47, 50, 51; Deleuze on, 47–51; depth of field and, 47–51, 49; *Rules of the Game*, 14, 41–51, 45, 49, 86, 121, 176
Renoir, Pierre-Auguste, 103–104
Resnais, Alain, 57, 58
Robbe-Grillet, Alain, 58–59
Rodowick, D. N., 7, 15, 20–21, 53, 60, 67–70; on Cavell, 110–111, 119; Deleuze and, 179; on digitization techniques, 8, 110–112, 122, 125; Marrati and, 187n17, 191n8; Martin-Jones on, 187n15; on *Matrix*, 192n14; on mind-game films, 120; on "will to control information," 125
Rohmer, Eric, 189n1
Rossellini, Roberto, 39
Rothman, William, 20
Rouch, Jean, 73
Rugo, Daniele, 18, 20, 178
Rules of the Game, The, 14, 41–51, 45, 49, 86, 121, 176
Rushton, Richard, 50
Ryle, Gilbert, 56

Sánchez, Eduardo, 113
Sayar, Vecdi, 168
Scatton-Tessier, Michelle, 83–84, 86
Schmerheim, Philipp, 6, 179; Cavell and, 109, 110, 192n13; Deleuze and, 53, 63–71; Früchtl and, 64, 68, 192n10

Sesonske, Alexander, 188n1, 193n7
Simons, Jan, 112
Singer, Alan, 74
Sinnerbrink, Robert, 7, 18, 20
skepticism, 6, 18, 27, 29–31; cinema and, 29–32; digital turn and, 109–114; intuition and, 26–28; literary, 7; philosophical, 1; threat of, 14
Spinoza, Benedict de, 62
Staiger, Janet, 112
Stimson, Blake, 20–21

Taghmaoui, Saïd, 100–102, *101*
Taubin, Amy, 131–132
Tautou, Audrey, *11*, 175
Taxi Driver, 131
Thirteenth Floor, The, 6, 71
Thompson, Richard, 76
Thoreau, Henry David, 29
Three Monkeys, 14–15, 125, 128–129, 151–174, *152–169* passim
Three-Sided Mirror, The, 55–56
3-Iron, 9, 118
Tilbe, Yildiz, 161
Treadwell, Timothy, *11*, 11–13, 75–82, *77*, 105–107, 113, 124–125
Trier, Joachim, 184n6
Truffaut, François, 189n1, 189n5
Truman Show, The, 6, 71
Turvey, Malcolm, 53–61, 63–65, 118, 179; on revelationism, 189n6, 190n6

Vaughan, Dai, 184n4
Vertov, Dziga, 54, 61, 190n6
virtual point of view, 132–135, 151–152, 154, 165
Vitti, Monica, 39

Wachowski brothers, 82

Washington, Denzel, 186n11
WAXWEB, 112
Wedel, Michael, 66
Weir, Peter, 184n6
Weltanschauungen, 46
Willemen, Paul, 184n4
Wittgenstein, Ludwig, 3–4, 29, 185n7; Austin and, 24; Cavell and, 17, 22–25; on time, 60

Wizard of Oz, 72
Wong Kar-wai, 9
world cinema, 8–11, 183n5

Y tu mamá también, 9

Zalewski, Daniel, 12
Zavattini, Cesare, 33, 39
Žižek, Slavoj, 196n9

www.ingramcontent.com/pod-product-compliance
Lightning Source LLC
Chambersburg PA
CBHW030648230426
43665CB00011B/1003